HD9710.G73 B67 2010

The impacts
automotive
2010.

The Impacts of Automotive Plant Closure

Economic restructuring has been a notable feature of so-called mature industrial economies such as the UK and Australia in the last two decades, with deregulation, privatisation, technological change and globalisation combining to reshape such economies. Some industries have grown, while others have declined. Moreover, while overall employment in the UK and Australia has grown, many newly-created positions require skills not found in the industries shedding labour, or are in casualised and low paid occupations. Many lesser-skilled workers leaving declining industries are therefore at risk of long-term unemployment or leaving the workforce entirely. Both mental and physical health can be affected after redundancy. It is therefore crucial that the measures put in place in many domains of social policy (such as formal health policy, employment assistance, community development, housing assistance and so on) to adequately address the difficulties confronting this group. This volume takes a closer look at the impact of manufacturing - notably automotive - plant closures in the UK (Birmingham) and Australia (Adelaide) in recent years and policy responses to those closures. It attempts to tease out differences in policy response and effectiveness, and attempts to identify areas where policy could be made to work better in terms of adjusting to large scale manufacturing change and resulting job losses. In so doing, it begins, for the first time we believe, to take a comparative approach to understanding the impact of plant closures and policy responses.

This book was published as a special issue of *Policy Studies*.

Andrew Beer is Professor in the School of Geography, Population and Environmental Management at Flinders University, Adelaide, Australia.

Holli Evans is a Lecturer in the School of Political Science and International Relations at the University of Queensland, Australia.

The Impacts of Automotive Plant Closure

A Tale of Two Cities

Edited by Andrew Beer and Holli Evans

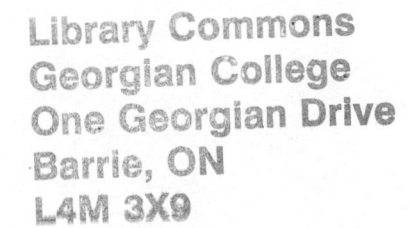

Routledge
Taylor & Francis Group
LONDON AND NEW YORK

First published 2010 by Routledge
2 Park Square, Milton Park, Abingdon, Oxon, OX14 4RN

Simultaneously published in the USA and Canada
by Routledge
270 Madison Avenue, New York, NY 10016

Routledge is an imprint of the Taylor & Francis Group, an informa business

© 2010 Taylor & Francis

Typeset in Times New Roman by Value Chain, India
Printed and bound in Great Britain by MPG Books Group

All rights reserved. No part of this book may be reprinted or reproduced or utilised in any form or by any electronic, mechanical, or other means, now known or hereafter invented, including photocopying and recording, or in any information storage or retrieval system, without permission in writing from the publishers.

British Library Cataloguing in Publication Data
A catalogue record for this book is available from the British Library

ISBN10: 0-415-54334-7
ISBN13: 978-0-415-54334-7

Contents

List of contributors		vii
Abstracts		ix
1.	Introduction: A tale of two cities: auto plant closures and policy responses in Birmingham and Adelaide *Andrew Beer and Holli Evans*	1
2.	Supply chains and locational adjustment in the global automotive industry *Ho-Yeon Kim and Philip McCann*	7
3.	Rover and out? Globalisation, the West Midlands auto cluster, and the end of MG Rover *David Bailey, Seiji Kobayashi and Stewart MacNeill*	19
4.	Birmingham: whose urban renaissance? Regeneration as a response to economic restructuring *Austin Barber and Stephen Hall*	33
5.	The housing and neighbourhood impacts of knowledge-based economic development following industrial closure *Alex Burfitt and Ed Ferrari*	45
6.	The impact of factory closure on local communities and economies: the case of the MG Rover Longbridge closure in Birmingham *Caroline Chapain and Alan Murie*	57
7.	Risk and return: housing tenure and labour market adjustment after employment loss in the automotive sector in Southern Adelaide *Andrew Beer*	71
8.	Closure of an automotive plant: transformation of a work-based 'community' *Fiona Verity and Gwyn Jolley*	83
9.	Auto plant closures, policy responses and labour market outcomes: a comparison of MG Rover in the UK and Mitsubishi in Australia *Kathy Armstrong, David Bailey, Alex de Ruyter, Michelle Mahdon and Holli Evans*	95

10. A tale of two regions: comparative versus competitive approaches to economic restructuring
   Holli Evans, Andrew Beer and David Bailey 109

   Index 123

Edited by ANDREW BEER AND HOLLI EVANS

List of contributors

KATHY ARMSTRONG, National Australia Bank.

DAVID BAILEY is Professor of International Business Economics and Strategy, Coventry University Business School, UK.

AUSTIN BARBER is a Lecturer in the Centre for Urban and Regional Studies, Birmingham Business School, UK.

ANDREW BEER is a Professor in the School of Geography, Population and Environmental Management, Flinders University, Adelaide, Australia.

ALEX BURFITT is a Research Manager at the Audit Commission, UK.

CAROLINE CHAPAIN is a Research Fellow in the Centre for Urban and Regional Studies, Birmingham Business School, UK.

ALEX DE RUYTER is Professor of Public Sector Management at the University of the West of Scotland.

ED FERRARI is a Research Fellow at the Department of Town and Regional Planning, University of Sheffield, UK.

STEPHEN HALL is Principal Lecturer in Planning, University of the West of England, UK.

GWYN JOLLEY is Senior Research Officer, SA Community Health Research Unit, Flinders University, Adelaide, Australia.

MICHELLE MAHDON is Senior Researcher at The Work Foundation, London, UK.

HOLLI EVANS is a Lecturer in the School of Political Science and International Relations at the University of Queensland, Australia.

SEIJI KOBAYASHI is Associate Professor at the Graduate School of Business, Nihon University, Tokyo, Japan.

STEWART MACNEILL is Senior Lecturer in Economic Development, Centre for Urban and Regional Studies, Birmingham Business School, UK.

PHILIP MCCANN is Professor of Economics, Department of Economics, The University of Waikato, Hamilton, New Zealand.

ALAN MURIE is Emeritus Professor of Urban and Regional Studies, Centre for Urban and Regional Studies, Birmingham Business School, UK.

FIONA VERITY is a Senior Lecturer at Flinders University, Adelaide, Australia.

HO YEON KIM is a Professor in the School of Economics, Sungkyunkwan University, Seoul, Korea.

Abstracts

Supply chains and locational adjustment in the global automotive industry
Ho-Yeon Kim and Philip McCann

This paper helps to set the scene for this special issue on automotive restructuring and policy responses. It starts by providing a brief introduction to the different inventory and supply-chain management approaches dominant within the industry at different stages of its evolution, before moving on to outline the spatial implications of these different approaches. The paper then presents a transactionscosts conceptual framework for analysing key features of the auto manufacturing and supply-chain system, using a taxonomy approach. The paper concludes by highlighting the spatial and policy implications for the auto industry which arise from such a transactionscosts analysis. Interestingly, the logic of both a transactionscosts approach and a consideration of knowledge spillovers both point towards the increasing spatial concentration of higher value-added activities. This may have a number of policy implications in terms of the industrial, technology and regional policies required to support and sustain such higher value-added activities. This is also consistent with the view that globalization leads to greater spatial dispersion, as the latter tends to be dominated by lower value-adding activities, with the core locations progressively moving towards higher value-adding activities. Overall, the opposing positive and negative impacts on regional 'winners' and 'losers' will be more greatly amplified than would previously have been the case. As such, regions benefiting from the immigration of integrated supply-chain networks will tend to maintain their advantageous position in the industry over time. On the downside, regions which lose such supply-chain systems, as seen over the last two decades in many regions in the US, UK and Australia, face a challenging situation, with very limited prospects for redeveloping such systems via policy initiatives.

Rover and out? Globalisation, the West Midlands auto cluster, and the end of MG Rover
David Bailey, Seiji Kobayashi, and Stewart MacNeill

This paper sets the scene for this *Policy Studies* special issue on plant closures by outlining the form of the auto cluster in the West Midlands, the nature of structural changes unfolding in the industry, and the decline and eventual collapse of MG Rover (MGR). Structural changes highlighted include: greater pressure on firms to recover costs when technological change has been intensifying, driving up the costs of new model development; increased international sourcing of modular components; and a shift of final assembly operations towards lower-cost locations. All of these make maintaining mature clusters such as the West Midlands more challenging for firms and policy-makers. The paper then looks at 'what went wrong' at MGR. Given long-run problems at the firm and its inability to recover costs, BMW's sale of the firm in 2000 left MGR virtually dead on its feet, and by 2002/2003 it was clear to many that the firm was running out of time. Whilst recognising that the firm's demise was ultimately a long-term failure of management, the paper also looks at other contributing factors, including government policy mistakes over the years, such as the misguided 'national champions' approach in the 1950s and 1960s, a failure to integrate activities under nationalisation in the 1970s, a mistaken privatisation to British Aerospace in the 1980s, and a downside of competition policy in 'allowing' the sale to a largely inappropriate owner in BMW in the 1990s. The considerable volatility of sterling in recent years hastened the firm's eventual demise.

Birmingham: whose urban renaissance? Regeneration as a response to economic restructuring
Austin Barber and Stephen Hall

This paper draws together two traditionally distinct discourses that have dominated debates over urban policy responses to economic restructuring, deindustrialisation, major plant closures and the rise of the service and knowledge-based economy over the past 20 years. It investigates the case of Birmingham, where the policy drive of city centre regeneration, flagship development and the re-making of central urban space for new economic activities has been accompanied by much acclaim and 'boosterist' hype. At the same time, the socio-spatial impact of economic restructuring and the resulting policy response has been extremely uneven. The economic difficulties and wider disadvantage experienced by much of the city's population and many of its neighbour-hoods, especially those inner city areas with large ethnic minority populations, have endured and even deepened since the early 1990s despite the efforts of numerous area-based regeneration programmes funded by central government. The paper reflects upon this dual narrative by asking the question *whose urban renaissance?* From this study it clear that the dominance of the 'boosterist' discourse is significantly tempered by the uneven and enduring socio-economic divides within the city and the partial nature of the city's overall recovery, particularly in terms of providing employment for its residents. In this sense, significant policy challenges remain despite the clear achievements of the past 20 years. The paper concludes by considering new spatial policy approaches that could bind together the dual imperatives of creating new economic opportunities, and addressing aspects of acute need among the local population.

The housing and neighbourhood impacts of knowledge-based economic development following industrial closure
Alex Burfitt and Ed Ferrari

Economic development initiatives following large-scale industrial closures often seek to regenerate the local economy through investment in technology and knowledge-intensive activities. The resulting changes in the make-up of the local workforce are in turn likely to generate new forms of demand for housing; demand that will not necessarily be met by the residential offer of the neighbourhoods worst affected by the initial closure. This paper explores these processes through a study of the proposals for a science park as a component of the programme to redevelop the Longbridge site in Birmingham in the UK, following the closure of the Rover automotive plant in 2005. The paper examines the capacity of local workers to take up the anticipated high-technology jobs; the likely configuration of an incoming workforce; and the fit between the housing requirements of these new workers and the residential offer of neighbourhoods in the Longbridge area. It concludes that there is likely to be a poor match between the housing and residential characteristics of neighbourhoods most closely associated with the plant closure and the requirements of an incoming high-tech workforce. This in turn raises a policy dilemma. On the one hand there is a necessity to secure economic diversification for the local economy as a whole, whilst on the other is the requirement to address the specific needs of the discrete neighbourhoods most affected by the closure and whose quality of place offer is often furthest from the requirements of the incoming workforce. A number of policy implications are discussed, drawing on the experience of recent housing and regeneration policy.

The impact of factory closure on local communities and economies: the case of the MG Rover Longbridge closure in Birmingham
Caroline Chapain and Alan Murie

Much of the recent literature concerned with the impacts of factory closure refers to closures occurring in the 1980s and 1990s and affecting heavy industry – coal, steel and shipbuilding. It also tends to focus on employment and labour market impacts assessed through the subsequent experience of workers made redundant following closures. It also tends to assume that these impacts are localized. Because of this much of the discussion of policy implications relates to the workers made redundant and to a very local economy. This paper refers to the closure of the MG Rover factory in Longbridge, Birmingham, UK. This closure was regarded as presenting a crisis for government and the local community. The paper responds to arguments in the research literature and explores the spatial and economic impact of the MG Rover closure in more detail. It complements other research which has focused on the experience of those made redundant in 2005 by referring to the loss of employment over a longer time period and identifying a wider impact spatially and socially. The paper draws upon different sources of evidence and concludes with a discussion of implications for policy and research.

Risk and return: housing tenure and labour market adjustment after employment loss in the automotive sector in Southern Adelaide
Andrew Beer

This paper examines the interaction between housing tenure and the propensity of displaced workers from the automotive sector to be employed one year to 18 months post-redundancy. It considers the 'Oswald thesis' that home ownership contributes to higher rates of unemployment in advanced economies and reviews this proposition using survey data from 314 households. The paper focuses on the experience of workers retrenched from the Lonsdale and Tonsley Park plants of Mitsubishi Motors Australia Ltd and, unlike some other research, finds general support for the Oswald thesis. It is suggested that a number of factors contribute to a lower rate of re-engagement with the formal labour market by home owners, including the absence of locally available employment, the high cost of transport to regions where employment is on offer and a strong sense of attachment to their region.

Closure of an automotive plant: transformation of a work-based 'community'
Fiona Verity and Gwyn Jolley

This paper is an exploration of one aspect of 'community' impacts of retrenchment, namely, what happens for a work-based 'community' when capitalist production decisions result in redundancies from a South Australian-based manufacturing plant. This work draws on longitudinal data and uses Ferdinand Tonnies' conceptualisation of types of social relations as a reference point in analysis. Accounts of retrenched workers suggest *Gemeinschaft*-type relations in the workplace that had developed and deepened over time. These connections, described repeatedly as like 'family relationships', had tentacles extending outside the workplace. With retrenchment many respondents identified a rupturing of valued social connections that had, for some, not re-formed beyond common employment. These social changes have been associated with loss and grief. Given the health-enhancing factors attributed to social connectivity and the evidence that disenfranchised grief is associated with psychosocial health issues, policy attention to 'community' impacts of retrenchments, including the transformation of work-based communities, seems warranted.

Auto plant closures, policy responses and labour market outcomes: a comparison of MG Rover in the UK and Mitsubishi in Australia
Kathy Armstrong, David Bailey, Alex de Ruyter, Michelle Mahdon, and Holli Evans

This paper provides a preliminary comparative longitudinal analysis of the impact on workers made redundant due to the closure of the Mitsubishi plant in Adelaide and the MG Rover plant in Birmingham. Longitudinal surveys of ex-workers from both firms were undertaken over a 12-month period in order to assess the process of labour market adjustment. In the Mitsubishi case, given the skills shortage the state of Adelaide was facing, together with the considerable growth in mining and defence industries, it would have been more appropriate if policy intervention had been redirected to further training or re-skilling opportunities for redundant workers. This opportunity was effectively missed and as a result more workers left the workforce, most notably for retirement, than could have otherwise been the case. The MG Rover case was seen as a more successful example of policy intervention, with greater funding assistance available and targeted support available, and with more emphasis on re-training needs to assist adjustment. However, despite the assistance offered and the rhetoric of successful adjustment in both cases, the majority of workers have nevertheless experienced deterioration in their circumstances particularly in the Australian case where casual and part-time work were often the only work that could be obtained. Even in the UK case, where more funding assistance was offered, a majority of workers reported a decline in earnings and a rise in job insecurity. This suggests that a reliance on the flexible labour market is insufficient to promote adjustment, and that more active policy intervention is needed especially in regard to further up-skilling.

A tale of two regions: comparative versus competitive approaches to economic restructuring
Holli Evans, Andrew Beer, and David Bailey

In April 2004 Mitsubishi announced the closure of its Lonsdale plant in South Australia. Almost a year later, MG Rover went into administration, resulting in the immediate closure of its Longbridge plant just outside Birmingham, England. Both closures were expected to have a considerable impact on their regional economies through the loss of employment and associated economic activity. However, governments in Australia and England responded in significantly different ways: in England the focus was on competitive advantage through the modernisation of the auto cluster and the diversification of the regional economy into new, high-technology industries. In Australia, the national and state governments introduced policy responses based on the pursuit of comparative advantage. This paper compares and contrasts the two sets of government responses and examines the capacity of each to deliver long-term benefits to their affected communities.

INTRODUCTION

A tale of two cities: auto plant closures and policy responses in Birmingham and Adelaide

Andrew Beer and Holli Evans

Economic restructuring has been a notable feature of so-called mature industrial economies such as the UK and Australia in the last two decades, with deregulation, privatisation, technological change and globalisation combining to reshape such economies. Some industries have grown, while others have declined. Moreover, while overall employment in the UK and Australia has grown, many newly-created positions require skills not found in the industries shedding labour, or are in casualised and low-paid occupations. Many lesser-skilled workers leaving declining industries are therefore at risk of long-term unemployment or leaving the workforce entirely. The research of our colleagues at Flinders University shows that the mental health of displaced workers plummets relative to their peers in the first 12 to 18 months of redundancy, followed by a recovery to population norms. Physical health, however, is high at the time of retrenchment but declines over time, which suggests that such events have both short-term and long-term impacts on affected individuals. It is therefore crucial that the measures put in place in many domains of social policy (such as formal health policy, employment assistance, community development, housing assistance and so on) adequately address the difficulties confronting this group. This book takes a closer look at the impact of manufacturing – notably automotive – plant closures in the UK (Birmingham) and Australia (Adelaide) in recent years and policy responses to those closures. It attempts to tease out differences in policy response and effectiveness, and attempts to identify areas where policy could be made to work better in terms of adjusting to large-scale manufacturing change and resulting job losses. In so doing, it begins, for the first time we believe, to take a comparative approach to understanding the impact of plant closures and policy responses.

Plant closures remain an important and topical issue in many developed economies, especially as the automotive sector has continued to restructure on a global scale. In the case of Australia, the plant closure discussed in this special issue has been followed by the announcement of the closure of Ford's engine-making plant in Geelong, Victoria; a reduction in the number of shifts worked at General Motors' Elizabeth plant; a commitment by Ford to produce a new four-cylinder car at Broadmeadows on the outskirts of Melbourne; and the announcement of the closure of Mitsubishi's remaining plant in South Australia, Tonsley Park. Such shifts have continued to challenge policy-makers at all levels, with the newly-elected Rudd Labour government exhibiting a greater commitment to the maintenance of the automotive industry than its predecessor and discussing new policy instruments, including an offer of AU$500m for Toyota to produce hybrid vehicles in Australia. At a more local level, the Government of South Australia is currently considering potential uses for Mitsubishi's soon-to-be-closed plant at Tonsley Park. It is significant that amongst other inputs, policy-makers will examine the

Longbridge experience and outcomes, thereby highlighting the value of comparative analysis and scholarship.

Overview

The book begins with two scene-setting chapters on restructuring in the car industry generally (by Kim and McCann) and the impact of such change on the West Midlands in particular (by Bailey, Kobayashi and MacNeill). These are followed by three chapters looking in detail at the experience of manufacturing decline and adjustment in Birmingham, with chapters by Barber and Hall, Burfitt and Ferrari, and Chapain and Murie. Experience in Adelaide is then examined by Beer and then Verity and Jolley. Finally, two chapters examine the comparative dimension, with Armstrong *et al.* providing a comparative longitudinal analysis of the impact on workers, and Thomas, Beer and Bailey comparing and contrasting the industrial policy responses in each case, and the capacity of each to deliver long-term benefits to their affected communities.

The first scene-setting chapter, by Kim and McCann, begins by providing a brief introduction to the different inventory and supply-chain management approaches dominant within the industry at different stages of its evolution, before moving on to outline the spatial implications of these different approaches. The chapter then presents a transactions–costs conceptual framework for analysing key features of the auto manufacturing and supply-chain system, using a taxonomy approach. Interestingly, the logic of both a transactions–costs approach and a consideration of knowledge spillovers both point towards the increasing spatial concentration of higher value-added activities. This may have a number of policy implications in terms of the industrial, technology and regional policies required to support and sustain such higher value-added activities. Overall, they suggest that the opposing positive and negative impacts on regional 'winners' and 'losers' will be more greatly amplified than would previously have been the case. As such, regions benefiting from the immigration of integrated supply-chain networks will tend to maintain their advantageous position in the industry over time. On the downside, regions which lose such supply-chain systems, as seen over the last two decades in many regions in the US, UK and Australia, face a challenging situation, with very limited prospects for redeveloping such systems via policy initiatives.

The second scene-setter, by Bailey, Kobayashi and MacNeill, follows on by outlining the form of the auto cluster in the specific case of the West Midlands, the nature of structural changes unfolding in the industry, and the decline and eventual collapse of MG Rover (MGR), one of the firms that this book examines. Structural changes highlighted include: greater pressure on firms to recover costs when technological change has been intensifying, driving up the costs of new model development; increased international sourcing of modular components; and a shift of final assembly operations towards lower-cost locations. All of these make maintaining mature clusters such as the West Midlands more challenging for firms and policy-makers. The chapter then looks at 'what went wrong' at MGR. Given long-run problems at the firm and its inability to recover costs, BMW's sale of the firm in 2000 left MGR virtually dead on its feet, and by 2002/2003 it was clear to many that the firm was running out of time. Whilst recognising that the firm's demise was ultimately a long-term failure of management, the chapter also looks at other contributing factors, including government policy mistakes over the years. The considerable volatility of sterling in recent years hastened the firm's eventual demise.

The broader impact of restructuring in Birmingham is then examined by Barber and Hall. They note that the economic difficulties and wider disadvantage experienced by much of the city's population and many of its neighbourhoods have endured and even deepened since the early 1990s, despite the efforts of numerous area-based regeneration programmes funded by central government. The chapter reflects upon this by asking the question *whose urban renaissance?* The authors make clear that the dominance of the 'boosterist' discourse is significantly tempered by the uneven and enduring socio-economic divides within the city and the partial nature of the city's overall recovery, particularly in terms of providing employment for its residents. In this sense, significant policy challenges remain despite the clear achievements of the past 20 years. The authors conclude by considering new spatial policy approaches that could bind together the dual imperatives of creating new economic opportunities, and addressing aspects of acute need among the local population.

Such spatial and social policy requirements are then highlighted by Burfitt and Ferrari in the specific context of the MG Rover closure at Longbridge. This is explored through a study of the proposals for a science park at the Longbridge site in Birmingham in the UK, following the closure of the MG Rover automotive plant in 2005. The chapter examines the capacity of local workers to take up the anticipated high technology jobs; the likely configuration of an incoming workforce; and the fit between the housing requirements of these new workers and the residential offer of neighbourhoods in the Longbridge area. It concludes that there is likely to be a poor match between the housing and residential characteristics of neighbourhoods most closely associated with the plant closure and the requirements of an incoming high-tech workforce. This in turn raises a policy dilemma. On the one hand there is a necessity to secure economic diversification for the local economy as a whole, whilst on the other is the requirement to address the specific needs of the discrete neighbourhoods most affected by the closure and whose quality of place offer is often furthest from the requirements of the incoming workforce. A number of policy implications are discussed, drawing on the experience of recent housing and regeneration policy.

The third chapter looking at the MG Rover closure, by Chapain and Murie, suggests that the spatial impact of the Rover closure has been much wider than would have been expected 20 or more years ago, owing to the development of longer-distance commuting and the restructuring of the housing market. They conclude that researchers should be cautious about dramatising a highly localised neighbourhood effect of a major factory closure, but that equally they should not swing to the opposite extreme and imply that there is no neighbourhood effect at all. Rather, the evidence points to a wider zone experiencing a 'relatively concentrated' impact. In addition, some two years after the closure, even though most Rover workers are officially recorded as having found new jobs, levels of long-term employment are still not back to their initial levels. The authors conclude by suggesting that there are second-wave effects from factory closures not picked up by methodologies that focus on short-term impacts or that are wholly focused on tracking individual redundant workers. Future research concerned with spatial as well as other impacts of factory closure should explore these issues as well as the relationship between the place of residence and the location of the factory that has closed.

The book then turns to look at experiences in the wake of the Mitsubishi plant closure in Adelaide. The chapter by Beer examines the interaction between housing tenure and the propensity of displaced workers from the auto sector to be employed one year to 18 months post-redundancy. It considers the 'Oswald thesis' that home ownership contributes to higher rates of unemployment in advanced economies and focuses on the experience of workers retrenched from the Lonsdale and Tonsley Park plants of Mitsubishi Motors Australia Ltd and, unlike some other research, finds general support for the Oswald thesis. The author suggests that a number of factors contribute to a lower rate of re-engagement with the formal labour market by home owners, including the absence of locally-available employment, the high cost of transport to regions where employment is on offer and a strong sense of attachment to their region.

The broader community impact of retrenchment at Mitsubishi is examined by Verity and Jolley. They explore one aspect of this community impact, namely what happens for a work-based community when capitalist production decisions result in redundancies from a South Australian-based manufacturing plant. This work draws on longitudinal data and uses Tonnies' conceptualisation of types of social relations as a reference point. Accounts of retrenched workers suggest *Gemeinschaft* (community)-type relations in the workplace that had developed and deepened over time. With retrenchment many respondents identified a rupturing of these valued social connections that had, for some, not re-formed beyond common employment. These social changes have been associated with loss and grief. The authors conclude that policy attention to the community impacts of retrenchments is required, given the health-enhancing factors attributed to social connectivity and the evidence that disenfranchised grief is associated with psychosocial health issues.

The final two chapters look specifically at comparative aspects of plant closure and policy responses in Birmingham and Adelaide. Armstrong *et al.* provide an initial comparative longitudinal analysis of the impact on workers made redundant in each case. Longitudinal surveys of ex-workers from both firms were undertaken over a 12-month period in order to assess the process of labour market adjustment. In the Mitsubishi case, given the skills shortage Adelaide was facing, together with the considerable growth in mining and defence industries, the authors suggest that policy intervention should been redirected to further training or re-skilling opportunities for redundant workers. This opportunity was effectively missed and as a result more workers left the workforce, most notably for retirement, than could have otherwise been the case. In contrast, the MG Rover case is seen as a more successful example of policy intervention, with greater funding assistance available and targeted support available, and with more emphasis on retraining needs to assist adjustment. However, despite the assistance offered and the rhetoric of successful adjustment in both cases, the majority of workers have nevertheless experienced a deterioration in their circumstances. This suggests that a reliance on the flexible labour market is insufficient to promote adjustment, and that more active policy intervention is needed, especially in regard to further up-skilling.

The final chapter, by Thomas, Beer and Bailey, examines the different policy responses to the two plant closures in Australia and England. The authors argue that governments in each case responded in significantly different ways: in England the focus was on competitive advantage through the modernisation of the auto cluster and the diversification of the regional economy into new, high-technology industries. In Australia, the national and state governments introduced policy responses based on the pursuit of comparative advantage, notably an emphasis on the growth of extractive industries. This chapter compares and contrasts the two sets of government responses and examines the capacity of each to deliver long-term benefits to their affected communities.

Background on the plant closures studied

Bailey *et al.* discuss the history of MG Rover and events surrounding the closure of its plant at Longbridge in Birmingham in this book.

The closure of the Lonsdale plant of Mitsubishi Motors Australia Limited (MMAL) and the voluntary redundancies from the Tonsley Park assembly plant, announced in April

2004, are briefly highlighted here to avoid repetition in later papers. These resulted in the loss of 1200 jobs in the southern region of metropolitan Adelaide. The factory had been in operation since the mid 1960s and had performed a number of roles, including foundry work and component assembly. Tonsley Park remained in operation as an assembly plant, but in February 2008 its closure was also announced by MMAL.

MMAL's operations in Australia had been in doubt for a number of years, with several rounds of bail-outs from state and federal governments. Since further tariff reductions were announced in the late 1990s, MMAL had been threatening closure of its operations. In 2001 Mitsubishi received AU$200m in federal assistance as well as a AU$20m interest free loan from the state government. In 2002 a further AU$85m package of assistance was received from state and federal governments. This was in addition to the funding available through the federal government's AU$4.2bn Automotive Competitiveness and Investment Scheme. Despite claims that this would secure Mitsubishi's future in Australia, with Mitsubishi pledging to employ extra workers, the reality was that between 1999 and 2002 Mitsubishi shed more than 1000 jobs. By 2004 MMAL was suffering falling domestic sales and declining exports. Meanwhile the parent company, Mitsubishi Motors Corporation, which was then 37% owned by Daimler Chrysler, announced a loss of nearly US$900 million in 2003. This forced Mitsubishi to restructure and consolidate its global production, with Daimler Chrysler announcing that it would sell off its stake in the firm; its withdrawal was completed by 2005.

The loss of employment from MMAL in 2004 can be seen as part of the longer-term restructuring of the automobile industry, and manufacturing more generally, in Australia (House of Representatives 2006). Where once car-making plants could be found in all state capitals except Perth, by 2000 motor vehicle production had consolidated into a few locations, with Toyota and Ford assembling vehicles in Melbourne, and Mitsubishi and General Motors Holden building cars in Adelaide. With MMAL's closure, in 2008 that list becomes even shorter.

Acknowledgements

The authors would like to thank Mark Evans for the opportunity to compile this special issue. They are especially grateful to referees who gave freely of their time and who provided much constructive comment on the papers in this volume.

Reference

House of Representatives Standing Committee on Employment, Workplace Relations and Workforce Participation, 2006. *Shifting gears: employments in the automotive components manufacturing industry.* Canberra: AGPS.

Supply chains and locational adjustment in the global automotive industry

Ho-Yeon Kim and Philip McCann

Introduction to the global automobile industry

The global automobile and truck industry has been transformed over the last three decades by three major phenomena. The first phenomenon is that of global restructuring amongst the major competitors mediated via a series of mergers, acquisitions and rationalizations. This process of restructuring amongst the US and European automobile industry was primarily in response to the rise of Asian manufacturers. The outcome of this industry restructuring is that the influence of nationally-oriented manufacturing firms has almost entirely waned, while the production of final outputs (Automotive News Europe 2006, 2007, Automotive World 2004, JAMA 2006a,b, PWC 2006a,b) as well as intermediate input supplies (Automotive News Europe 2006, Deloitte 2006, PWC 2006a, 2006b) has become ever more concentrated in the hands of genuinely global organizations.

The second major phenomenon within the automobile industry is that of changes in the overall geography of production. While the widespread entry of foreign direct investment (FDI) by Asian vehicle manufacturing producers into the US, European (Sadler 1994) and developing-country (Barnes and Kaplinsky 2000, Black 2001) markets are well documented (Automotive News Europe 2006, 2007, JAMA 2006a, 2006b), the actual logic of these geographical relocations remains little understood. Overall, Europe has exhibited a general southward (Lagendijk 1993) and eastward (Sadler and Swain 1994, Automotive News Europe 2006, PWC 2006b) drift in automotive industry in response to increasing European integration. Similarly, the United Sates has also exhibited a general southwards drift of the automobile industry (Klier and Rubinstein 2006a,b) away from the traditional centre of vehicle manufacturing around the Great Lakes region. At the most general level we can say that firms are investing in production sites which are not only relatively close to their markets, but also where supply–cost conditions and the infrastructure for market accessibility (Rubinstein 1986) are favourable.

The third major phenomenon within the auto industry concerns the way in which vehicle manufacturing is itself undertaken. Nowadays, vehicle manufacturing firms focus on maintaining lean production systems with minimum inventories held within the whole supply chain, thereby allowing for increases in the flexibility (Nishiguchi 1994) and productivity (Lieberman and Demeester 1999) of production. Since the mid-1980s these changes have been a direct response to the principles of Just-In-Time (JIT) manufacturing and Total Quality Management (TQM) developed by Japanese automobile producers (Schonberger 1981, 1996), which were demonstrated to provide for radically higher levels of final output product quality than existing Western mass-production techniques had previously allowed for. The general themes and techniques of these innovations are by now well known (Schonberger 1981, 1996, Best 1990) and involve high frequency shipments between supplier and buyer firms, and in Japan these production systems were characterized by extreme geographic localization. In the case of Western economies, however, the particular organizational and geographical implications of these supply-chain issues are still relatively under-researched. Incumbent firms in the countries where Japanese auto producers located began learning many of the new production techniques directly from the new immigrant firms (Ali *et al.* 1997), and part of this learning process also involved changes in the nature of knowledge-sharing (Sako *et al.* 1994). Indeed, trust between buyer and supplier firms is a much more important component of Japanese types of auto production than traditional Western systems (Sako and Helper 1994) and along with the increasing frequency of shipments, these more intensive buyer–supplier networks point towards a logic of increasing geographical localization within the industry even in Western countries. However, these new supply-chain systems and their management were grafted onto the existing historical, industrial (Carroll *et al.* 1996), organizational and spatial structure of the Western auto industry (Sadler 1994, Zirpoli and Caputo 2002). The resulting outcomes appear to be somewhat different in different contexts (Koste and Malhotra 2000). As such, it is not clear exactly how these changes impact on the economic geography of auto-production regions (Bordenave and Lung 1996). The reason is that the actual outcomes of these changes also depend on many other issues such as the purchasing autonomy of the plants (Kamp 2007), the history (Helper 1991), nature (Dussauge *et al.* 2004), and hierarchical structure (Belis-Bergouignan *et al.* 2000) of the buyer–supplier relationships, and the particular forms of modular (Collins *et al.* 1997, Friedriksson 2002) supply systems developed.

The relationships between globalization and regionalization (Schlie and Yip 2000) in the global automotive industry have therefore become very complex over the last two decades as these buyer–supplier systems have evolved. The aim of this paper is to provide a framework for analysing these issues within a geographical setting. Monteverde and Teece (1982) and Langlois and Robertson (1989) argue that transactions–costs explanations rather than asset stock explanations are crucial for understanding the long-term evolution of the auto industry, while Friedlaender *et al.* (1983) argue that any such explanations must analyse costs, technology and performance at the level of the firm rather than just the individual establishment. Therefore, in order to do this we adopt a transactions–costs taxonomy which allows us to explicitly examine the organizational and network environment within which buyer–supplier relations operate, and to identify the particular spatial arrangements appropriate under different organizational arrangements.

The paper is organized as follows. The next section provides a brief introduction to the different inventory and supply-chain management approaches dominant within the automotive industry at different stages in its evolution, and Section 3 outlines the spatial implications of these different approaches derived from various model frameworks. Section 4 presents a transactions–costs conceptual framework for analysing many features of the automotive manufacturing and supply-chain system. Finally, Section 5 discusses the spatial and policy implications for the automotive industry which arise from transactions–costs analysis.

Inventory management systems and the geography of vehicle manufacturing supply-chain systems

In traditional Western production techniques, input ordering was focused on ensuring the cheapest delivered price, while the organization of input supply deliveries was based on the principle of the economic order quantity (Love 1979), generally referred to as the EOQ. Basically, EOQ models focus on the relationship between fixed ordering costs and inventory costs that increase with order size. Goods are typically ordered in batches, and gradually sold off until the cycle is repeated. The order cost is incurred each time a batch is ordered. It is generally not associated with the quantity ordered, but with activities required to process the order, such as entering the purchase order, invoice processing, and incoming inspection. On the other hand, inventory holding cost includes interest, insurance, and storage costs that are directly associated with the inventory levels on hand. Thus, there is a trade-off between total ordering cost and inventory holding cost. The EOQ model therefore determines the shipment size and shipment frequency which minimizes the sum of order costs and inventory holding costs. Under this regime, the location of the supplier with respect to the assembly firm is largely irrelevant, as long as the delivered prices of inputs are minimized. Detailed explanations of these EOQ formulae set in the explicitly spatial setting of delivered prices are given in McCann (1998).

A basic problem with the EOQ system is that the management of inventories can lead to many types of cost increases (Schonberger 1981, 1996, Best 1990). Overproduction generates waste because it creates unnecessary stock on hand. Different processing times over successive stages cause a backlog to build up, and batch production leads to even more waste due to rigidity in die changes. In contrast, the Just-In-Time (JIT) delivery system, pioneered by the Toyota Motor Company in Japan and dubbed the 'kanban' (sign plates) system, eliminates back-up inventory in every stage. By delivering parts only when they are needed, and only in the precise amount needed, defects are revealed and the need for warehousing space and associated costs are reduced. Before the early 1980s, $600–$800 of capital was tied up in per car inventory in the US, compared with only $75–$150 in

Japan. Consequently, the average Japanese assembly plant was 600,000 ft^2 smaller than its American counterpart.

The JIT system is designed to expose all inventory-related problems instead of concealing them. Each station replenishes only the amount that has been taken, and treats the next station down the line as a customer. In this way, JIT simulates in-house sourcing while avoiding the lack of tension that may hamper work morale and efficiency. However, the transplantation of JIT lean manufacturing systems to Western industry was not without problems. The Japanese tradition of tight linkages is not just based simply on trust, but rather on the sharing of mutual benefits such as the joint analysis of costs, a fair determination of prices, and the sharing of profits (Aoki 1988). Under perfect JIT, all set-up, ordering, and holding costs are eliminated for all parties involved (Nishiguchi 1994). In Western firms, however, the burden of ordering activity and inventory management was often passed onto suppliers and this compromised their profits. Some critics argued that JIT delivery forced suppliers to make their products and store them, delivering to the assembly plants only upon demand (Trevor and Christie 1988). There were also the major obstacles to avoiding increased costs, such as the increased transport costs due to geographical dispersion, the old habit of pursuing the maximum possible output, and adversarial relationships between assemblers and suppliers. Notwithstanding these major challenges, however, since the mid-1980s, the widespread adoption of JIT principles had led to dramatic reductions in inventory levels, and associated increases in the rates of inventory turnover, not only in much of Western industry, but in particular, in the vehicle manufacturing industry (Schonberger 1996).

The implications of these changes from EOQ to JIT are that while the decisions of the vehicle manufacturers, often termed OEMs (original equipment manufacturers), are still determined primarily by cost and profitability considerations, as has always been the case, in the modern business environment of JIT and TQM, OEM profitability issues are interrelated with the performance of the whole supply chain in a manner which was not previously so prior to the mid-1980s, except for the case of Japanese firms. The reason for this is that in order for such high-frequency shipments to be viable, increasing proximity is required between the OEM assembly firm and its suppliers (McCann 1998). As such, the performance of the manufacturing supply chain nowadays depends critically on the spatial structure and organization of the whole system of suppliers to an extent which was simply not so prior to the late 1980s, except once again for the case of the Japanese manufacturers. The result, therefore, is that the fundamental changes in production techniques and philosophy which have emerged in the global automobile industry over the last two decades have also radically changed the geography of the relationships between vehicle assembly firms and their suppliers.

The first work to coherently document the spatial impacts of JIT production systems within the vehicle manufacturing industry was undertaken by Sheard (1983). The very high degree of spatial concentration amongst Japanese buyer–supplier systems, in which the degree of proximity between the supplier and the assembler also increases with the tier rank of the supplier, provided a marked contrast with the spatial organization of supply systems amongst Western vehicle manufacturers. The spatial structure of the Western automotive industry was highly diverse and very spatially dispersed. Traditional Western supply chains tended to exhibit complex global webs of supply links, with little obvious observable spatial logic to them (Bloomfield 1981). The reason for this is that under the traditional logic of Western inventory and supply-chain management, input supply choices depended primarily on ensuring the cheapest delivered prices, irrespective of location. On the other hand, the highly rationalized Japanese JIT supply chains generally exhibited far fewer suppliers than Western supply chains, of which the vast majority of the suppliers would be located within close proximity of the assembly plant. The reason for this spatial structure was that the logic of the JIT systems was not primarily based on ensuring the cheapest delivered price, but rather on ensuring frequent and timely flows of inputs to the plant.

The transition in Western production and supply systems to more of a JIT type of model therefore has had major cost implications not only for the choice of production processes within the OEM establishments, but also for the geographical organization of the input supply chains, and by implication, the location and relocation decisions of the assembly firms themselves. The reason is that attempting to implement JIT principles within the existing automotive supply-chain structure implies an attempt to graft a different geography of production, based on extreme spatial concentration, onto an existing widely-distributed spatial structure. By 1982, Ford's Dearborn engine plant supplied the Wayne assembly plant on a daily basis. Chrysler's Kokomo plant supplied the Belvidere facility with transaxles daily by truck, instead of every four days by rail. Chevrolet's Morraine assembly plant even stipulated that suppliers should locate in town. Haimson (1992) found that supplier–assembler proximity grew substantially during the 1980s; assemblers with smaller inventories and higher productivity, in particular, became closer to supplier plants. As these changes have become increasingly widespread and embedded in the wider vehicle manufacturing industry, the geography of buyers and suppliers within the Western automotive industry has become increasingly dominated by spatial proximity (Klier 1998, Klier and McMillan 2005), and this is true for older as well as the newer plants, irrespective of nationality (Klier et al. 2004). The need to maintain proximity between the assembly firm and its suppliers is now the single most important consideration for supply systems in the US (Kim 2005), Europe (Larsson 2002), and even in developing countries (Gulyani 2001, Lecler 2002).

On the other hand, the enormous challenges associated with having to graft the logic of a spatially-concentrated geography of production onto an inherited supply system which is spatially diffuse, has led to the emergence of something of a hybrid geography of production amongst the Western automotive industry, which is a mixture of the older spatially-diffuse supply system and the newer spatially-concentrated logic (Sadler and Swain 1994). While a tendency towards increasing spatial concentration is widely observed in the Western automotive industry, it is still nowhere nearly as spatially concentrated as the Japanese systems within Japan. The reason is that the inherited diffuse geography of the Western automotive supply system means that the Western firms cannot operate all input delivery systems in the form of pure JIT. As such, Western firms are still required to trade off the cost advantages associated with high-frequency JIT shipments with less frequent bulk deliveries associated with the EOQ logic. This trade-off poses both significant cost challenges, and also significant location choice challenges, to the automotive firms. Analysing these trade-offs is the issue to which we now turn.

Modelling the interaction between firm location behaviour and JIT supply chains

The theoretical implications of the previous sections imply that we cannot begin to understand the location and relocation behaviour of the OEM automobile assembly firms without understanding of the simultaneous choices of production techniques, locational opportunities and supply-chain arrangements which they nowadays face. Yet, except for the work of a very few authors (McCann 1993, 1998, Lovell 2003, Harrigan and Venables 2006, Kim 2007) there has still been almost no theoretical work undertaken regarding the location behaviour of OEM vehicle assembly firms, when the supply-chain cost considerations are themselves also an explicit location decision-making criterion. The problem is that traditional location theory focuses on the role played by transportation costs in determining location behaviour. In this approach, the optimum location of a firm is generally deemed to depend primarily on transport costs, regardless of output level. However, once considerations of input delivery costs and the frequency of input delivery shipments become a major consideration, then it is necessary to adopt a much broader concept of spatial costs, which also incorporates inventory holding costs (McCann 1993, 1998). This approach provides for a much richer and more complex analysis of the interaction between location behaviour and supply-chain issues. Although the mathematics of these models are outside of the scope of this paper, a few points are worth highlighting regarding some of their major analytical conclusions.

First, high value-adding OEM assembly firms are found to be relatively more market-oriented in terms of their location as the greater frequency of output shipments associated with the higher value-added requires increased spatial proximity (McCann 1998). Similarly, from the perspective of supplier firms, if an increase in profits due to the reduced output transport markup more than offsets the loss caused by higher land and wage costs close to the OEM, the suppliers will also move towards the assembler (Kim 2007). This increased clustering behaviour can be shown to be optimal in terms of profit generation by the supplier firms as the required shipment frequencies associated with JIT practices increase. As such, supplier firms will also tend to congregate in more or less the same location close to the OEM, even though they have no direct relationships among themselves, and this is perfectly consistent with what is predicted by location theory when the optimal location problem is set within a hierarchical supply-chain structure (McCann 1995). This phenomenon has already been empirically observed in the European automotive sector (Larsson 2002, Kamp 2007), and provides a pure profit rationale for increased clustering as shipment frequencies are increased.

Second, if on the other hand, the cost advantages associated with lower local labour prices outweigh the perceived quality advantages associated with spatial concentration, then the economic geography of the system will still remain somewhat more dispersed (Kim 2007). This trade-off largely accounts for the fact that both the US and European automotive production systems have become more spatially concentrated than previously, although still remaining much less so than their counterparts in Asia, while at the same time, the industry as a whole is increasingly moving away from its traditional heartlands to lower wage regions. There will be regional winners and regional losers from this process of spatial reorganization.

Third, in addition to these pure profit-based location optimization considerations, there are also other buyer–supplier considerations regarding knowledge spillovers, such as information-sharing and the development of trust relations, all of which are likely to be fostered by proximity. If geographical proximity is indeed associated with such knowledge spillovers and trust relations, then this would provide an additional argument as to why such clustering is advantageous for the auto industry. Note, however, that the arguments above suggest that these new production systems imply increasing advantages associated with clustering even without such knowledge exchanges. Therefore, if such knowledge exchanges are also increasingly fostered, then the clustering logic will be further reinforced. In order to discuss these issues we need to employ a framework which allows us to integrate the locational and organizational aspects of buyer–supplier relations with knowledge transfer issues. The framework we adopt is the transactions–costs taxonomy of hierarchies and clusters (Gordon and McCann 2000) which has subsequently been extended to include innovation and cluster evolution (Iammarino and McCann 2006). The next section briefly discusses this taxonomy and we then apply this approach to the automotive sector. More detailed discussions of this taxonomy can be found in McCann and Sheppard (2003), McCann and Shefer (2004) and Iammarino and McCann (2006).

A taxonomy of cluster types and application to the automotive industry

Adopting the transactions–costs framework approach, we can see from the literature that there are three broad typologies of agglomerations and industrial clusters, defined in terms of the features they exhibit (Gordon and McCann 2000). These are the pure agglomeration, the industrial complex, and the social network. The key feature which distinguishes each of these different ideal types of spatial industrial cluster, is the nature of the relations between the firms within the cluster. The characteristics of each of the cluster types are listed in Table 1, and as we see, the three ideal types of clusters are all quite different.

First, in the model of pure agglomeration, knowledge inter-firm relations are inherently transient, firms are essentially atomistic, and there is no loyalty between firms. There are no free riders, access to the cluster is open, and the external benefits of clustering are the tacit informal knowledge spillovers which accrue to all local firms simply by reason of their local presence. Consequently it is the growth in the local real estate rents which is the indicator of the cluster's performance, and this type of clustering only exists in individual cities.

The second model, the industrial complex model, is characterized primarily by long-term stable and predictable relations between the firms in the cluster. Component firms within the spatial grouping each undertake significant long-term investments, particularly in terms of physical capital and local real estate, in order to become part of the grouping. Access to the group is therefore severely restricted both by high entry and exit costs, and the rationale for spatial clustering in these types of industries is that proximity is required primarily in order to minimize inter-firm transport transactions–costs. Neither rental

Table 1. Industrial clusters.

Characteristics	Pure agglomeration	Industrial complex	Social network
Firm size	Atomistic	Some firms are large	Variable
Characteristics of relations	Non-identifiable, fragmented, unstable	Identifiable, stable trading	Trust, loyalty, joint lobbying, joint ventures, non-opportunistic
Membership	Open	Closed	Partially open
Access to cluster	Rental payments, location necessary	Internal investment, location necessary	History, experience, location necessary but not sufficient
Space outcomes	Rent appreciation	No effect on rents	Partial rental capitalisation
Notion of space	Urban	Local but not urban	Local but not urban
Example of cluster	Competitive urban economy	Steel or chemicals production complex	New industrial areas
Analytical approaches	Models of pure agglomeration	Location production theory, input–output analysis	Social network theory (Granovetter)

appreciation nor tacit knowledge spillovers are major features of the cluster. The key issue here is that the industrial structure within the complex exhibits primarily oligopolistic characteristics, and the notion of space in the complex model is local, but not necessarily urban.

The third type of spatial industrial cluster is the social network model. This model is predicated on the view that mutual trust relations between key decision-making agents in different organizations mean that inter-firm cooperative relations may differ significantly from the organizational boundaries associated with individual firms, and that these relations may be continually reconstituted. The social network model is essentially aspatial, but from the point of view of geography, it can be argued that spatial proximity will tend to foster such trust relations, thereby leading to a local business environment of confidence, risk-taking and cooperation.

These three generic cluster types based on a transactions–costs framework appear rather static. However, each of these three cluster types can also be shown to exhibit direct analogues in terms of generic innovation types (Iammarino and McCann 2006), such that the sources of innovation and the mode of cluster emergence are different in each case. Moreover, it is perfectly possible for a particular geographical cluster to evolve over time both in terms of its transactions–costs structure and also its innovation processes. In reality, however, at a particular point in time, all spatial concentrations of economic activity will exhibit at least one of these cluster types, and the case of large cities will exhibit aspects of all three models (see Bailey *et al.* in this special issue on the West Midlands Auto cluster). Analytically, the most important point is to determine which mode of transactions–costs relations and innovation processes is dominant in the particular geographical–organizational structure.

The emerging geographical–organizational logic of the automotive industry and policy implications

The traditional organizational structure which emerged in the automotive sectors of the US and Europe in the first half of the twentieth century was based primarily on the industrial complex model, whereby oligopolistic producers undertook major long-term location-specific investments, and the relations between the final assemblers and their top-level supplier firms were long-term, predictable, stable and primarily local regional. On the other hand, the relationships between these higher-level firms and the lower-level supplier firms were very much arm's length, competitive, short-term contracting relations typical of the pure agglomeration model in densely populated regions such as Detroit, Birmingham and Turin. In contrast, the structure of the Japanese automotive industry which emerged in the second half of the twentieth century placed much more emphasis on loyalty. Once again, the relations between the top-level assemblers and their suppliers were primarily on the industrial complex model, but the relations between these firms and the lower-level suppliers was based much more on mutual trust relations, of the type evident in social network structures (Banerji and Sambharya 1998).

As the production approaches of the Japanese auto manufacturers became progressively grafted on to the existing systems of the Western automotive industry, there has emerged something of a hybrid organizational–geographical structure which is the result of a partial convergence of the two systems. Many Western firms have tried to develop more long-term relations with lower-level supplier firms than had previously been typical, in order to promote long-term innovation and quality improvements.

European firms have therefore progressively adopted the types of organizational–geographical structures reminiscent of the Japanese firms (Pavlinek and Janak 2007). At the same time, Japanese firms locating in the US and Europe have aimed to develop more of a network approach to their supply chains. In order to do this, one of their typical responses has been to bring supplier firms with them, which then locate in close proximity to the assembler (Banerji and Sambharya 1996). In addition, a second typical response has been to move away from the core of the traditional automobile-producing urban regions in order to set up new supplier–buyer relations based more on the social network frameworks that they operate in their home regions. Such firms have far fewer suppliers than traditional Western systems exhibited and many of these supplier firms are encouraged to relocate close to the new production locations of the assemblers. As we have seen, in the case of the US this has entailed a southwards drift from the mid-west (Klier 1998, Klier et al. 2004, Klier and McMillan 2005, Klier and Rubinstein 2006a,b). Yet, the difficulties of grafting the Japanese business model onto the Western model ensure that Japanese overseas subsidiaries must allow for a greater level of arm's length contracting than their parent organizations typically allow for, although similar changes along these lines are now increasingly evident even within Japan itself (Ahmadjian and Lincoln 2001, Schaede 2007).

In terms of innovation and survival, geographically clustered systems have always been advantageous in automotive production (Klepper 2002, Boschma and Wenting 2007), and R&D activities in the auto industry appear to be becoming even more spatially concentrated as product life-cycles get shorter (Miller 1994). As such, the logic of both the transactions–costs considerations and knowledge spillover considerations appear to point in the same direction, namely towards the increasing spatial concentration of the higher value-added activities of the automotive industry. Such trends may have a number of consequences for policy approaches in terms of training and education, and science and technology policy. This observation is not inconsistent with the argument that globalization is also leading to greater spatial dispersion, because such dispersion processes will tend to be dominated by lower value-adding activities whereas the core locations will progressively move towards higher value-adding activities (McCann 2008).

A final policy-related point to mention is that the increasing spatial concentration of buyer–supplier firms in the automotive sector will also tend to increase the value of regional multipliers. Moreover, this argument can be shown to apply not only to the automotive sector, but to any high value-adding industry sector which adopts JIT-type thinking in the management of its supply chains (McCann and Fingleton 1996). The implication here is that the opposing positive and negative impacts on the regional winners and losers will therefore be greatly amplified from what would previously have been the case. As such, the regions which benefit from the immigration of these integrated supply-chain networks will tend to maintain their advantageous position in this industry over a long period, as such clustered systems will be much less sensitive than standalone facilities to factor price variations in other locations. For these 'winner' regions, this is obviously a positive development. On the other hand, however, because of the long-term nature of the contracting relations in these highly-integrated local supply-chain systems, the possibilities for other local firms to gain access to these local clusters may actually be much more limited than under the traditional agglomeration models (Larsson 2002). On the downside, for regions which lose these supply-chain systems, as has been the case over the last two decades for many areas of the US, UK and Australia, the prospects for redeveloping such systems via policy initiatives look very limited indeed. Some of the difficulties and challenges faced in such situations are teased out by contributions in this special issue.

References

Ahmadjian, C.L. and Lincoln, J.R., 2001. Keiretsu, governance and learning: case studies in change from the Japanese automotive industry. *Organization science*, 12 (6), 683–701.
Ali, F., Smith, G., and Saker, J., 1997. Developing buyer–supplier relationships in automobile industry. *European journal of purchasing and supply management*, 3 (1), 33–42.
Aoki, M., 1988. *Information incentives and bargaining in the Japanese economy*. Cambridge: Cambridge University Press.
Automotive News Europe, 2006. Global market data book [online]. Available from: www.autonewseurope.com
Automotive News Europe, April 2007. Market data: North America production. Crain Communications Inc. [online]. Available from www.autonewseurope.com/2007marketdata
Automotive World, 2004. *The world's truck manufacturers*. 8th ed. [online]. London: Synthesis Media. Available from: www.awresearcher.com
Banerji, K. and Sambharya, R.B., 1996. Vertical keiretsu and international market entry: the case of the Japanese automobile ancillary industry. *Journal of international business studies*, 27 (1), 89–113.
Banerji, K. and Sambharya, R.B., 1998. Effect of network organization on alliance formation: a study of the Japanese automobile ancillary industry. *Journal of international management*, 4 (1), 41–57.
Barnes, J. and Kaplinsky, R., 2000. Globalization and the death of the local firm? The automobile components sector in South Africa. *Regional studies*, 34 (9), 797–812.
Belis-Bergouignan, M-C., Bordenave, G., and Lung, Y., 2000. Global strategies in the automobile industry. *Regional studies*, 34 (1), 41–53.
Best, M., 1990. *The new competition: institutions of industrial restructuring*. Cambridge: Polity Press.
Black, A., 2001. Globalization and restructuring in the South African automotive industry. *Journal of international development*, 13, 779–796.
Bloomfield, G.T., 1981. The changing spatial organisation of multinational corporations in the world automotive industry. *In*: F.E.I. Hamilton and G.R. Linge, eds. *Spatial analysis, industry and industrial environment vol. II: international industrial systems*. Chichester: John Wiley.
Bordenave, G. and Lung, Y., 1996. New configurations in the European automobile industry. *European urban and regional studies*, 3, 305–321.
Boschma, R.A. and Wenting, R., 2007. The spatial evolution of the British automobile industry: does location matter. *Industrial and corporate change*, 16 (2), 213–238.
Carroll, G.R., Bigelow, L.S., Seidel, M-D.L., and Tsai, L.B., 1996. The fates of De Novo and De Alio producers in the American auto industry 1885–1981. *Strategic management journal*, 17, 117–137.
Collins, R., Bechler, K., and Pires, S., 1997. Outsourcing in the automotive industry: from JIT to modular consortia. *European management journal*, 15 (5), 498–508.
Deloitte Consulting LLP, 2006. *The road ahead 2006*. Automotive suppliers information technology survey.
Dussauge, P., Garrette, B., and Mitchell, W., 2004. Asymmetric performance: the market share impact of scale and link alliances in the global auto industry. *Strategic management journal*, 25, 701–711.
Friedlaender, A.F., Winston, C., and Wang, K., 1983. Costs, technology and productivity in the US automobile industry. *Bell journal of economics*, 14 (1), 1–20.
Friedriksson, P., 2002. Modular assembly in the car industry – an analysis of organizational forms' influence on performance. *European journal of purchasing and supply management*, 8, 221–233.
Gordon, I.R. and McCann, P., 2000. Industrial clusters: complexes, agglomeration and/or social networks? *Urban studies*, 37 (3), 513–532.
Gulyani, S., 2001. Effects of poor transportation on lean production and industrial clustering: evidence from the Indian auto industry. *World development*, 29 (7), 1157–1177.

Haimson, J., 1992. *Just-In-Time and vertical agglomerations.* PhD dissertation. Yale University, New Haven.
Harrigan, J. and Venables, A.J., 2006. Timeliness and agglomeration. *Journal of urban economics*, 59, 300–316.
Helper, S., 1991. Strategy and irreversibility in supplier relations. *Business history review*, 65 (4), 781–824.
Iammarino, S. and McCann, P., 2006. The structure and evolution of industrial clusters: transactions, technology and knowledge spillovers. *Research policy*, 35, 1018–1036.
JAMA, 2006a. New plants, new jobs, new vehicles, Japanese automakers in America [online]. Japan Automobile Manufacturers Association Inc. Available from: www.jama.org
JAMA, 2006b. The motor industry of Japan [online]. Japan Automobile Manufacturers Association Inc. Available from: www.jama.org
Kamp, B., 2007. *Location behaviour and relationship stability in international business networks.* London: Routledge.
Kim, H.Y., 2005. The locational and functional behavior of US autoparts suppliers. *Small business economics*, 24, 79–95.
Kim, H.Y., 2007. Modeling Just-In-Time manufacturing in a vertically-integrated industry. *In*: J. Johansson, ed. *Entrepreneurship and development: local processes and global patterns, research reports 2007:01.* Trollhättan, Sweden: University West.
Klepper, S., 2002. The capability of new firms and the evolution of the US automobile industry. *Industrial and corporate change*, 11 (4), 645–666.
Klier, T., 1998. *Geographic concentration in US manufacturing: evidence from the US auto supplier industry.* Federal Reserve Bank of Chicago Working Paper 1998–17, Chicago.
Klier, T. and McMillan, D.P., 2005. *Clustering of auto supplier plants in the US: a GMM spatial logit for large samples.* Federal Reserve Bank of Chicago Working Paper 2005–18, Chicago.
Klier, T. and Rubinstein, J.M., 2006a. *The US auto supplier industry in transition.* Federal Reserve Bank of Chicago essays on issues no. 226, May, Chicago.
Klier, T. and Rubinstein, J.M., 2006b. *The US auto supplier industry in transition: the new geography of auto production.* Federal Reserve Bank of Chicago essays on issues no. 229b, August, Chicago.
Klier, T., Ma, P., and McMillan, D.P., 2004. *Comparing location decisions of domestic and foreign auto supplier plants.* Federal Reserve Bank of Chicago Working Paper 2004–27, Chicago.
Koste, L.L. and Malhotra, M.K., 2000. Trade-offs among the elements of flexibility: a comparison from the automotive industry. *Omega*, 28, 693–710.
Lagendijk, A., 1993. The internationalisation of the Spanish automobile industry and its regional impact. *Tinbergen Institute Research Series 59*, Amsterdam.
Langlois, R.N. and Robertson, P.L., 1989. Explaining vertical integration: lessons from the American automobile industry. *Journal of economic history*, 49 (2), 361–375.
Larsson, A., 2002. The development and regional significance of the automotive industry: supplier parks in Western Europe. *International journal of urban and regional research*, 26 (4), 767–784.
Lecler, Y., 2002. The cluster role in the development of the Thai car industry. *International journal of urban and regional research*, 26 (4), 799–814.
Lieberman, M.B. and Demeester, L., 1999. Inventory reduction and productivity growth: linkages in the Japanese automotive industry. *Management science*, 45 (4), 466–485.
Love, S., 1979. *Inventory control.* New York: McGraw-Hill.
Lovell, M.C., 2003. Optimal lot size, inventories, prices and JIT under monopolistic competition. *International journal of production economics*, 81, 59–66.
McCann, P., 1993. The logistics-cost location-production problem. *Journal of regional science*, 33 (4), 503–516.
McCann, P., 1995. Rethinking the economics of location and agglomeration. *Urban studies*, 32 (3), 563–577.
McCann, P., 1998. *The economics of industrial location: a logistics-costs approach.* Heidelberg: Springer.
McCann, P., 2008. Globalization and economic geography: the world is curved, not flat. *Cambridge journal of regions, economy and society*, forthcoming.
McCann, P. and Fingleton, B., 1996. The regional agglomeration impact of Just-In-Time input linkages: evidence from the Scottish electronics industry. *Scottish journal of political economy*, 43 (5), 493–518.

McCann, P. and Shefer, D., 2004. Location, agglomeration and infrastructure. *Papers in regional science*, 83 (1), 177–196.
McCann, P. and Sheppard, S.C., 2003. The rise, fall and rise again of industrial location theory. *Regional studies*, 37, 6–7, 649–663.
Miller, R., 1994. Global R&D Networks and large scale innovations: the case of the automobile industry. *Research policy*, 23, 27–46.
Monteverde, K. and Teece, D.J., 1982. Supplier switching costs and vertical integration in the automobile industry. *Bell journal of economics*, 13 (1), 206–213.
Nishiguchi, T., 1994. *Strategic industrial sourcing: the Japanese advantage*. Oxford: Oxford University Press.
Pavlinek, P. and Janak, L., 2007. Regional restructuring of the Skoda auto supplier network in the Czech Republic. *European urban and regional studies*, 14 (2), 133–155.
PWC, 2006a. *Global automotive financial review: an overview of industry data. Trends and financial reporting practices* [online]. Price Waterhouse Coopers. Available from: www.pwc.com/auto
PWC, 2006b. *The automotive and general manufacturing industry* [online]. Price Waterhouse Coopers. Available from: www.pwc.com/auto
Rubinstein, J.M., 1986. The changing distribution of the American automobile industry. *Geographical review*, 76 (3), 288–300.
Sadler, D., 1994. The geographies of just-in-time: Japanese investment and the automotive components industry in Western Europe. *Economic geography*, 70 (1), 41–59.
Sadler, D. and Swain, A., 1994. State and market in Eastern Europe: regional development and workplace implications of foreign direct investment in the automobile industry in Hungary. *Transactions of the Institute of British Geographers*, 19 (4), 387–403.
Sako, M. and Helper, S.R., 1994. Determinants of trust in supplier relations: evidence from the automotive industry in Japan and the United States. *Journal of economic behavior and organization*, 34 (3), 387–417.
Sako, M., Lamming, R., and Helper, S.R., 1994. Supplier relations in the UK car industry: good news – bad news. *European journal of purchasing and supply management*, 1 (4), 237–248.
Schaede, U., 2007. Globalization and the Japanese subcontractor system. *In*: D. Bailey, D. Coffey and P. Tomlinson, eds. *Crisis or recovery in Japan: state and industrial economy*. Cheltenham: Edward Elgar.
Sheard, P., 1983. Auto-production systems in Japan: organisational and locational features. *Australian geographical studies*, 21 (1), 49–68.
Schlie, E. and Yip, G., 2000. Regional follows global: strategy mixes in the world automotive industry. *European management journal*, 18 (4), 343–354.
Schonberger, R.J., 1981. *Japanese manufacturing techniques: nine hidden lessons in simplicity*. New York: Free Press.
Schonberger, R.J., 1996. *World class manufacturing: the next decade*. New York: Free Press.
Trevor, M. and Christie, I., 1988. *Manufacturers and suppliers in Britain and Japan*. London: Policy Studies Institute.
Zirpoli, F. and Caputo, M., 2002. The nature of buyer–supplier relationships in co-design activities: the Italian auto industry case. *International journal of operations and production management*, 22 (12), 1389–1410.

Rover and out? Globalisation, the West Midlands auto cluster, and the end of MG Rover

David Bailey, Seiji Kobayashi, and Stewart MacNeill

Introduction

The structural changes and shifts unfolding in the auto industry have been vividly illustrated through recent events in the West Midlands. These have included the collapse of MG Rover in 2005 and closures of Jaguar's Brown's Lane plant in Coventry and Peugeot's Ryton plant. Add in continuing uncertainty over the future of the Jaguar and Land Rover plants given (at the time of writing) Ford's attempt to sell off the brands owing to ongoing losses at Jaguar, and fears over a 'meltdown' of assembly activity in the region seem justified. These events have also highlighted the difficulties involved in supporting and developing the auto 'cluster' in the region.

This paper explores the background to the MG Rover (MGR) collapse and sets the scene for this special issue. In the second section it outlines the form of the auto cluster in the West Midlands, putting this into broader context by examining structural changes in the industry. These include: greater pressure on firms to recover costs when technological change has been intensifying, driving up the costs of new model development; increasingly global sourcing; and the growth of assembly operations in lower-cost locations in South and Eastern Europe. All of these make maintaining the West Midlands cluster both more necessary and yet also more difficult for policy-makers.

The paper then looks a 'what went wrong' at MGR, agreeing with the analysis of Holweg and Oliver (2005) which stressed long-term problems, the 'cycle of doom' at the firm and its inability to recover costs for new model development. Given this position, BMW's sale of the firm in 2000 left MGR in an unsustainable position, with only a very limited time horizon in which to find an investment partner. Indeed, by 2002/2003 it was clear that the firm was running out of time. The paper goes further, however, and examines wider environmental factors contributing to the demise of MGR, in particular government policy mistakes over the years, including a misguided 'national champions' approach involving forced mergers in the 1950s and 1960s, a failure to integrate activities under nationalisation in the 1970s, a mistaken privatisation to British Aerospace in the 1980s, and a clear downside of competition policy which resulted in the sale to an inappropriate owner in BMW in the 1990s. Add in the considerable volatility of sterling in recent years, and the firm's eventual demise came as no surprise to many analysts.

The West Midlands auto 'cluster' in a restructuring global industry
Shifts in the global auto industry

In the course of its history the auto industry has arguably undergone radical changes described as three 'revolutions' by Womack *et al.* (1990), the first two being the introduction of assembly line production by Ford and so-called 'lean production' by Toyota.[1] In the past four decades, further radical changes have affected the entire value chain, from manufacturers and suppliers to service providers and dealers (Chanaron 2004, MacNeill and Chanaron 2005)[2] and, since the mid-1990s, a 'third revolution' has focused on change through flexibility, with consequent effects on product creation, production and life cycle.

The main drivers of this development are the pressures of cost recovery which, together with intense competition, has led car-makers to seek economies of scale by increasing production volumes, standardising platforms and components and outsourcing 'non-core' activities. In addition, increasing regulatory pressures and consumer demands for quality and capability have led to the development of new technologies for more efficient powertrains, reduced weight, hybrid/electric vehicles and bio-fuels, as well as high-value electrical, electronic and communications componentry. Finally, market pressures have led to the growth of new segments, such as minivans or small 'city' cars, and the need to offer increasing numbers of radical variations whilst still maintaining common 'under-skin' platforms.

One result of these developments is too much overall assembly capacity, with around 25% under-utilisation in Western Europe and more than 30% in the developing markets of Central and Eastern Europe. Thus the weakest firms are under intense pressure, and although MGR was the first to go under others have also struggled. For example, Fiat was in such difficulties that GM paid $1.5 billion in a divorce settlement in 2005 (although new model launches have since helped the company). More recently Peugeot–Citröen has seen disappointing sales and declining profits, such that in late 2007 the company announced

8000 job cuts across Europe. A second outcome has been the rising costs of new model development. In contrast with what is expected under the 'life cycle' model of industry development, the 'crisis of cost recovery' facing firms has intensified over time. In today's prices, the cost of getting a genuinely new model to market lies somewhere between £400 million and £1 billion. As a result, large-scale production over different models and brands using a platform-sharing approach is vital to generate the cash for future model development, yet at the same time carries with it the risk of diluting brand image, as evidenced by Jaguar's problems with the X-type model, which shared the same platform with the Ford Mondeo and Mazda 6.[3]

Simultaneously, major manufacturers are developing assembly operations in low-cost locations in emerging markets such as Central/Eastern Europe, or the southern states of the US. Indeed, as well as declining profitability, a key factor in the recent decision by Peugeot–Citroën to close its Ryton plant near Coventry with 2300 immediate job losses was the opening of a new plant in Slovakia, where labour costs are around one quarter those in Britain. Once the decision was taken to expand capacity in Eastern Europe, Ryton was particularly exposed for a number of reasons. Firstly, it was a small plant assembling only the Peugeot 206 from parts brought in from France, and secondly cutting each job in France would have been up to three times as expensive (Bailey and Cowling 2006). The UK's flexible labour markets make it as easy to destroy jobs as to create them and the lack of significant domestically-owned manufacturing means that activities in Britain are exposed when transnationals look to cut auto assembly capacity.

Restructuring at a local level

With the collapse of MG Rover, and the closure of the Ryton plant, volume assembly in the region has in effect ended. Remaining activity is high-value luxury branded niche production under the current control of Ford, notably Land Rover and Jaguar in Birmingham/Solihull, with smaller-scale production by a newly independent Aston Martin at Gaydon and at a range of other less-known but still significant producers such as LDV Vans (commercial vehicles), Morgan and Westfield (sports cars) and Carbodies (taxis). However, much of the 'old' high-volume supply matrix still remains with manufacturing concentrated in the main conurbations.

With losses of over $12 billion in 2006, Ford announced in 2007 its intention to sell Jaguar and Land Rover, prompting fears about further capacity cuts and the future of 17,000 Jaguar and Land Rover jobs if a private equity firm acquires them (although at the time of writing, the Indian firm Tata seems the most likely buyer). Meanwhile, Nanjing Auto has plans to re-start small-scale MG sports car assembly at Longbridge in late 2007 with complete 'knock-down' kits shipped in from China (although eventual production volumes are uncertain). Longer term there is much scepticism over Nanjing's ability to develop new models and their commitment to production in the West Midlands, especially given plans to produce and develop models in Oklahoma. However, the takeover in late 2007 of Nanjing by the larger state-owned Chinese firm Shanghai may offer more hope in this regard, given Shanghai's much larger size and its commitment to R&D activities in the region through its joint venture with Ricardo.

Amongst first-tier suppliers there has also been a process of concentration and specialisation around global players, a process accelerated by recent takeover activity. In the West Midlands this leaves first-tier firms such as GKN (drivelines), Dana (axles), Bosch (lighting), Delphi (engine management), Johnson Controls (air conditioning and heating), Faurecia (seating), Lear (seating and interiors), Denso (starters and alternators), TRW (steering, and safety systems), Rockwell (chassis,) and Siemens–VDO (instrumentation). Significant second-tier suppliers include Sarginsons Precision Components and Zeus (aluminium castings), Brandaur (pressings), Radshape (sheet metal forming) and Premier Stampings (die forgings) amongst many others.

The cluster is underpinned by research, consultancy and support organisations including Ricardo (engine and drivetrain), Prodrive (performance engineering and motor sport) MIRA (research development and testing centre), the Warwick Manufacturing Group, and the Society of Motor Manufacturers and Traders (SMMT) Industry Forum. The region also benefited from the decision by Ford in 2006 to invest £1 billion in research and development into cleaner technology and hybrid engines, with significant funding coming to Ford's development centres at Gaydon and Whitley, although there are question marks as to the future if Ford sells Jaguar and Land Rover. Finally, a joint R&D venture ('Ricardo 2010') between Ricardo and Shanghai continues to develop the model initially envisaged as the replacement for the Rover 45, reflecting the ongoing R&D strengths of the region's auto cluster despite the MGR collapse. Strengths also remain in engine production and research, as evidenced by the number of patents in this area and BMW's investment in its Hams Hall engine plant near Birmingham.

Not surprisingly, despite recent plant closures, the West Midlands is still seen as the core of the British automotive industry with some 53,000 jobs (ONS 2005) under the NACE (EU) industry classification code for motor vehicle and component manufacture, (approximately 30% of the UK total, and around 6% of regional GVA (EMCC 2004). Local activity includes the manufacture of electrical equipment, around half of UK tyre production and some 20% of jobs in processing and shaping glass (e.g. windscreens) as well as retail sales and the distribution of spares and parts (often more profitable than assembly itself) (DTI 2001). The metal, plastics and rubber products clusters also support the industry and a significant proportion of jobs in the wider manufacturing sector are also automotive-related. The industry has also been a major focus for inward investment over the last decade, with nearly 40% of all jobs created by FDI being in auto or auto-related industries (RTF 2000).

However, recent assembly plant closures and job losses in the components industry have had a major impact. Indeed, from 1998 from 2005 employment in the region under NACE Code 34 declined by 32% compared with a 23% decline in Great Britain as a whole (ABI 2005).[4] In a sense every maturing economy witnesses a shift from manufacturing to services and therein a process of natural 'de-industrialisation', with a fall in manufacturing's share in total employment (Rowthorn and Wells 1987). However, using Rowthorn and Wells' (1987) classification, we can differentiate between 'positive' and 'negative' variants of de-industrialisation. The 'positive' type is associated with the 'normal' process of industrial dynamism in a 'developed' economy, where rapid manufacturing productivity growth releases workers who are absorbed by an expanding service sector. Major auto manufacturers, for example, generally operate on the basis of a 5% productivity rise per year. In this positive scenario, unemployment remains low and is frictional in nature as workers search and/or retrain for new service sector employment in an expanding economy where real incomes are rising. In contrast, the 'negative' variety is a sign of economic distress; manufacturing is in difficulty and displaced workers are unable to take up employment in the service sector. This is associated with rising unemployment and the stagnation of real incomes. Whilst unemployment in the West Midlands is just below the UK average at around 5.3% (on a Labour force survey measure), in Birmingham it remains significantly higher, at around 7.5%. In this sense the auto sector and manufacturing more generally have exhibited signs of both types of de-industrialisation.

An inter-regional network?

Whilst centred in the West Midlands, the 'cluster' connections clearly extend to adjacent English regions and Wales. For example, in 2001 there were over 40,000 employees in the neighbouring East Midlands region with some 9000 in auto assembly (including the Toyota plant at Burnaston) and 8000 in manufacturing parts and accessories. Another 20,000 were employed in manufacturing autos, parts and accessories in the South East region (plus 1600 in the motor sport cluster); 13,000 in the South West (which includes the Honda plant at Swindon); 12,000 in Wales (suppliers for Honda and engine manufacturing for Ford and Toyota); and 24,000 in the North West (15,000 in motor vehicle assembly via GM and Jaguar/Land Rover in Merseyside, VW Bentley at Crewe and Congleton and Paccar trucks in Leyland, and 9000 in manufacturing parts and components). Whilst the North West is seen by the DTI (2001) as a 'distinct' cluster, component manufacturing is under-represented, indicating supply from elsewhere (notably the West Midlands), and that these are inter-related clusters or even part of a single national cluster. This has implications for the region given, for example, recent uncertainty over GM production at the Vauxhall plant at Ellesmere Port.[5] If a West Midlands 'cluster' can be identified, in reality it forms part of an inter-regional or national auto network extending into several other regions. Indeed, the transfer of some Land Rover production by Ford from Birmingham to its Halewood plant on Merseyside, and the sourcing of engines by Ford from Wales and by BMW from Birmingham for Mini production in Oxford are all indicative of the interlinkages across administrative regions.

Diversity and challenges to the WM auto 'cluster'

The diversity of component manufacturing in the region is a strength that enables it to supply a wide range of products, as noted by Tilson (1997,1997a) decade ago. At that time many component manufacturers were dependent on local assemblers, with 70% selling their products in the region (Tilson 1997, RTF 2000). With the decline in volume production, suppliers have had to seek markets elsewhere. In this regard, the inter-connected nature of the industry and the reach of purchasing provide opportunities. However, most local activities are in the traditional mechanically based areas of vehicle engineering with relatively little involvement in the new high-value electronic and electrical componentry making up an increasing proportion of the value of a new car (EMCC 2004). The lack of a significant 'home-owned' electronics or telemetry industry puts the region, and the UK as a whole, at a disadvantage.

Tilson (1997) also found, perhaps unsurprisingly, that many companies were experiencing reduced profits through downward pressure on costs from the vehicle-makers and major suppliers. The so-called 'lean paradigm' which seeks to squeeze out costs and improve productivity has since intensified, leading to significant consolidation at all levels in the supply matrix. Thus only those companies able to innovate and adapt are able to survive. However, firms' differing levels of competencies are not only reflected in their technological and organisational trajectories, but also in the way they are networked, engage in collaboration, the markets they serve and their openness beyond the cluster. Tully and Berkeley (2004), drawing on Gordon and McCann's work on cluster types, identify three groupings of firms in the West Midlands auto 'cluster'. The first (30% of the sample) does not cooperate or interact with competitors or customers, reflecting a 'pure agglomeration model'. Firms here are atomistic, and their co-location is in line with a Marshallian view of urban-based firms co-locating to access labour, infrastructure and a flow of ideas and information. The second group (45%) cooperates up and down the supply chain, with more sophisticated, stable and long-term relationships with customers and suppliers underpinned by OEM-driven schemes to drive up quality and productivity. A final group (25%) also collaborates with competitors and agencies in a Granovetter-type 'social network model', characterised by trust and a lack of opportunism. This group encompasses more complex interpersonal relationships, reflecting a recognised need to work together for common, beneficial goals. As Tully and Berkeley (2004) stress, the more sophisticated a firm's relationships, the more positive is their outlook, the more informed they are about market trends and the more likely they are to have links with universities. Such firms also invest more in new technologies, have better extra-regional links, and are more likely to be market leaders. They are also more likely to have shifted from high-volume, low-value standardised production towards higher-value, customised and design-led niche activity. Given the structural changes in the industry, such strategic moves are seen by many as vital for firms to survive yet are also risky. As Donnelly *et al.* (2005) highlight, many regionally-based SMEs 'lack the capacity to upgrade their skills, processes or R&D capacities on their own', noting that 'outside assistance is required otherwise many small firms will fail'.

Modularisation, post 'Japanisation' and the end of a 'geography of proximity'?

These global trends threaten established local production systems such as those in the West Midlands. Under the 'lean manufacturing' model, OEMs demand high 'QCD' (quality, cost and delivery) performance and deal with fewer suppliers to ease coordination costs in managing the supply chain (in effect passing these to first-tier suppliers). The overall effect has been to force suppliers to become 'world class', leading to a wave of consolidation similar to that for OEMS, with first-tier suppliers taking on greater R&D roles (Bergner 2000) and, in some cases, responsibility for whole systems (e.g. drives or steering), modules (e.g. interiors, 'front ends' or 'corners') or even assembly work,[6] as witnessed, for example, at Jaguar's Birmingham facility where assembly of the aluminium XJ model is undertaken in a joint venture with Stadco. In turn they exert greater power over lower-level suppliers (McIvor *et al.* 1998) as they themselves outsource a range of design and development functions. Thus a 'post-Japanisation' phase characterised as 'at supplier cost' is emerging where innovative capability is required at all levels in the value chain (see Wells and Rawlinson 1994). In addition, the internationalisation of component-sourcing by assemblers has accelerated (Sadler 1999, RTF 2000). Thus, GKN, the region's largest auto business, has more than 80% of purchasing outside the UK, BMW shifted £1 billion of Rover's £4 billion annual components spend out of Britain (*Financial Times 1999, 2002*), and even MGR was planning significant sourcing from China before its collapse. Of course modularisation, and the outsourcing of bulky components, inevitably results in major suppliers setting up in geographic proximity to the vehicle-makers. Thus the list of major suppliers is replicated in most automotive regions, including where there is new assembly capacity in Central and Eastern Europe, China and India. However, component-sourcing for these plants enables low-cost imports to Western Europe and changes the supply 'filiere' (Lagendijk 1997). Those West Midlands firms that concentrate on high-volume, single-material and single-process parts are at risk in this scenario. As Larsson (2002) notes, first-tier suppliers may have little incentive to source components locally for the modules they prepare.

The key points to emerge from this brief overview of the industry and 'cluster' are threefold. First, increasingly global sourcing, and a shift to lower wage-cost locations, threatens established 'clusters' such as the West Midlands, making a cluster policy in this area simultaneously more necessary but more difficult to sustain. The ending of volume car production in the West Midlands through the collapse of MGR and the closure of the Peugeot plant, and the shift to smaller-scale higher-value production is itself evidence of this. Second, even major firms are under intense pressure given the rising costs of new model development, necessitating large-scale production, platform-sharing strategies and/ or joint ventures in order to survive. Thirdly, at the local level, the West Midlands cluster ranges from low-tech 'metal bashing' to high-tech composite materials, engines and environmental technologies, with a series of interlinked networks ranging from local supply to global supply chains dominated by the big players. However, as we have highlighted a number of technological and organisational trends pose both opportunities and threats and raise a number of crucial points about the role for policy.

MG Rover: a brief anatomy of failure

At the time of its collapse in 2005 MGR was producing just over 100,000 units a year, when it needed to be in the 2–3 million range to generate enough cash for new model development. Not surprisingly, much media attention focused on the short-term failure of the Phoenix management over the preceding five years and the tiny size of the firm. However, from a wider perspective MGR can be viewed as the unsustainable rump of a government-created giant which never sufficiently integrated activities and which was never in a position to recover the rising costs of new model development. Its long-term decline and ultimate collapse is tied up in a complex vortex of long-running and inter-related factors, including macro-economic instability, the particular short-termism of British finance–industry relations, fratricidal industrial relations, misguided government policy interventions, and above all the firm's perennial inability to generate the cash needed for new model development (Williams *et al.* 1994a). As noted, this 'crisis of cost recovery' has actually intensified over time.

Long-running problems and the failure of a 'national champion'

MG Rover itself was the remnant of a government creation of the 1950s and 1960s, the British Leyland Motor Corporation (BLMC, later BL, Austin Rover and finally Rover). As Williams *et al.* dryly observed, the name often changed but the underlying problems remained the same (Williams *et al.* 1994b). The firm was brought together by the government in effect merging smaller auto manufacturers (Austin, Morris, Triumph, Rover and Jaguar[7]) through various stages into a single firm, in probably the most prominent and infamous example of the misguided policy of creating so-called 'national champions'. As Owen (1999) commented, the merger 'was a mistake both in concept and in execution, reflecting a naïve belief in the advantages of size and in the ability of charismatic individuals to revive declining companies'. Rather than a 'champion', a mega-merger was forced on reluctant and resistant incumbent managers. Not surprisingly, suspicion and rivalry across brands hampered efforts to integrate activities, share high-value components and to strip-out costs leading to continued loss-making. This inability to recover development costs, or the 'cycle of doom' as Holweg and Oliver (2005) term it, went back to the 1950s and 1960s, and plagued the firm across decades. After the oil-price shock of the early 1970s, nationalisation in 1975 cost the government, and British taxpayers, billions of pounds in subsidies which went in buying industrial-relations peace and limited new model development.

By 1978, the then Austin Rover still assembled over 600,000 units, and exported 40% of them. Its UK market share (for Austin, Morris, Rover and Triumph) was 23.5%, or almost a quarter of all cars sold in the UK that year (Williams et al. 1987). Exports collapsed after this point, however, and never recovered, falling from 40% of Austin Rover output to just 20% in the mid-1980s when the firm assembled around 300,000 cars. This export collapse was linked to the ending of assembly operations by Austin Rover on the continent and the high value of sterling during the early 1980s. Under Thatcher, the company was privatised in 1985 through a sale to British Aerospace (BAe) which was diversifying away from aircraft. After the failure of its regional jet business, BAe sold Rover to BMW for £800 million. As Hutton (1999) noted, the sale of Rover to a foreign firm reflected the twin factors of British short-termism (BAe's desire for cash) and the openness of British industry and government to penetration by foreign investment. Thereby Rover became part of BMW, but probably for the 'wrong' reasons. BAe needed cash and BMW wanted the four-wheel-drive Land Rover division – as at that time the company did not have the resources to develop its own model to compete in an expanding market segment – and also to double production volume (at the time both had annual sales of around 440,000.) At the time, many commentators recognised the difficulties of achieving economies of scale whilst the cars were so different in design and driveline (Bailey et al. 1994). Although some criticism has also been levelled at the government's failure to heed these warnings, it is noteworthy that the Rover Management Board were in favour of a BMW purchase since there was an historic connection between the companies[8] and they saw the possibility of joining BMW in the profitable premium segment.

Life under BMW: the 'English Patient'

Whatever the precise reasons for BMW's acquisition, problems were immediately apparent. Rover under government, and then BAe, ownership had relied heavily on a joint venture (JV) with Honda through which Honda designs were badged and sold as Rovers to European markets, saving Rover considerable R&D costs and periodically enabling it to make modest profits. Honda executives were unimpressed when Rover was abruptly sold to a competitor, and Honda subsequently sold its 20% stake. As commentators warned at the time, it was not clear what BMW would actually make after the JV with Honda was terminated. Thus, although one joint Honda–Rover model programme, the Honda Civic–Rover 400/45 continued into production, BMW was now on its own. As observed by Williams et al. (1994b), BMW did not have the capacity to develop the Rover brand and style of car and therefore jobs were at risk. Logic suggested that, since the UK was the company's second market after Germany, the BMW-3 series should be made at Longbridge. However, concerns about quality and worries about dilution of the BMW brand prevented this ever happening.

Not surprisingly, through a combination of model obsolescence (as BMW struggled to bring new models on line), marketing mistakes, and macro-economic factors such as the rise in the value of sterling, Rover sales declined and losses grew to £500 million a year by the late 1990s. Whilst BMW invested heavily in the Land Rover plant at Solihull (Birmingham) and at Cowley (Oxford), the position of Longbridge was always vulnerable, with BMW threatening early on to switch production of the new Mini elsewhere if productivity did not improve and deals on working conditions were not agreed (Bailey 2003). Similarly, in March 1999 BMW threatened to shift production to Hungary if a state aid package was not agreed by the government to build a new model, the R30. A £152 million subsidy package was agreed with the government in mid-1999 in return for a planned £1.7 billion investment by BMW in Longbridge. After a complaint by Porsche, however, the European Commission decided to investigate the aid package under EU state aid rules. Before the prolonged investigation was finished, however, BMW announced in March 2000 that it was pulling out, leading to the buy-out by Phoenix.

It was clear to several commentators (Bailey *et al.* 1994, Williams *et al.* 1994a) that BMW's purchase of Rover in 1994 was a corporate mistake for BMW and likely to cause severe problems for Rover.[9] As Wolf later commented (*Financial Times* 1999): 'BMW did not realise how bad a buy Rover would be'. The 'failure' of competition policy contributed to this problem by allowing BMW to buy Rover when it was clear to many that it was an inappropriate owner (Bailey *et al.* 1994). It is widely accepted that local production systems can be improved by firms – whether domestic or foreign – that bring new technology and investment but can also be damaged through takeovers (Harrison 1994). Whilst BMW was seen by many as an inappropriate owner at the time of its takeover of Rover, Volkswagen (which had earlier shown interest) might have been much more suitable in that it could have extended its strategy of sharing platforms across brands to MGR as had worked so well with VW, Audi, Seat and Skoda. It should be stressed that the case here is not anti-inward investment *per se* but rather focuses on the suitability of acquiring firms (whether domestic or foreign) for the local production system. None of this, of course, was considered by the government, as the only perceived role for intervention was on a narrow competition basis.

Not surprisingly, despite the substantial investment in the late 1990s, BMW decided in 2000 to break up the company, selling Land Rover to Ford, retaining the Cowley factory in Oxford (for the new Mini) and the Hams Hall engine plant and selling the remaining Rover division with its Longbridge factory for a symbolic £10 to the Phoenix consortium. Despite the hopes raised in 2000, BMW's withdrawal left MGR virtually dead on its feet. The cancellation of the R30 project, which was the key mid-sized model being developed under BMW as a replacement for the R45, meant that a whole cycle of model development had been missed (Holweg and Oliver 2005). The firm was now brutally exposed as its aging model line became increasingly unattractive to buyers and it had only a very limited time horizon in which to find a partner; by 2002/2003 it was clear to many that the firm was running out of time (Bailey 2003). The unsustainable position of the firm was evidenced by the way it consumed what assets it had.

Exchange rate volatility

Another view is that BMW acquired Rover not only for its 4WD competencies but also to obtain a manufacturing base 'in a country which had lower labour costs than Germany and ... a stable labour relations climate' (Owen 1999). Any such relative unit–labour cost advantage was soon eliminated by the sustained and marked appreciation in the value of sterling from 1994 onwards. At the time of the takeover in 1994, sterling was valued in the range DM2.40–2.50, making auto assembly in the UK attractive to firms such as BMW.

BMW budgeted for a turnaround plan at Rover with sterling at around DM2.90, yet by January 2000 sterling had risen to DM3.20, and Church (1999) estimated that by July 1999 the sterling effective exchange rate was overvalued by around 20%. This over-appreciation exacerbated Rover's problems, making exports (of increasingly aging models) extremely difficult at a time when the company was losing home sales and trying to reorientate its sales towards export markets.

Such exchange rate volatility continues to make conditions for the region's manufacturers extremely difficult and has accelerated the shift to sourcing overseas, as Bailey (2007) notes. At the time of writing, sterling is at a 26-year high against the dollar of over $2. This weak dollar makes selling to the US very difficult and has impacted severely on firms such as Jaguar, as over a half of its sales are in the US market, especially for the large XJ model. As much as a half of Ford's Premier Auto Group's losses in recent years could be down to this exchange rate issue. This exchange rate pressure accelerates the trend towards smaller-scale luxury branded production as noted in the second section. More broadly, cluster policies and development goals in a manufacturing-orientated region can be undermined by such major exchange rate fluctuations. There may be good reasons for Britain remaining outside of the Eurozone, but the 'cost' of exchange rate volatility has not gone away, and MGR's most recent difficulties are a stark illustration of this – the story could have been quite different in the absence of such sterling over-appreciation. Indeed, the reduction of exchange rate risk through Euro membership could be a significant benefit to auto assemblers based in the UK, although this would not help Jaguar and Land Rover in selling to the key US market.

Phoenix: an unsustainable strategy

On taking over in 2000, the Phoenix management set four strategic objectives for the firm: maintaining production at 200,000 units; bringing a new model to market (the replacement for the medium-sized R45); finding a partner for new model development; and returning to profit. But with a limited and aging product range, and in particular the lack of models in key growth segments (such as compact cars, people carriers and sports utility vehicles), this was always going to be a huge challenge. Whilst sales held up reasonably well in 2000, thereafter they declined rapidly and by 2002/2003 it became increasingly clear to commentators that the firm had limited time in which to find a partner to bring new models to market (Bailey 2003).

Some imaginative re-badging of aged Rover designs as MGs bought a little time, but over the next few years MGR sold off its only real assets (land, the profitable parts business and finance arm and later its intellectual property rights) in an increasingly desperate attempt to keep going. By 2004, output had dwindled to around 115,000 units and R&D spending had dried up. No partnership deal had been delivered other than an agreement with Tata to supply the small 'City Rover' model – which was marketed at an uncompetitive price and failed to sell in significant numbers. With limited room for manoeuvre in that many of the big players had already entered partnership deals, it became clear that the very survival of MGR depended on a deal with Shanghai Automotive to jointly develop models. However, Shanghai became increasingly concerned about the financial viability of MGR and feared picking up sizeable redundancy and pensions liabilities, and talks dragged on for several months before ending in failure in April 2005. At that point the firm was forced into administration, with the remaining assets later bought for £60 million by Nanjing, another Chinese firm. All but two production lines, along with the Powertrain engine production plant, were then stripped out from Longbridge in a 'lift and shift' move to China.

New hopes or false dawn?

Nanjing aimed to re-start small-scale production of MG TF sports cars at Longbridge in late 2007, with complete knock-down kits being imported from China. However, production has been delayed given quality concerns, and to date only a very limited number have been made. The eventual production volume is as yet unclear and likely to be far smaller than the 100,000 units a year initially suggested by Nanjing at the time of takeover. Thus whilst of considerable significance in terms of redeveloping the Longbridge site, only 'a few hundred' jobs at best will be created. Initially it seemed that there would also be no substantial R&D centre, with the latter likely to be located at Nanjing's new MG plant in Oklahoma. This represented something of a missed opportunity when compared with what was potentially on offer from a Shanghai Auto takeover of MGR. More recent developments look more promising, however. Shanghai Auto (which brought the intellectual property rights to the Rover 25 and 75 and the replacement model for the R45 in development at the time of the MGR collapse) has developed a joint venture with Ricardo to develop the new model. Nanjing has also reversed its previously-announced strategy and has stated that it will bring its R&D base to Longbridge. Most recently, in late 2007, Shanghai acquired the car-making operations of Nanjing with Chinese government encouragement; this is likely to strengthen the likelihood of genuine R&D coming back to Longbridge. Auto assembly (even if on a small scale) and R&D may therefore be returning to Longbridge, albeit under Chinese state ownership.

Summary and conclusions

A number of technological and structural changes are unfolding in the auto industry, including: more rapid technological change which has driven up the costs of new model development, in turn increasing the pressure on firms to recover costs; more international sourcing of components with a greater role for larger first-tier suppliers; and a shift of labour-intensive assembly operations towards lower-cost locations as trade barriers have come down and as globalisation proceeds. All of these make maintaining the West Midlands cluster more challenging for firms and policy-makers through cluster policy. Manufacturers and policy-makers are aware of the 'threat' from low-cost competitor locations in Central and Eastern Europe, and in the longer term, from India and China. At the same time, possibilities for cooperation are evident in the recent Shanghai–Ricardo R&D venture in the West Midlands.

Within this broader context, MGR was the unprofitable rump of a former giant which for years had struggled to generate cash for new models owing in part to a lack of integration across the firm. The firm became reliant on Honda for new models in the 1980s before being acquired by BMW. The latter's withdrawal from the firm in 2000 left MGR virtually dead on its feet, and by 2002/2003 it was clear to many that the firm was running out of time. Also significant in the firm's demise, however, were a number of government policy mistakes over the years, including a misguided 'national champions' approach, a failure to integrate activities under nationalisation, a mistaken privatisation, and the downside of competition policy which saw the sale to an inappropriate owner (in BMW) in the 1990s. Add in the considerable volatility of sterling, and the scene was set for the firm's demise. The impact of this collapse and policy responses will be explored in papers in this issue. This will include a comparative analysis, comparing policy responses (see Thomas *et al.*) and labour market outcomes (Armstrong *et al.*) in the case of MGR in Birmingham and Mitsubishi in Adelaide.

Notes
1. Coffey (2006) is critical of what he terms the 'myth of Japanese efficiency'.
2. See Clark (2006) who draws on Abernathy's work highlighting the unexpected and significant increase in the level of innovation at Ford in the 1960s.
3. A key issue for the future is what effect the anticipated shift to more specialised 'short-run' production, including electric/hybrid powered autos, will have on development costs, minimum efficient scales and the players involved.
4. Taking a broad definition of the filiere to include auto-related industries gave a figure of around 120,000 people in 2001, higher than the 100,000 figure given in RTF (2000). More recently, Donnelly *et al.* (2005) put the numbers of workers in the *broadly* defined auto industry in the region as low as 65,000. If correct, this would signify as many as 35,000 job losses over 2000–2005.
5. Although in 2007 GM announced that the new model would be assembled there, safeguarding 2200 direct jobs and more in the supply chain.
6. Bergner (2000) notes that between 1988 and 1998 the global number of direct component suppliers to OEMs and the aftermarket shrank from 30,000 to 8000. This number is expected to fall considerably in the future. For example, McIvor *et al.* (1998) argue that 50% of European suppliers will cease to exist in their current form owing to pressure from OEMs to reduce costs and innovate.
7. Jaguar was separated and privatised in the 1980s, acquired by Ford in 1989 and sold again to Ford's US parent in 1991, later being sold to the Indian conglomerate Tata in 2008.
8. For example, in the 1920s BMW had manufactured versions of the Austin 7 under licence.
9. Although BMW was able to access Land Rover's four-wheel-drive (4WD) technology and was later able to produce its own 4WD models.

References
Bailey, D., 2003. Globalisation, regions and cluster policies: the case of the Rover task force. *Policy studies*, 24 (2/3), 67–83.
Bailey, D., 2007. Globalisation and restructuring in the auto industry: the impact on the West Midlands auto cluster. *Strategic change*, 16, 137–144.
Bailey, D., and Cowling, K., 2006. *The lesson Peugeot has taught Britain*. Parliamentary brief, June.
Bailey, D., Harte, G., and Sugden, R., 1994. British Policy towards inward investment. *Journal of world trade*, 28 (2), 113–138.
Bergner, R., 2000. Responding to the challenges: demands from vehicle manufacturers towards suppliers are ever-increasing [online]. Available from: http://www.autoindustry.co.uk/library
Chanaron, J.J., 2004. Relationships between the core and the periphery of the European automotive system. *International journal of automotive technology and management*, 4 (2/3), 198–222.
Church, K.B., 1999. Properties of the fundamental exchange rate in the treasury model. *National Institute economic review*, 169, 96–104.

Clark, P., 2006. Superfactuals, structural repertoires and productive units: explaining the evolution of the British auto industry. *Competition and change*, 10 (4), 393–410.
Coffey, D., 2006. *The myth of Japanese efficiency. The world car industry in a globalising age*. Cheltenham: Edward Elgar.
Department of Trade and Industry (DTI) , 2001. *Business clusters in the UK – a first assessment, volumes 1 and 2*. London: The Stationery Office.
Donnelly, T., Barnes, S., and Morris, D., 2005. Restructuring the automotive industry in the English West Midlands. *Local economy*, 20 (3), 249–265.
EMCC, 2004. *The automotive sector at a crossroads*. Dublin: European Monitoring Centre on Change.
Financial Times , 1999. Rover suppliers warned to be more competitive. *Financial Times*, 24 June, p. 9.
Financial Times , 2002. Defiant carmaker foresees a positive route to the future. *Financial Times*, 27 April, p. 3.
Harrison, B., 1994. *Lean and mean. The changing landscape of corporate power in the age of flexibility*. New York: Basic Books.
Holweg, M. and Oliver, N., 2005. *Who killed MG Rover?* Cambridge: The Cambridge–MIT Institute.
Hutton, W. , 1999. Why Rover was driven out of UK hands. *In: The stakeholder society. Writings in politics and economics*. Oxford: Polity Press.
Lagendijk, A., 1997. Towards an integrated automotive industry in Europe: a 'merging filiere' perspective. *European urban and regional studies*, 4 (1), 5–18.
Larssen, A., 2002. The development and regional significance of the automotive industry: supplier parks in Western Europe. *International journal of urban and regional research*, 26 (4), 767–784.
MacNeill, S. and Chanaron, J.J., 2005. Trends and drivers of change in the European automotive industry: mapping the current situation. *International journal of automotive technology and management*, 5 (1), 83–106.
McIvor, R.T., Humphreys, P.K., and McAleer, W.E., 1998. European car makers and their suppliers: changes at the interface. *European business review*, 98 (2), 87–99.
Office of National Statistics (ONS), 2005. *Annual business inquiry 2005*. London: ONS.
Owen, G., 1999. *From empire to Europe. The decline and revival of British industry since the Second World War*. London: Harper Collins.
Rover Task Force (RTF1) , 2000. *Final report and recommendations to the Secretary of State for Trade and Industry*. Birmingham: Advantage West Midlands.
Rowthorn, B. and Wells, J.R., 1987. *Deindustrialisation and foreign trade*. Cambridge: Cambridge University Press.
Sadler, D., 1999. Internationalization and specialization in the European automotive components sector: implications for the hollowing out thesis. *Regional studies*, 33 (2), 109–119.
Tilson, B., 1997. *Survey of firms in the automotive components sector in the West Midlands region. Final report for the West Midlands Development Agency*. Birmingham: Centre for Urban and Regional Studies, University of Birmingham.
Tully, J. and Berkeley, N., 2004. Visualising the operating behaviour of SMEs in sector and cluster: evidence from the West Midlands. *Local economy*, 19 (1), 38–54.
Wells, P. and Rawlinson, M., 1994. *The new European automobile industry*. New York: St Martin's Press.
Williams, K., Williams, J., and Haslam, C., 1987. *The breakdown of Austin Rover*. Leamington Spa: Berg.
Williams, K., Haslam, C., Johal, S., and Williams, J., 1994a. *Cars. Analysis, history, cases, providence*. Providence: Berghahn Books.
Williams, K., Haslam, C., and Johal, S., 1994b. *Who's responsible? BAe: BMW: Honda: Rover*. Public interest report from the Centre for Empirical Research in Accounting and Finance, University of Manchester, and the Business Policy Unit, East London Business School, University of East London.
Womack, J.P., Jones, D.T., and Roos, D., 1990. *The machine that changed the world*. New York: Rawson Associates.

Birmingham: whose urban renaissance? Regeneration as a response to economic restructuring

Austin Barber and Stephen Hall

Introduction

The economic and social composition of cities in the developed world has been profoundly transformed in the past two decades by the processes of globalisation, deindustrialisation and tertiarisation (Fothergill *et al.* 1986, Sassen 2006). A key contemporary challenge for city governments and their partners, arising from this transition, is balancing an aspiration for economic competitiveness, i.e. promoting a better mix of attributes for business and business success (cf. Boddy and Parkinson 2004), with an imperative to promote social inclusion, i.e. seeking to reintegrate those households and individuals excluded from mainstream prosperity and opportunity by poverty, inequality and social deprivation. These two models have tended, since the 1980s, to be subject to *separate* policy regimes and different practitioner, media and academic discourses in the United Kingdom.

A distinctive 'entrepreneurial' model of urban economic development has evolved worldwide (Harvey 1989). This involves investment in service-sector physical infrastructure, promotion of 'creative' industries, 'boosterist' city marketing campaigns, development of up-market housing in the central business district (CBD), hosting internationally-important sporting and leisure-related events, and 'themed' neighbourhood regeneration (Smyth 1994, Hall and Hubbard 1998). These interventions are designed to reinvigorate economically urban areas and, thus, contribute to economic competitiveness. They are commonly branded as examples of 'urban renaissance'. In reality, the links between urban renaissance and competitiveness are ambiguous (ODPM 2004a, 2004b). These entrepreneurial strategies are typically conceived, funded and implemented by coalitions of local government and business stakeholders and are characterised by exclusive, corporatist forms of political process (Davies 2001). High-profile examples include the redevelopment of the Bullring shopping centre in Birmingham, Manchester's hosting of the Commonwealth Games in 2002 and associated developments, and Liverpool's acquisition of the title of European Capital of Culture 2008.

The pursuit of social inclusion is associated with area-based and client-targeted initiatives, conceived and funded by central government but implemented at a local level. These polices seek to address the acute, localised socio-economic problems that arise from economic restructuring (e.g. poverty, deprivation, social exclusion). They are characterised by a more inclusive form of political process, albeit one that has met with uneven success. The most important recent examples include the Single Regeneration Budget, New Deal for Communities, Sure Start and the Housing Market Renewal Areas (Brennan *et al.* 2003, Imrie and Raco 2003).

The discourse of the so-called 'urban renaissance' has become dominant to the extent that claims of economic and social transformation are made in respect of entire cities on the basis of developments in their CBDs. In a global context, Baltimore and its harbourfront redevelopment is often cited as a pioneer of urban renaissance. In Europe, Barcelona has become an icon of urban renaissance, following its successful exploitation of the 1992 Olympic Games. However, in both cases, this apparent success is not reflected in terms of improved competitiveness or inclusion as expressed in positive economic and social outcomes (Levine 1987, ODPM 2004a, 2004b).

In 2000, the Urban White Paper *Our towns and cities – the future* noted that, while the major conurbations had performed relatively poorly on most socio-economic indicators, there were some embryonic signs of urban revival during the previous decade in the form of overall employment and population growth (DETR 2000). More recently, the government has been more forthright in extolling the virtues of the urban renaissance:

> Our cities are back and the reasons are simple. They remain centres for wealth creation, trade and culture, and are cleaner, safer and greener ... The Core Cities have turned the corner ... Economic success, social justice and sustainable communities are being created through leadership and partnership. (ODPM 2004a)

Birmingham is regarded as a paradigmatic example of an entrepreneurial 'renaissance' city and is described as:

> A trendsetter in urban renaissance, having transformed its open spaces into plazas, its arcades into shopping experiences. Last month, the new Gaudi-like Selfridges was unveiled, trumpeting the city's transformation from concrete jungle to model of creative urban design. (www.newstartmag.co.uk)

Indeed, local business and political elites have argued that, as a result of recent investment in city-centre redevelopment, brownfield regeneration and economic diversification, leave

Birmingham in a strong position to 'weather the storm' of the MG Rover crisis (Building 2000, Birmingham Post 2005).

Conversely, sceptical accounts (e.g. Turok and Edge 1999) emphasise the relative decline of the employment base of Britain's major conurbations (a net loss of 500,000 jobs, between 1981 and 1996, in Britain's 20 largest urban areas, compared to a net gain of 1.7 million elsewhere) and, thus, a transition in the role of cities from centres of employment to centres of non-employment, under-employment and social crisis.

In reality, 'urban renaissance' is *selective* both geographically and socially. This paper seeks to address the question of *whose urban renaissance* in the context of the City of Birmingham. We compare and contrast the key differences (and commonalities) between the discourse of economic restructuring espoused by policy elites and the reality of everyday life in Birmingham's diverse neighbourhoods. The objective of this paper is not to analyse plant closures *per se* but to provide a critique of urban regeneration policy pursued during a period during which plant closures have fundamentally altered the economic composition of Birmingham.

Economic context and crisis in Birmingham

The long decline of MG Rover and the closure of the Longbridge plant in 2005 are analysed elsewhere in this volume. In the section, we consider the decline of the manufacturing base in Birmingham and the West Midlands in an historical context and, in so doing, highlight the magnitude of the economic challenge facing local policy-makers during the 1980s and beyond.

During the Industrial Revolution, Birmingham and the West Midlands became the pre-eminent manufacturing region of the UK and developed an industrial structure based on small firms with highly-skilled workers. This enabled the region to attract new investment in consumer goods industries, especially automotive production (Gwynne 1996) during the first half of the twentieth century. The region is, thus, clearly differentiated from the manufacturing regions of northern England – the latter based on large factory organisation and low-skilled mass labour in steel, shipbuilding, textiles and coal – that had been in (relative) decline for much of the twentieth century (Martin and Rowthorn 1986).

The economic heyday of Birmingham and the West Midlands coincided with the zenith of the Fordist system of industrial production (Bryson *et al.* 1996). In 1961, some 65% of employment in Birmingham and the West Midlands was in the manufacturing sector, compared to around 39% nationally (Bryson *et al.* 1996). The most important industrial sector, by far, was automotive production. In 1971, some 151,000 people in the region were employed in motor vehicle manufacture (*excluding* the supply chain) representing nearly 20% of all employment in manufacturing (Spencer *et al.* 1986). Between 1951 and 1966, total employment in the region increased by 14%, compared to 8.5% nationally, including an additional 360,000 jobs in manufacturing (Spencer *et al.* 1986). By the mid-1960s, the regional economy was characterised by higher participation rates and wage levels than the national economy (Spencer *et al.* 1986). Gross domestic product per capita was 10% above the UK average and second only to London and the South East (Spencer *et al.* 1986).

However, the post war boom was followed by an equally precipitous economic collapse. Indeed, since the late 1960s, Birmingham and the West Midlands have performed poorly on all economic indicators (Spencer *et al.* 1986). This is indicative of long-term structural decline rather than a cyclical problem (Spencer *et al.* 1986). The concentration of employment in the automotive sector which gave Birmingham and the West Midlands their dynamism during the post-war period and, especially, the relatively low levels of investment and productivity therein, were significant contributors to the decline (Spencer et al. 1986, Bryson et al. 1996).

Between 1965 and 1981, Birmingham and the West Midlands lost some 370,000 manufacturing jobs (Spencer et al. 1986). In the decade, 1971 to 1981, alone, more than 40% of employment in the motor industry was lost (Spencer et al. 1986). By 1981, gross domestic product per capita of the region had fallen to 10% *below* the UK average, making Birmingham and the West Midlands the second poorest region in the UK, after Northern Ireland (Spencer et al. 1986). By the mid-1980s, then, this rapid decline had created a sense of political urgency in the city around the need to generate a proactive response to economic crisis. The following section examines the ambitious policy initiatives led by Birmingham City Council (BCC) in conjunction with partners in the public and private sectors.

The policy response: towards an urban renaissance in Birmingham

In March 1988, BCC convened the first 'Highbury Symposium', a conference of local stakeholders and international urban experts, to consider an appropriate response to the decline of local industry. The resulting strategy, informed by the experience of US 'rust belt' cities such as Baltimore, was premised on a spatial argument that posited the CBD as a key potential setting for attracting modern urban economic sectors and fashioning a more progressive, attractive image of Birmingham. In practice, the strategy consisted of three complementary components: a cluster of flagship projects; a new spatial vision and related environmental investments; and, the promotion of 'city living'. The first major set of initiatives comprised the development of a cluster of flagship projects designed to lead Birmingham's move into international business tourism and related leisure sectors. The main elements were:

- International Convention Centre/Symphony Hall (ICC): a £180 million conference and concert facility opened in April 1991.
- National Indoor Arena (NIA): a £57 million, 13,000-seat sports venue opened in October 1991.
- Hyatt Hotel: a £31 million four-star, 319-room hotel with extensive leisure facilities.

The primary objective of these investments was to generate an important new business tourism sector for Birmingham and, thus attract visitors with trickle-down effects through the local economy. The projects were also designed to promote further new private investment in services and amenities in the surrounding areas, and to create a new visual identity for Birmingham that could form the basis of a proactive place-marketing campaign.

The most important spatial planning objectives set out at Highbury were the breaking of the 'concrete collar' – the post-war Inner Ring Road that constrained the growth of the CBD – the promotion of greater pedestrian priority and the development of a series of distinctive quarters (e.g. the Jewellery Quarter) surrounding the main core, along the lines of central districts found in many European cities. Important investments in this domain included the downgrading of the inner ring road, the pedestrianisation of New Street, linking to two new traffic-free public squares, and the extensive upgrading of the canal network environment in the surrounding area. The flagship projects, the environmental investments and the accompanying spatial policy framework, created the conditions for a reinvigoration of the CBD. Accordingly, the CBD has experienced a steady increase in private-sector investment since the mid-1990s. The main elements of this investment include:

- Brindleyplace: a £300 million mixed-use development adjacent to the International Convention Centre (ICC), combining offices, restaurants, shops, cultural amenities and private-sector housing.
- Broad Street Leisure Area: a multitude of new bars, clubs, restaurants and leisure/cultural amenities also in the immediate ICC/Brindleyplace area. Broad Street has recently been designated as a US-style Business Improvement District which provides increased municipal services financed through a supplementary business tax.
- The Mailbox: a major canalside mixed-use development comprising offices, restaurants, high-value retailing and hotels.
- The Bullring: a £500 million redevelopment of an outdated 1960s centre to provide a retail complex of regional importance, completed in September 2003.

The final element of the strategy was to encourage the growth of a CBD residential population by creating the conditions for new private housing investment. In the early 1990s, Birmingham's city-centre population was limited primarily to residents of post-war social housing. However the physical investments and transformation of the 1980s and 1990s created a conducive climate for new private housing development. Following the completion of the first major scheme at Brindleyplace in 1996, residential development grew slowly but steadily in subsequent years (Barber 2007).

The first wave of BCC's CBD regeneration strategy, as outlined above, had been driven by strong political consensus in the 1980s and the close working relationship between the Labour-led BCC and business interests which has seen Birmingham characterised as a prime example of a pro-growth urban regime (DiGaetano and Klemanski 1993). However, direct public investment in the CBD agenda declined from 1994, and much of the continued investment in the urban realm was funded by private developers or other external sources, including the European Union or National Lottery funds. However, the political commitment to developing business tourism, CBD regeneration and diversifying the economy has remained a key strand of city policy, enduring intact through a change of city-council political leadership from Labour to a Conservative–Liberal Democrat coalition in 2004.

This continued emphasis on the CBD regeneration agenda is reflected in the ambitious plans for the 180-hectare Eastside district, immediately adjacent to the city core. The proposals launched in 1999 are anchored around the themes of learning, technology and heritage, with a less specific but prominent ambition to see the district grow as one of Birmingham's main creative or cultural quarters. The main initial public investment included the demolition of the inner ring road in the vicinity and land assembly for disposal of large sites to private developers as well as for a new library (designed by Richard Rogers) and a City Park. The Eastside project is still in its infancy. However, evidence suggests that, while private development is beginning on the CBD fringe, some difficulties in achieving less commercial elements (including the abandoned library plans) have been encountered and there is growing controversy about the displacement of existing businesses and community networks amid the large-scale assembly and clearance processes led by public agencies (Barber 2006, Porter and Barber 2006).

The vigour and scale of Birmingham's regeneration strategy in the 1980s and 1990s, and the city's high profile relative to its counterparts during this period, gave rise to the beginning of a lively, highly polemical debate. The following section discusses the main thrust of this critique.

The critical debate

Entrepreneurial strategies such as that pursued by Birmingham in the 1980s and 1990s are commonly accompanied by 'boosterist' hype about the extensive physical transformation, the revival of city fortunes and associated reawakening of civic pride. This is evident in the proclamations of city's political and business leaders, as well as official marketing campaigns. Indeed, at the time of the G8 Summit, hosted by Birmingham at the ICC in 1998, the US President, Bill Clinton, was recruited to the cause:

> I was astonished how beautiful Birmingham was. The buildings, the art, the use of water. It is an extraordinary jewel of a city. I was bowled over when I was there. (Bill Clinton, *The Times*, 2 October 2002)

In 2001, BCC was designated, by central government, a 'Beacon Council' (a formally-sanctioned example of 'best practice') in the domain of 'town centre regeneration'.

However, these narratives were challenged in early 1990s by an academic critique developed by Loftman and Nevin (1992, 1994, 1996). They criticised the apparent lack of employment benefit for the city's deprived populations – for example, noting that, in 1991, 42% of employment at the ICC and 71% at the NIA were in low-paid, insecure cleaning, catering and security classifications (Loftman and Nevin 1994), and that substantial local-authority funds used to build the ICC were diverted from front-line services, such as education and housing which were most heavily used and needed by Birmingham's poorer communities. For example, they argue that, during the construction of the ICC and NIA (1986 to 1992), BCC spent £120 million less on housing than the average for all local authorities in England (Loftman and Nevin 1996). One consequence of this under-investment in front-line services is Birmingham's categorisation (until recently) as a 'weak' council in the Audit Commission's Comprehensive Performance Assessment, especially in respect of housing and children's social services (Audit Commission 2004).

Henry and Passmore (1999, p. 61) summarise the case against the city's entrepreneurial strategy as follows: 'To many, the flagship projects have created an elite international enclave within Birmingham city centre: a space for the national and international tourist/business class, which is increasingly divorced from its regional and local context'. This attack on the economic rationale and value behind the strategy prompted a polemical response from city politicians at the time. They argued that the critics' approach was too selective, and that it was too early to undertake any robust economic evaluation. Bloomfield (2001), a former senior local authority official argued that 'to call this an "elite international enclave" beggars belief'. Perhaps most interestingly, critics had attributed distributional objectives to projects which were not part of the core rationale in the first instance. As another academic commentator observed in 1994:

> The main aims were to create a new economic base to the other key industries in the region. This excluded the incorporation of the local population into the urban regeneration strategy in

a central position. Any trickle-down effect was perceived as a benefit, yet was secondary. It is ironic, although not surprising, that it is on the basis of the 'sub-goals' that the city is facing criticism. (Smyth 1994)

BCC also commissioned two reports by consultancy KPMG to quantify the economic impact of the NEC Group venues. Their second report, published in 1993, estimated that Birmingham's principal business tourism venues attracted 4.5 million visitors in 1992/1993. This generated an estimated net income of £180 million pounds (32% to Birmingham, the balance to the rest of the West Midlands region) and supported 16,800 jobs (35% in Birmingham, the balance in the West Midlands region) (KPMG 1993).

The debate on the 'urban renaissance' of Birmingham has stalled somewhat since the late 1990s. It is appropriate, then, to take a balanced view of Birmingham's experience that can add a more considered perspective to the 'boosterist' hype and the short-term critiques. In the following section, and with the benefit of several years' reflection, we pose the question: whose urban renaissance?

Whose urban renaissance in Birmingham?
A decade after the first polemical debate it is evident that Birmingham has enjoyed significant growth in financial and professional services since the early 1990s. These sectors include a significant proportion of high-skilled, high-value jobs. The CBD is the focus of this growth and has seen the sector develop a critical mass of activity, despite continuing decentralisation pressures (such as relocation of back-office functions). There are some 115,000 jobs in the Ladywood ward, which incorporates most of the expanded CBD, representing more than a quarter of total employment in Birmingham. Employment in financial, professional, and business services in Ladywood increased from 32,000 in 1991 to more than 50,000 in 2002, and is estimated to rise to 59,000 by 2015 (BEIC 2005). This CBD sector represents nearly half of the entire jobs growth in the city over this period. Birmingham and the CBD cluster, in particular, have strengthened their role as a regional centre in this field and firms in the legal, property and accountancy sectors have driven their growth by an increased presence in national and international markets.

The 'visitor' economy – including retail, hospitality and leisure – has also emerged as a driver of employment growth. The number of jobs in tourism-related industries grew by 24% to nearly 31,000 between 1991 and 2002 (BEIC 2005). This was still below the regional and national levels as a proportion of total employment but exceeded the regional and national growth rates over that period. This employment again has been focused strongly on the CBD and the business tourism activities developed as part of the regeneration initiatives of the 1980s and 1990s. The most notable increase in visitors has been from overseas with visitor totals increasing from 390,000 to 670,000 between 1991 and 2002 (BEIC 2005); a performance that improved Birmingham's relative standing, rising to the UK's third most-visited destination behind London and Edinburgh.

In the retail sector, the opening of the Bullring centre and events including the Frankfurt Christmas Market have strengthened the city's stature as a day-trip destination. In 2006, retail consultancy Experian ranked Birmingham as the country's third most dynamic retail centre after it had trailed 13th (and behind all other major regional cities) at the beginning of the decade. The city is now playing a greater role as a regional centre, as more than a quarter of Bullring shoppers come from beyond the immediate urban area (Birmingham Alliance 2006).

Alongside this economic transition, the 'city living' strategy has developed into a significant driver of change in Birmingham's housing markets since the mid-1990s. More than 9000 new city-centre homes, 85% for private sale, were completed from 1995 to 2007. This new market began as an integral part of the city-centre regeneration initiatives outlined above, and has since expanded outwards into adjacent, previously industrial, districts of the enlarged city centre. New completions in the CBD currently exceed 1500 dwellings per year and there is growing evidence that these are adding to the diversity of housing options within Birmingham for middle- and high-income households, and is contributing (albeit modestly) to first signs of a re-urbanisation process and supporting service provision in the inner city. However, 'city living' remains a narrow market, dominated by young professional residents, investor purchasers and rental occupation, a highly transient population and a preponderance of small one- and two-bedroom apartments. The process is also beginning to exert some gentrification or displacement pressures on nearby communities, most of which are characterised by high levels of deprivation, as well as mainly industrial enterprises in areas such as Ladywood and Digbeth (Barber 2007).

However, beneath these outwardly impressive changes, there remains evidence of more problematic economic and social circumstances amid the restructuring process. By 2005, the conurbation had a proportion of its workforce in manufacturing (15.0%) that was little higher than that of the UK as a whole (11.15) (BEIC 2005). This might suggest a successful transition from an industrial past to a post-industrial present. However, these figures obscure the fact the Birmingham's manufacturing base remains dominated by low-growth sectors. For example, in 2004, relative employment in the automotive sector in Birmingham was still more than three times the national average (BCC 2006). Conversely, employment in computer manufacture, other electronic industries and pharmaceuticals was 18, 29 and 61% of the national average respectively (BCC 2006). The most striking feature of the contemporary Birmingham economy, perhaps, is not the distribution of workers between sectors but the fact, at the time of the 2001 Census, a total of 350,658 Birmingham residents were in employment; a figure nearly 40% below the post-war peak (Office for National Statistics). Thus little has changed in the decade since Bryson *et al.* (1996) argued that 'Birmingham is far from being a post industrial city founded on a strong and diverse service economy with a relatively small (but high value added) manufacturing sector' (p. 166).

It is notable that despite the national acclaim for its CBD development strategy, Birmingham has performed poorly compared to its peer cities (which, themselves, may be considered to under perform economically in a European context). In December 2007, the (claimant) unemployment rate for Birmingham (8.1%) was the second highest for all the core cities. Elsewhere, unemployment rates varied from 8.4% (Liverpool) to 2.5% (Bristol) (BEIC 2007).

Birmingham has benefited from substantial central government investment in area regeneration and neighbourhood renewal in the past decade. This has included some £140 million in Single Regeneration Budget (SRB) programmes, mostly in inner-city neighbourhoods, since 1995; £100 million in two New Deal for Communities (NDC) areas (Aston in the inner city and Kings Norton in the southern suburbs); and, a variety of programmes financed via the Neighbourhood Renewal Fund (NRF). Moreover, a third 'Highbury Symposium', convened in February 2005, identified as the top priority for the city's future development the need to raise the quality of life and to 'shift the balance of priorities in regeneration and renewal by replicating the success of city centre regeneration in local neighbourhoods' (BCC 2004).

Notwithstanding this state investment (a number of BCC reports have noted its failure to reduce unemployment differentials throughout the city or, indeed, to have a notable impact on 'headline' unemployment figures in target neighbourhoods; BCC 2003, 2006) and that expended in the CBD, Birmingham remains a highly polarised city in terms of social and economic indicators. Analysis of the spatial distribution of deprivation at neighbourhood level in Birmingham between 1991 and 2001 shows that in both years, a 'collar' of deprivation around the CBD is very marked. It is also noticeable that there has been a decline in absolute levels of deprivation in Birmingham. That is, in 2001, fewer neighbourhoods exhibited deprivation levels above the top quartile threshold than in 1991. However, this has led to a 'residualisation' of deprivation. In light of the general increase in standards of living nationally, during the decade, it is possible to argue that the neighbourhoods identified as the most deprived in 2001 are relatively more deprived than in 1991.

Birmingham remains a highly polarised city in terms of the distribution of economic and social opportunities between social groups. In 2001, a white Birmingham resident was less than half as likely to be unemployed (an unemployment rate of 7.4%) than one of a minority ethnic background (unemployment rates exceed 15% for all other ethnic groups).

Finally, with regard to the significant new job opportunities that have been created in and near the CBD since the early 1990s, it is well established that in-commuting from beyond the city boundaries is highest among the high-value occupations that have driven the CBD economic revival in recent years. Indeed, between 44% and 51% of managerial and professional jobs in Birmingham are filled by individuals living outside the city.

In this respect, then, it is evident that the partial economic revival spurred by the regeneration strategy has brought significant benefits primarily to in-commuters, professionals and the small but growing population of mainly young professionals living in the new city-centre housing. But at the same time, large segments of Birmingham's population, notably those in outlying council estates and the inner-city districts with high black and minority ethnic (BME) and recent migrant populations, have been bypassed by the achievement of the city's response to economic restructuring over the past 20 years.

Conclusions

This paper has sought to bring together two separate discourses that have dominated debate about urban policy responses to economic restructuring, deindustrialisation, major plant closures and the rise of the service and knowledge-based economy over the past 20 years. In the case of Birmingham, the policy drive of city-centre regeneration, flagship development and the re-making of central urban space for new economic activities has been accompanied by much acclaim and 'boosterist' hype, while proving highly influential on other cities as well. At the same time, the socio-spatial impact of economic restructuring and the resulting policy response has been extremely uneven. The economic difficulties and wider disadvantage experienced by much of the city's population and many of its neighbourhoods, especially those inner-city areas with large BME populations, have endured and even deepened since the early 1990s despite the efforts of numerous area-based regeneration programmes funded by central government.

In response to our core question (whose urban renaissance?) it is clear that the dominance of the 'boosterist' discourse is significantly tempered by the uneven and enduring socio-economic divides within the city and the partial nature of the city's overall recovery, particularly in terms of providing employment for its residents. In this sense, significant policy challenges remain despite the clear achievements of the past 20 years.

An imperative for Birmingham policy-makers, then, is to find ways of binding together the dual imperatives of creating new economic opportunities, and addressing aspects of acute need among the local population. It is not the purpose of this paper to provide detailed policy prescriptions, but we can offer a broad overview of some alternative options open to policy-makers in Birmingham and other restructuring cities. The first two options concern ways of adapting the city-centre redevelopment agenda, and the third represents a more fundamental shift in the spatial focus of economic restructuring strategy.

First, measures are required to directly connect new employment opportunities created in city-centre regeneration with the communities and areas of need. A precedent for such action was provided by the opening of the Bullring retail centre in 2003. This was accompanied by an extensive public–private initiative to encourage unemployed residents in deprived areas of Birmingham to apply for the 5500 new jobs being created. Some 2230 of these posts were taken by people who took advantage of this initiative; more than 1000 of these individuals were previously unemployed and approximately half were from ethnic minority groups disproportionately affected by worklessness (Barber 2004). Extending such an initiative to more typically disparate regeneration processes (rather than a one-off development project) is a more complex task, but it is worth pursuing.

Second, there is an opportunity to adapt the city-centre regeneration agenda to encompass a broader range of objectives, activities and beneficiaries. There are two possible variations on this theme. The first one is to re-orientate ongoing city-centre regeneration around developments that would encourage a more bottom-up approach to economic renewal that can draw upon the interests and skills of its young people, such as through the provision of start-up and small business premises, education and training facilities, and the linking of these through targeted policy for important growth sectors such as in the creative industries. In Birmingham the first seeds of this approach have been evident in some of the thinking behind the Eastside district, although the realisation of such ambitions has been slow to emerge. The second variation is to harness the momentum of the city living development to guide a sustainable restructuring of adjacent inner-city districts, many of them experiencing high levels of deprivation. With proactive planning approaches, it is possible to encourage new private housing and economic functions into such areas without generating substantial displacement effects, combining this with regeneration programmes that can link new employment opportunities and local residents in a focused manner.

A third, more ambitious, alternative is to fundamentally alter the spatial approach to economic regeneration policy. This would entail focusing new service-sector business and employment growth in a small number of suburban centres closer to the communities and neighbourhoods disadvantaged by the restructuring of the 1980s and 1990s. Such centres and concentrations of new opportunities would need to be anchored by much improved public transport access, and accompanied by continued investment in education and skills training for residents of these nearby areas.

All of these policy possibilities are variations on the core imperative to link the creation of new economic opportunities with the addressing of socio-economic needs through proactive, innovative spatial policy initiatives. All are emerging onto the policy agenda in Birmingham, to varying degrees, but have yet to be applied with sufficient weight. The latter two possibilities in particular require the public sector to exert a strong role in shaping market conditions, influencing the character and mix of new development, rather than relying overwhelmingly on market forces and private-sector investment as has often been the case in the past. This is a formidable task for policy-makers in Birmingham and other restructuring cities, but an essential one to grasp if their strategic response to economic upheaval is to provide sustainable, lasting benefits for all of their residents.

Acknowledgements

The authors wish to acknowledge the support of the ESRC under award number RES-000-22-2478.

References

Audit Commission, 2004. *Annual audit and inspection letter*. London: Audit Commission
Barber, A., 2004. *Birmingham's city centre strategy and policies to extend its benefits to wider communities*. Paper presented to Asian Development Bank seminar, Manila, Philippines, 10–12 Oct.
Barber, A., 2006. *Reconciling competitiveness and inclusion in the heart of the entrepreneurial city? Planning for new central districts in Lyon and Birmingham*. Paper presented to the World Planning Congress, Mexico City, 11–16 July.
Barber, A., 2007. Planning for sustainable re-urbanisation: policy challenges and city centre housing in Birmingham. *Town planning review*, forthcoming.
BEIC, 2005. *Birmingham and Solihull economic review 2005/6*. Birmingham: Birmingham Economic Information Centre.
BEIC, 2007. *Unemployment briefing – December 2007*. Birmingham: Birmingham Economic Information Centre.
Birmingham Alliance, 2004. *Bullring halts city's shopper export*. Birmingham: Birmingham Alliance.
Birmingham City Council (BCC), 2003. *The effectiveness of Birmingham SRB programmes in getting people into work*. Scrutiny report to City Council. Birmingham: Birmingham City Council.
Birmingham City Council (BCC), 2004. *Flourishing neighbourhoods: Birmingham's neighbourhood renewal strategy 2003/4*. Birmingham: Birmingham City Council.
Birmingham City Council (BCC), 2006. *Information briefing: employment. Reducing the differentials.* Birmingham: Birmingham City Council.
Birmingham Post, 2005. Region is more attractive since MG Rover crash. *Birmingham Post*, 1 July.
Bloomfield, J., 2001. Rethinking global city centres – a rejoinder to Henry and Passmore. *Soundings: a journal of politics and culture*, 17, 154–157.
Boddy, M. and Parkinson, M., eds., 2004. *City matters, competitiveness, cohesion and urban governance*. Bristol: Policy Press.
Brennan, A., Rhodes, J., and Tyler, P., 2003. New developments in area-based initiatives in England: the experience of the single regeneration budget. *Urban studies*, 40 (8), 1399–1426.
Bryson, J., Daniels, P., and Henry, N., 1996. From widgets to where? The Birmingham economy in the 1990s. *In*: A. Gerrard and T. Slater, eds. *Managing a conurbation: Birmingham and its region*. Studley: Brewin.
Building, 2000. Crisis, what crisis? *Building*, 22.
Davies, J., 2001. *Partnerships and regimes: the politics of urban regeneration in the UK*. Ashgate: Aldershot.
DETR, 2000. *Our towns and cities the future – delivering an urban renaissance*. London: Department for the Environment, Transport and the Regions.
Digaetano, A. and Klemanski, J., 1993. Urban regime capacity: a comparison of Birmingham, England and Detroit, Michigan. *Journal of urban affairs*, 15 (4), 367–384.

Fothergill, S., Gudgin, G., Kitson, M., and Monk, S., 1986. The de-industrialisation of the city. *In*: R. Martin and B. Rowthorn, eds. *The geography of de-industrialisation*. Basingstoke: Macmillan.

Gwynne, R., 1996. From craft to lean: technological change and the motor vehicle industry in the West Midlands. *In*: A. Gerrard and T. Slater, eds. *Managing a conurbation: Birmingham and its region*. Studley: Brewin.

Hall, T. and Hubbard, P., 1998. *The entrepreneurial city: geographies of politics, regime, and representation*. Chichester: Wiley.

Harvey, D., 1989. From managerialism to entrepreneurialism: the transformation in urban governance in late capitalism. *Geografiska annaler B*, 71, 3–17.

Henry, N. and Passmore, A., 1999. Rethinking global city centres – the example of Birmingham. *Soundings: a journal of politics and culture*, 13, 60–66.

Imrie, R. and Raco, M., 2003. *Urban renaissance? New Labour, urban policy and community*. Bristol: Policy Press.

KPMG, 1993. *The economic impact of the ICC, NIA and NEC on the West Midlands*. London: KPMG.

Levine, M., 1987. Downtown redevelopment as urban growth strategy. *Journal of urban affairs*, 9 (2), 103–123.

Loftman, P. and Nevin, B., 1992. *Urban regeneration and social equity: a case study of Birmingham 1986–1992*. Occasional Paper No. 8, Faculty of the Built Environment, University of Central England, Birmingham.

Loftman, P. and Nevin, B., 1994. Prestige project development: economic renaissance or economic myth? A case study of Birmingham. *Local economy*, 8 (4), 307–325.

Loftman, P. and Nevin, B., 1996. Going for growth: prestige projects in three British cities. *Urban studies*, 33 (6), 991–1019.

Martin, R., and Rowthorn, B., eds., 1986. *The geography of deindustrialisation*. Basingstoke: Macmillan.

ODPM, 2004a. *Making it happen: urban renaissance and prosperity in our core cities*. London: Office of the Deputy Prime Minister.

ODPM, 2004b. *Competitive European cities: where do the core cities stand?*. London: Office of the Deputy Prime Minister.

Porter, L. and Barber, A., 2006. Closing time: state-led gentrification and the meaning of place in Birmingham's Eastside. *City*, 10 (2), 215–234.

Sassens, S., 2006. *Cities in a world economy*. Thousand Oaks: Pine Forge Press.

Smyth, H., 1994. *Marketing the city: the role of flagship developments in urban regeneration*. London: Spon.

Spencer, K., *et al.*, 1986. *Crisis in the industrial heartlands: a study of the West Midlands*. Oxford: Clarendon.

Turok, I. and Edge, N., 1999. *The jobs gap in Britain's cities – employment loss and labour market consequences*. Bristol: Policy Press.

The housing and neighbourhood impacts of knowledge-based economic development following industrial closure

Alex Burfitt and Ed Ferrari

Introduction

The regional response to the Rover 'crisis' has been multifaceted, with aspects of success (Bailey 2003, House of Commons 2006). The 'Rover Task Force' (RTF) has on the one hand pursued policies of economic diversification, while on the other enabled significant investment in personal support, re-skilling and education for former Rover employees. The long-term economic prospects of neighbourhoods around the factory, however, will also be determined by what happens subsequently on the Rover site (Regeneris Consulting 2005).

Economic development proposals for the site envisage a variety of economic and residential uses. Although these are being articulated with increasing precision through the planning framework (BCC and BDC 2007), a core original component of the proposals is the development of a science and technology park on part of the Longbridge site. This development also represents one element of the Central Technology Belt (CTB), a 'high-technology corridor' running from the centre of Birmingham to the south of the adjoining county of Worcestershire. This economic development initiative is overseen by Birmingham City Council, the Regional Development Agency (RDA) and other local partners. Its objectives are to exploit knowledge assets in local firms, universities and hospitals in order to foster the development of high technology and knowledge-intensive enterprises. Whilst the proposals for other components of the Longbridge site are likely to outweigh the technology park in terms of land usage or direct job creation it is the CTB proposals that represent the greatest break from the economic traditions of the local economy and the most significant effort to establish a new, sustainable economic base for the area.

This paper is concerned with one of the key policy questions arising from this proposed switch in local economic activity. How can the development of the CTB site at Longbridge ensure appropriate and commensurate benefits for the local area and its residents? There are two fundamental components to this dynamic. The first relates to direct and indirect labour market impacts, such as the likely propensity for existing local residents to take up employment on the CTB Longbridge site or to benefit from the local secondary employment it generates. The second component involves the broader neighbourhood benefits to be gained from anchoring highly-skilled incoming workers within nearby communities, or alternatively, the potential costs of failing to achieve this. Given the nature of the CTB proposals for its Longbridge site and their marked divergence from the area's economic traditions, this latter aspect is likely to be especially relevant and challenging. In particular, the objective of diversifying the local economy from a long-standing history of medium-technology to a high-tech and knowledge-intensive future is likely to generate restructuring in the local labour force with concomitant changes in patterns of housing and neighbourhood demand.

Florida (2001), for example, has argued that the growth of high-technology centres is strongly related to the capacity of an area to attract and retain a highly skilled, 'creative' and mobile component of the workforce. Crucially, he has suggested that these workers are especially attracted to places demonstrating marked social diversity and characterised by high-quality housing and residential areas – factors often grouped within the concept of 'quality of place'. This insight has acted to recast residential factors, such the quality of local housing and the nature and internal diversity of neighbourhoods, as fundamental components of local economic competitiveness, bringing them into the mainstream of economic development policy and investment. Wong (2001) and Andrews (2001), for instance, argue that quality of place is an important factor underpinning competitiveness, especially where the aspiration is to develop the knowledge economy. Likewise LDY (2006) assert that:

> the literature, though not conclusive, suggest[s] that those economies seeking to grow the Knowledge Economy sector, would benefit more from Quality of Place investment and there may be a disproportionate benefit from those locations with a limited base. (LDY 2006, p. 38)

Cambridge Econometrics *et al.* (2003) also cite housing and local facilities alongside the more traditional forms of communicative infrastructure as being important regional factors of competitiveness. Furthermore, they note that these factors are more important (and consequently a higher investment priority) in what they term 'hubs of knowledge' (highly urbanised and cosmopolitan regions with high levels of gross value added) than in other regions.

It is perhaps questionable as to whether Birmingham or the West Midlands could be classed as such a 'hub'. Nevertheless, from the perspective of the preceding literature it appears that the policy of promoting the growth of a knowledge-intensive workforce through the development of the CTB technology park at Longbridge will raise questions over the quality of place offered by local housing and neighbourhoods. A particular concern in this context is the likelihood that the characteristics of the housing and neighbourhoods that surround this industrial site will be mismatched with the demands of a high-technology workforce. Two scenarios unfold from this. Either the local economy as a whole lacks the necessary quality of place to attract and retain a knowledge workforce at all; or there is a sufficiently attractive offer but the nature of housing and neighbourhoods in the immediate vicinity of the site are such that incomers choose other locations to live in, either immediately or over time. The potential benefits of a highly-skilled incoming workforce will therefore not accrue to the communities most directly affected by economic decline.

These scenarios in turn generate a dilemma for local policy-makers. On the one hand there is a necessity to secure economic diversification for the local economy as a whole, whilst on the other is the requirement to address the specific needs of the discrete number of neighbourhoods and communities most adversely affected by the initial closure; neighbourhoods whose quality of place offer is also likely to be furthest from the requirements of the incoming workforce. Policy makers must therefore construct housing and regeneration policies at the scale of the local housing market that are capable of securing the required diversification of the local economy and its workforce. Yet at the same time these policies must also be relevant to existing residents in the particular neighbourhoods affected by the closure. In particular, they must not subvert their needs in meeting the demands of a new economy. Equally, they must seek to maximise the regenerative benefit of an in-migrating workforce for existing communities. This can be a difficult balance to achieve, as recent experience of the Housing Market Renewal programme in the UK suggests (Cameron 2006).

The remainder of this paper examines the labour market and associated housing demand changes that are likely to emerge as a consequence of the CTB technology park on the Longbridge site. After presenting the research methodology the paper reviews the history, objectives and structure of the CTB. In the third substantive part of the paper, the potential labour market, housing and neighbourhood impacts of the CTB proposals for its Longbridge site are examined. The paper concludes by considering the implications of these developments for the policy framework in place following the closure of Rover.

Methodology

Several methods are used to address each of the paper's main research questions. First, potential labour market impacts are assessed through an analysis of national data sets including the Annual Business Inquiry (ABI) and the Labour Force Survey (LFS).[1] Second, the socio-economic characteristics of communities in the south of Birmingham are examined using small-area data from the 2001 Census of Population. Third, a review of the housing characteristics of a proxy high-tech workforce is provided through an analysis of the housing choices and priorities of members of the University of Birmingham science deaneries collected through a survey.[2] Finally, these requirements are compared to the patterns of housing and neighbourhood supply in the south of the city based again on small-area data from the Census.

Given the need to identify the impacts of the CTB at a neighbourhood level, a standard set of sub-local authority spatial units have been used throughout the research. These are the nine Housing Market Areas (HMAs) defined in Birmingham City Council's Housing Strategy (BCC 2005). These delineate areas within the city that have a certain level of commonality in factors such as house price activity, social housing turnover and tenure profile and also demonstrate a degree of cohesion across a range of socio-economic factors.

Two HMAs are of particular significance as these respectively contain and abut the Longbridge site: South West Birmingham (SWB), a peripheral zone running along the south-eastern boundary of the city, and containing the Longbridge site and a number of major areas of social housing; and the Suburban Ring South (SRS), a residential zone between SWB and the City Centre containing the university and characterised by more affluent neighbourhoods.

Data from the Index of Deprivation show that SWB has a significantly higher level of socio-economic deprivation than the SRS, which, considering its urban location, demonstrates relatively low levels of deprivation.[3] Furthermore, SWB is significantly more exposed to the labour market consequences of the closure of Rover. Some 28% of Rover employees in 2004 were resident in this neighbourhood; equivalent to 1.8% of total residence-based employment in the area. In contrast, only 6.2% of Rover employees lived in the SRS; equal to 0.4% of total residence-based employment.

The central technology belt

The development of the CTB predates the final closure of Rover in 2005. Its roots can be traced back to the sale and break-up of the Rover Group by BMW in early 2000. In response the Government set up the Rover Task Force (RTF) to consider the potential impacts of the closure and to put in place measures to deal with any likely fallout (Bailey 2003). The RDA, Advantage West Midlands (AWM), took the lead. Alongside administering a number of grant programmes, the RTF commissioned a series of reports focused on identifying innovative ways to compensate for the possible loss of Rover employment and to diversify the local economy from an over-reliance on the automotive sector. One of these, *Regenerating the West Midlands region: a study to consider opportunities for high technology corridors/clusters* (SQW 2001) argued that a 'corridor of regeneration', based on spillovers from the region's science and technology knowledge base, might take place along the A38 road running from central Birmingham to Malvern in the south of the region. Along this route in Birmingham lie not only the Longbridge site but also Birmingham and Aston universities and the Queen Elizabeth 'super-hospital'. Beyond the city boundary the route includes University College Worcester and Qinetiq, the former Ministry of Defence research centre in Malvern.

The recommendation for a high-technology corridor was supported by the RTF, which led to its inclusion in AWM's second Regional Economic Strategy (RES) published in 2004 (AWM 2004). High-technology corridors were enshrined as one of three key delivery mechanisms for the strategy alongside industrial clusters and regeneration zones. AWM established the CTB Company in January 2004 as a company limited by guarantee with a board chaired by the Pro-Vice Chancellor of the University of Birmingham and with members from relevant local authorities, public bodies and science parks. The objectives of the Company are to stimulate a more diverse economy by capitalising on the knowledge-intensive opportunities afforded by universities and research centres in the area. Overall, the CTB Company's ambition is to 'create technology rich business opportunities and bring about key economic benefits for people living and working in the [West Midlands] region' (CTB 2007).

Interventions are a mixture of infrastructure projects and investment in business support, research funding, public service improvements and the attraction of inward investment to the area. A key delivery vehicle is the coordination and development of several new science and technology parks on the sites of existing redundant economic uses. Indicative plans suggest that the CTB Company is targeting the creation of some 75 acres across three sites for the development of science and technology parks in south Birmingham, with a total direct employment target of 6300 jobs. The CTB's portion of the Longbridge site is significant among these. Here there will be a focus on the development of nanotechnology engineering and R&D, and environmental technologies, expected to directly create 4400 jobs on up to 58 acres. However, the Company has as yet to set out an explicit strategy or set of mechanisms that will allow local communities currently characterised by an absence of these high-tech skills to connect with CTB employment opportunities – a process that is unlikely to occur if left to its own devices. It appears, for instance, that former Rover employees are finding jobs in traditional manufacturing sectors rather than significantly penetrating new, knowledge-intensive sectors (Armstrong 2006).

Labour market and neighbourhood impacts

This section of the paper considers the likely impact of the CTB, first in terms of the employment opportunities it hopes to bring about and, second, the consequent impact on the local neighbourhood, its housing and communities.

New economy, new workforce?

Table 1 demonstrates that the region's current high-tech workforce is distinct not only to the regional workforce as a whole but also to its medium-tech comparator along a number of axes. First, there is a demographic difference with a propensity towards an older and disproportionately male workforce. Second, there are clear differences in working arrangements and remuneration levels, with the high-tech workforce characterised by higher rates of full-time and highly-paid employment. Third, the most substantial differences are in the educational characteristics of each component of the labour force.

Table 1. Key statistics for high-tech and comparator workforces in the West Midlands, 2004.

	High-tech labour force	Medium-tech labour force	Rest of regional labour force
Modal age group	40–44 years	35–39 years	35–39 years
Male (%)	73.0%	66.5%	51.9%
Full time (%)	93.4%	83.8%	71.6%
Gross hourly pay (£s)	£12.25	£10.40	£8.72
Post 16 education (%)	67.0%	41.9%	40.8%
No educational qualifications (%)	3.7%	12.8%	13.7%
Degree or equivalent (%)	30.6%	17.4%	14.7%
Managerial and professional occupations (%)	48.4%	27.4%	22.6%
Elementary occupations	1.2%	12.7%	13.0%
Commute >30 min (%)	30.3%	22.7%	16.5%
Inter-regional commuters (%)	9.5%	6.2%	4.9%
Inter-regional move in last year (those in current job <1 yr) (%)	35.8%	17.1%	9.5%

Source: Quarterly Labour Force Survey.

The tendency for high-tech workers to have stayed in education post-16 and to have gained formal educational qualifications, frequently at degree level, at a much higher rate than medium-tech and other workers is clear. Fourth, the educational achievements of the high-tech labour force are associated with a substantially greater proportion of higher-order managerial and professional jobs and conversely a lower level of unskilled elementary occupations. Finally, high-tech workers have markedly higher levels of mobility, not only in terms of commuting but also in terms of geographical labour market mobility. Data from the LFS suggest that 35.8% of high-tech workers in post for less than 12 months also undertook an inter-regional move in this period, over twice the rate of the medium-tech workforce.

Taken together, the labour market profile suggests that the CTB workforce will be disproportionately male, full-time, white collar, highly educated and highly skilled. It also appears that the residential geography of workers will be more dispersed and less centred on work locations. Finally, given the high degree of geographical mobility it is also likely that CTB employment will be associated with a large number of incomers from outside the region. However, as job-related inter-regional migration is predicated on the occupations of workers rather than sector *per se*, the rate of in-migration will differ markedly across different job types (Dixon 2003). It is likely that a disproportionate amount of in-migrants will be in managerial and professional occupations. This will create a distinct segmentation in the labour market for CTB employment opportunities based on levels of skills within the workforce. Lower-skilled positions will be filled predominantly from workers already in place in local and regional labour markets, whilst there will be national and international competition for higher-skilled positions resulting in a far higher number of these types of workers migrating into the region.

With this template of the likely CTB workforce in mind it is interesting to examine its fit with the characteristics of the resident workforce in the south of Birmingham. Table 2 demonstrates that there are marked differences between the resident workforces in the two HMAs in south Birmingham. In particular, it is clear that it is the SRS's workforce that is characterised by the high rates of educational performance that are definitive of the high-tech sector. Equally, the SRS has markedly higher levels of employment in highly-skilled managerial and professional occupations. In contrast, SWB's workforce performs at a rate below that of the city as a whole.

This comparison indicates that there is a distinct mismatch between the CTB proposals for its Longbridge site and the workforce in certain neighbourhoods in this part of the city. In particular, whilst communities in SWB have been most affected by the Longbridge closure they are least aligned to the opportunities presented by the CTB proposals. Clearly

Table 2. Key statistics for Birmingham workforce by Housing Market Area, 2004.

	SWB	SRS	B'ham	West Midlands
Full time worker*	77.4%	80.8%	78.4%	77.1%
Degree or equivalent**	13.2%	27.3%	16.6%	16.2%
No educational qualifications**	38.3%	27.0%	37.1%	34.0%
Managerial or professional occupations***	19.9%	32.3%	23.3%	24.0%
Elementary occupations***	14.2%	10.6%	13.6%	13.0%

*Proportion of employed population aged 16–74, excluding self-employed.
**Proportion of population aged 16–74.
***Proportion of employed population aged 16–74.
Source: ONS 2001.

there will still be some opportunities for these workers, but as a whole the CTB proposals do not appear to reflect the requirements of many workers in SWB. In contrast, it appears that it is the workforce resident in SRS, based on university, healthcare and professional employment, that is better equipped to access planned CTB employment. Furthermore, there is strong alignment of the population immediately to the south of Birmingham with the characteristics of a high-tech workforce. Consequently, the CTB proposals for its Longbridge high-tech park present the possibility that this significant portion of the site, once so central to employment provision for local residents, will instead provide employment predominantly for residents from the relatively affluent SRS and commuter areas south of the city.

Housing market impacts – anchoring incoming workers

Existing communities in SWB are poorly aligned to CTB opportunities and hence are less likely to benefit *directly* from CTB employment compared to other surrounding communities. However, the likelihood that the CTB will generate significant levels of in-movement of highly skilled workers creates the possibility of capturing *indirect* benefits through the attraction of these workers to SWB neighbourhoods. This can lead to wider socio-economic and housing benefits for existing communities including viable local services, higher levels of social capital, and other benefits associated with mixed communities (Berube 2005).

The propensity for incoming high-tech workers to locate in Longbridge neighbourhoods was examined through a survey of a proxy local knowledge-intensive workforce: members of the University of Birmingham's two science deaneries. The survey was predicated on the assumption that there will be a number of distinct components to the workforce taking up CTB employment. First, there will be workers taking up new employment and undertaking a job-related move into the region as a result. Second, there will be workers taking up new CTB employment who are already resident in the region, and therefore not required to undertake a job-related move. Finally, there will be workers in existing jobs in local firms that have relocated to the CTB sites. This is transferred rather than new employment, and also does not involve job-related movement. Given the anticipated demographic and socio-economic differences between these segments, it is likely that they will have distinct housing characteristics (Clark and Huang 2004). Consequently, the analysis of the university survey data reflects this diversity by employing three distinct labour market segments: new workers at the university (in post for less than five years) who have moved into the region in association with taking up employment (Group 1); new workers who were already resident in the region (Group 2); and a mature component who had been in post for over five years (Group 3).

Analysis of the socio-economic characteristics for each of the three workforce groups demonstrates that whilst the workforce as a whole is characterised by high levels of higher-order employment, this is especially marked in relation to Group 1 workers (93.1% of workers are in managerial and professional occupations). As would be expected, Group 3 workers are noticeably older (89.3% are aged 35 or over) than the two groups of recent recruits, but there is no significant age difference between Group 1 and Group 2 workers (42.9% and 43.1% aged 35 or over, respectively). Given the age differentials it is also not surprising that new workers (Groups 1 and 2) are also less likely to have a partner or children than the mature workforce (Group 3). However, Group 1 workers are more likely to be single (39.1%) and without children (21.1%) than those in Group 2 (26.7% and 31.6%, respectively). Overall, it appears that the CTB is likely to be associated with a highly skilled workforce in general, but that Group 1 workers (incomers) will form a distinct highly-skilled and less socially-constrained component.

The socio-demographic characteristics of each group also appear to be associated with particular patterns of housing consumption. Residence in flats is markedly higher amongst Group 1 workers (22.5%) compared to Group 2 (10.8%) and Group 3 (5.9%). This is related to marked differences in tenure patterns for both houses and flats. Group 1 workers are substantially more likely to take up private rented accommodation (37.4%) compared to Group 2 (13.3%) and Group 3 (3.9%). As incoming workers progress through their housing careers their patterns of consumption will begin to resemble those of the mature workforce (Group 3), 90% of whom live in owner-occupied houses. Consequently, in the long run the CTB is likely to generate increased demand for this type of accommodation. Yet, in the short term the initial formation of the CTB workforce is likely to be associated with an increased demand for privately rented flats. There is a complete absence of demand for social (public) housing across all three groups.

The survey of the proxy high-tech workforce also indicated that there were spatial differences in the geographical choices of the different workforce segments. In particular, it was clear that Group 1 workers were more likely to be located within 5 km (66.2%) of their workplace than Group 2 (52.7%) or Group 3 (48.0%) workers. There was also a very marked relative drop in Group 1 workers located between 5 km and 10 km from their work. This suggests that the objective for these workers is not simply to be close to work, but to be as close as possible. The outcome of this residential geography is that the median distance to work figure for Group 1 workers (3.3 km) is noticeably lower than for their counterparts (5.2 km and 5.6 km, respectively).

The survey explored the underlying reasons for the distinctive housing profile of in-movers by examining the decision-making processes behind the most recent move made by Group 1 and Group 2 workers. This therefore contrasted inter-regional job-related moves with intra-regional non-job-related or 'adjustment' moves. Respondents were asked to identify the extent to which they agreed or disagreed with a series of 41 statements relating to their most recent housing and neighbourhood choice. These scores were then aggregated in order to give a series of ranks of preferences for each workforce segment.

This analysis showed that flexibility in tenure arrangements ranked 14 places higher in shaping the decision of incomers (Group 1) to take up their current property compared to non-incomers (Group 2). In contrast, a desire to stay in the area or be near family and friends was ranked 13 and 10 places higher, respectively, by non-incomers. Overall, the analysis demonstrates a picture whereby the housing and neighbourhood decisions of incomers (Group 1) are driven to a greater extent by flexible tenure arrangements and proximity to work and suburban and city-centre facilities (Burfitt et al. 2006). Issues relating to social and cultural facilities, friendship networks, house type and design, and neighbourhood diversity are not as important as they are for groups already located in the region (Group 2). This is not to say that incoming workers do not value these features – and they are generally important – but these are the areas where there is most significant difference. In contrast, those already in the region prioritise housing characteristics, the desire to become an owner-occupier, the availability of schooling and the maintenance of social and family networks. They are already socially embedded in the area whereas incomers are not constrained by these ties and make their decisions on a narrower range of factors.

These findings perhaps present a window of opportunity for policy-makers to influence the location choices of a group of workers that has limited knowledge or prejudices of an area, has few social constraints, and has modest housing requirements beyond a desire to be close to work. They could form the basis of a new population in redeveloped areas in previously deprived neighbourhoods. In contrast, encouraging the existing workforce to relocate there might be more difficult.

Housing and neighbourhood supply

The remainder of this section examines the degree to which different neighbourhoods in the south of Birmingham are able to meet the particular requirements of incoming high-tech workers. Table 3 shows the housing type and tenure profiles for the two south Birmingham HMAs and also for Birmingham as a whole. It demonstrates that SWB is markedly less diverse in its offer than the SRS and arguably – at least in terms of tenure and type offer – is not immediately attractive to the incoming population associated with high-technology employment due to a paucity of rental accommodation or flats for rent or sale. The prevalence of social rented accommodation may also make it unattractive to an incoming workforce. The implication here is that the potential of SWB to capitalise on an incoming workforce whose housing choices are governed to a large extent by a desire for co-location to their place of work may well be lost due to the absence of an appropriate housing offer. The nature of local housing stock and neighbourhoods may also mean that incoming workers that do locate here initially quickly choose to relocate as their housing careers progress (Clark and Huang 2004).

The likelihood that SWB will ultimately prove unattractive to high-tech inter-regional movers can be further demonstrated through analysis of migration data from the 2001 Census. This indicates that SWB was relatively unpopular as a destination for households involved in inter-regional moves. Only 0.45% of households in SWB were there as a result of an inter-regional move into the area in that year. In contrast the SRS had an aggregate rate of in-movement of 0.59% as a share of households, some 31.1% higher than SWB. Crucially, the SRS has also been highly successful at attracting the managerial and professional workers that are so characteristic of the high-tech workforce. Some 67.1% of regional incoming households had a head of household drawn from this category, compared to only 17.8% in SWB.

Policy implications

Taken together, this analysis of high-tech workers' housing choices and the profile of existing housing suggests that the aspirations of households associated with the high-tech sector are remote from south Birmingham's offer and that, consequently, neighbourhoods

Table 3. Housing tenure and type combinations by HMA.

	SWB Owned	SWB Private rented	SWB Social rented	SRS Owned	SRS Private rented	SRS Social rented	Birmingham Owned	Birmingham Private rented	Birmingham Social rented
Houses	56%	5%	19%	57%	10%	11%	56%	7%	15%
Flats	3%	3%	13%	6%	7%	10%	5%	5%	13%
Total	59%	8%	32%	63%	17%	21%	61%	12%	28%

Note: 'Owned' means owner-occupied; 'house' includes bungalow; 'flat' includes maisonette. The table excludes 'other' categories hence some rows may not sum to 100%.
Source: ONS 2001.

in adjoining districts (and beyond) will routinely be considered by new households to the region as well as existing households. This is particularly the case in SWB where the willingness of incoming workers to locate in neighbourhoods close to their employment at the Longbridge site may be stymied by a lack of an appropriately-aligned housing offer – the area particularly lacks an appropriate supply of private rented accommodation, for example. This in turn may fuel location either in the SRS or outside the city in nearby settlements such as Bromsgrove or Solihull: areas that have a similar travel-to-work journey to Longbridge compared to the SRS. As such there is the possibility that as the high-tech workforce matures and undertakes secondary housing moves, it will disproportionately eschew south Birmingham in favour of more affluent surrounding areas. Such 'second wave' effects will thus jeopardise the ability for any long-term benefits from the CTB to be secured for those areas and communities most affected by the Rover closure.

When former industrial plants like Longbridge are redeveloped, there can be a strong mismatch between the demands of an envisaged replacement workforce and the characteristics of the housing and neighbourhoods that surround their workplaces. This suggests that, at the very least, housing and regeneration policies need to be complementary to the likely labour market pattern of the new economy. The most important components of such policies are likely to be housing and tenure diversification (notably encouraging a larger and higher-quality private rented sector); the application of mixed communities principles to new developments and remodelling activity; a focus on high quality local services; improvements to accessibility and transport infrastructure (both to workplace sites and to the city centre); and the development of sufficient housing choices within the area to meet the aspirations and needs of workers as their lifestyles and housing needs evolve.

But there is an attendant danger that such housing and neighbourhood policies can lose sight of the needs of existing residents. The need to maintain local relevance while reshaping the nature of an area's housing offer and overall character is quite clearly a question of balance. Recent experience of the UK's Housing Market Renewal (HMR) policy – where housing-led regeneration explicitly aims to cater for an aspired-for future population – proves that the practice of implementing such policies is fraught with difficulty and the justification is far from uncontested (Cameron 2006). The interim lessons learned from HMR such as those highlighted by Leather et al. (2007) seem particularly pertinent. These include the need to engage with residents early and in a transparent way. They also highlight the importance of setting out regeneration policies within a framework of long-term funding certainty wherever possible. The HMR experience suggests that regeneration partnerships can suffer from a 'credibility problem' (Leather et al. 2007, p. 152) at the local level if initial portents of difficult changes within communities prove to be unfounded. The importance of dealing with tangible assets such as land at an early juncture and in an unambiguous way is implied by this. The need for certainty and transparency within economic development initiatives, wherever feasible, seems to be the general rule. We would contend that this applies as much to the housing and neighbourhood implications of economic development as it does to the jobs-creation aspect.

Conclusions

Our analysis demonstrates that the type of workforce associated with high-technology employment growth has characteristics that predispose it to certain housing and neighbourhood choices. These are a poor match to the housing and neighbourhood characteristics of areas where large-scale manufacturing industry has declined. There are broadly two processes that disadvantage these areas. First, workers who move to the region will initially prioritise proximity to work, but also need a flexible supply of rented accommodation, with good access to central services and facilities. Neighbourhoods in peripheral areas have little high-quality rented housing and do not provide good accessibility. Second, even when new workers locate close to their work, the literature on mobility and our findings specific to a high-tech workforce suggest that the residential pattern of workers as their housing career matures will favour more affluent neighbourhoods, often at some distance from their workplace.

This raises a number of related policy implications. First is that economic development strategies need to be partnered with complementary housing and neighbourhood policies. These might necessitate tenure restructuring or other adjustments to supply, although it is clear that such policies require careful and sensitive treatment. Second, there are possible negative outcomes associated with the development of high-tech jobs such as increased commuting and segregation, which might run counter to local policy agendas. Third, the nature of the balance between high-tech jobs growth and other strands of economic development strategy is clearly of importance. Much of what we have concluded in this paper is particularly pertinent to strategies that emphasise high-tech jobs at the expense of others. Where high-tech jobs growth is envisaged as part of a broader set of economic development objectives, the negative impacts may be lessened. In the context of the CTB, this elevates the importance of the wider planning framework for the area and the relationship between the CTB and the strategy underpinning the development of the whole Rover site. But at the broadest level, our conclusion is that securing the success of a high-tech strategy using local resources such as land must not lead to us losing sight of how its wider impacts might affect local communities over the longer term.

Acknowledgements

The authors would like to thank John Gibney and Andrew Tice for their contributions to the research underpinning this article and for their insights into its subject matter. They are particularly grateful to the editors of this special issue and to two anonymous referees for their helpful comments on an earlier draft. The authors of course remain responsible for any errors. Census output is Crown copyright and is reproduced with the permission of the Controller of HMSO and the Queen's Printer for Scotland.

Notes

1. To analyse the high-tech workforce, we amalgamated the generic *high-technology manufacturing industries* classification identified by OECD with a subgroup of the OECD's *knowledge-intensive service sectors*, based on their fit with CTB objectives. Readers should, however, be aware of the imperfect fit between OECD classifications and the actual workforce. For comparison, a 'medium-tech' sector was also analysed, again based on OECD classifications. The 'rest of the regional economy' was retained as a second comparator.
2. Primary survey data have been collected from a 'proxy' local high-tech workforce composed of employees of all types in the University of Birmingham's two science deaneries. A postal survey generated some 688 responses: a response rate of 29.5%. This survey permitted the construction of detailed profiles of mobility and housing consumption amongst different components of this workforce.
3. Some 33.3% of Census Super Output Areas (SOAs) in SWB fall in the 10% most deprived in England and Wales. Only 7.3% of SOAs in the SRS are similarly deprived (ODPM 2004).

References

Advantage West Midlands (AWM), 2004. *Delivering advantage: the West Midlands economic strategy and action plan 2004–2010*. Birmingham: Advantage West Midlands.

Andrews, C.J., 2001. Analyzing quality-of-place. *Environment and planning B*, 28, 201–217.

Armstrong, K., 2006. *Life after MG Rover: the impact of the closure on the workers, their families and the community*. London: The Work Foundation.

Bailey, D., 2003. Globalisation, regions and cluster policies: the case of the Rover Task Force. *Policy studies*, 24 (2/3), 67–85.

Berube, A., 2005. *Mixed communities in England*. York: Joseph Rowntree Foundation.

Birmingham City Council (BCC), 2005. *Housing strategy 2005/6*. Birmingham: Birmingham City Council.

Birmingham City Council (BCC) and Bromsgrove District Council (BDC), 2007. *Longbridge area action plan: preferred options report*. Birmingham: Birmingham City Council.

Burfitt, A., Ferrari, E., Gibney, J., and Tice, A., 2006. *Connecting technology and regeneration aspirations: the potential impact of the Central Technology Belt on residents and communities in South Birmingham*. Report for Birmingham City Council, January, University of Birmingham.

Cambridge Econometrics, Ecorys, and Martin, R.L., 2003. *A study on the factors of regional competitiveness*. Brussels: European Commission.

Cameron, S., 2006. From low demand to rising aspirations: housing market renewal within regional and neighbourhood regeneration policy. *Housing studies*, 21 (1), 3–16.

Central Technology Belt (CTB), 2007. *Welcome to the Central Technology Belt* [online]. Birmingham: Central Technology Belt. Available from: http://www.centraltechnologybelt.com [Accessed 2 May 2007].

Clark, W.A.V. and Huang, Y., 2004. Linking migration and mobility: individual and contextual effects in housing markets in the UK. *Regional studies*, 38 (6), 617–628.

Dixon, S., 2003. Migration within Britain for job reasons. *Labour market trends*, April, 191–201.

Florida, R., 2001. Competing in the age of talent. *Greater Philadelphia regional review*, Summer, 10–17.

House of Commons, 2006. *The closure of MG Rover. Fifty-seventh report of Session 2005–06 of the House of Commons Committee of Public Accounts*. HC 1003. London: The Stationery Office.

Leather, P., Cole, I., and Ferrari, E., 2007. *National evaluation of housing market renewal: baseline report*. London: Communities and Local Government.

Llewelyn Davies Yeang (LDY), 2006. *Quality of place: the North's residential offer*. Newcastle-upon-Tyne: The Northern Way.

Office for National Statistics (ONS), 2001. *Census: standard area statistics (England and Wales)* [computer files]. ESRC/JISC Census Programme, Census Dissemination Unit, Mimas (University of Manchester).

Office of the Deputy Prime Minister (ODPM), 2004. *The English indices of deprivation 2004 (revised)*. London: Office of the Deputy Prime Minister.

Regeneris Consulting, 2005. *Closure of MG Rover: economic impact assessment*, Stage 2 report. Birmingham: Advantage West Midlands.

SQW, 2001. *Regenerating the West Midlands region – a study to consider opportunities for high technology corridors/clusters*. Birmingham: Advantage West Midlands.

Wong, C., 2001. The relationship between quality of life and local economic development: an empirical study of local authority areas in England. *Cities*, 18 (1), 25–32.

The impact of factory closure on local communities and economies: the case of the MG Rover Longbridge closure in Birmingham

Caroline Chapain and Alan Murie

Introduction

Plant closures were studied intensively in the 1970s and the 1980s. Pinch and Mason (1991) argued that these studies were generally derived from a restricted geographical base: they were mostly concerned with redundancies among manufacturing workers in older industrial regions. In order to redress this geographical bias, Pinch and Mason looked at two case studies in the South East and showed that the impact of plant closure redundancies in terms of rates of pay, working conditions and level of job satisfaction may differ in a more buoyant labour market.

More recent studies include Hinde (1994), Tomaney et al. (1997, 1999), Kirkham and Watts (1998), Shutt et al. (2003), Henderson and Shutt (2004) and Pike (2002, 2005). These studies have followed two major research and theoretical strands (Tomaney et al. 1999). The first looks at the plant closures themselves (origin, closure proposal, response) with some particular emphasis on multi-plant closures. The second looks at the aftermath of the closures and their impact on the local economy and/or labour market. Because these two strands are rarely combined in the literature, Tomaney et al. (1999) and Pike (2005) called for a more holistic perspective on closure. However a more holistic view would also need to address a further issue which few of the existing studies engage with – the extent of the spatial and longer-term impacts of closure.

Existing studies of factory closure usually have a strong focus on the workers made redundant and on their work trajectories, but neglect the spatial or neighbourhood impact and the effect on other workers and households living in the same areas as the redundant workers. Hinde's (1994) insightful study of the labour market experiences of redundant workers over a 29-month period in Sunderland following the end of shipbuilding in 1989 looked at placement rates, migration, job-quality issues but only considered the local economic environment as a factor affecting chances of reemployment. Tomaney *et al.* (1997, 1999) studied the case of Swan Hunter in Tyneside. Again, their focus was on the shipbuilding industry and the work trajectory of redundant workers. Shutt *et al.* (2003) and Henderson and Shutt (2004) adopted a wider perspective when looking at the Selby coalfield closure in Yorkshire and Humber in 2002. Their papers look at the causal factors behind the closure, the regional impact and the regeneration needs arising as well as the holistic approach adopted on the policy response side. This more holistic approach was taken into consideration because 'past regeneration experience suggests that socially related problems occur 18 months to two years after mining ceasing' (Henderson and Shutt 2004, p. 34). Their approach to analysis of regional impact was however limited and did not provide a detailed account of the spatial and long-term impact of closure. Finally, Pike (2005), referring to the closure of an R&D company in the North East in 1998, called for 'building a Geographical Political Economy of Closure', looking more broadly at the 'social process of production that unfolds over time, across space and in place'. His paper, however, does not detail the spatial and long-term impact.

Building on Pinch and Mason (1991) and recent calls for a more holistic approach to plant closure, this paper explores the spatial and economic impact of the MG Rover closure at Longbridge over time from 1998 to 2007. The closure at Longbridge represents the largest corporate closure (loss of 6000 jobs) in Britain since that of British Steel at Shotton in 1980. It is one of a number of major closures in the automotive sector occurring in Britain in recent years: Ford in Dagenham (1100 jobs) and Vauxhall in Luton (1900 jobs) in 2002, Jaguar in Coventry (2200 jobs) in 2004, and most recently (2007) Peugeot in Ryton, Coventry (2300 jobs). This paper adds a more recent example of factory closure and refers to a different industry and region compared to much of the existing literature. The data used also enable analysis of the geography of the impact of closure and question the implicit or, at times explicit, assumption that impacts are highly localized. The paper draws on new research which has included analysis of the places of residence of MG Rover workers, use of census data and local employment data as well as published material related to the closure.

The paper reviews the evidence produced so far on the impact of the MG Rover closure and goes on to outline the methodology used to produce new evidence of long-term spatial and economic impacts.

Long-term impacts of the MG Rover closure – the evidence so far

The MG Rover factory in Longbridge, Birmingham closed in April 2005 with the immediate loss of some 5900 jobs. Over 100 years of manufacturing at the old Austin works came to an abrupt end when MG Rover went into administration and its remaining assets were sold to Nanjing Automobile Corporation (see Bailey *et al.* in this issue). Only a skeleton staff remained working at Longbridge. The closure of the last British-owned mass car producer aroused considerable media and political anxiety, not least because it occurred in the middle of the general election campaign taking place that year. The Prime Minister and Chancellor of the Exchequer were among those expressing concern at the closure and leading action to mitigate its impact. The closure of the MG Rover works in Birmingham conjured up an image of job loss, a sudden increase in unemployment and an immediate shock impact on households and local communities. The policy responses were high profile and centred on actions by government and its agencies and partners to help MG Rover workers to find new jobs. In particular a new Rover Task Force was set up with a focus on the Longbridge and Northfield wards and a wider strategic remit to achieve recovery of the local economy, mainly through actions directed at workers and suppliers. An earlier Task Force had been set up in 2000 (Bailey 2003).

Given the large number of redundancies and the iconic symbol that MG Rover represented for the UK automotive industry, various reports have presented short-term evaluations of the policy response to closure and its impact on workers (RC 2005a,b, MG RTF 2005, 2006, Amicus the Union 2006, Armstrong 2006, House of Commons 2006, 2007, NAO 2006). These are valuable reports but their limitations include a short-term focus on the situation immediately before closure and on the impacts since. They also concentrate on the workers made redundant and their experience in finding employment and the impact on businesses in the supply chain linked to production at Longbridge. They mostly consider the impact on the immediate locality – the Longbridge ward and adjacent wards within Birmingham. Any evaluation of the impact of the closure of the Longbridge works should include these elements, but a more detailed and comprehensive approach would go beyond this. In particular, it would: take account of the major job losses from Longbridge that had occurred in the period 1998 to 2005; adopt an evidence-based approach to spatial impact; and consider data related to local employment and unemployment. Rather than focusing on redundant workers alone, this would raise questions about displacement and wider employment effects.

The remainder of this paper focuses on these issues using three major datasets. First, we use a payroll dataset of employees at MG Rover at two points in time (1998 and 2005) to analyse the extent of the spatial impact of the closure of the MG Rover works. Both datasets provide postcodes for the home addresses of most of MG Rover's employees working at Longbridge. We have been able to map these data in detail. The 1998 dataset also comprises information on age, type of occupation for each employee (executive, hourly workers, managerial staff, general staff and trainees). Second, in order to estimate the economic impact of the closure over the longer term, we analysed the monthly claimant count database for claimants of unemployment-related benefits. These are currently the Jobseeker's Allowance (JSA) and National Insurance (NI) unemployment credits. Unemployment-related benefit claimants do not exactly correspond to unemployment as defined by the International Labour Organization.[1] For example, claimant counts exclude unemployed people who do not claim or are not eligible for benefits, whilst they include inactive claimants and some employed claimants. That is why the two measures of unemployment are not comparable. Usually the claimant count data are less accurate than other measures of unemployment (ONS 2006). However, claimant counts can be more reliable at sub-regional level than estimates of unemployment from the Labour Force Survey, given the larger numbers involved. Claimant count data have been available at ward level since 1996. In addition, analysis of the claimant count is available in some detail. For example, analysis of claimants by age, duration of claim and occupation has been available since 2004. We use these data to estimate the long-term economic impact of the closure of the MG Rover works. Finally, we complement these two datasets with data from the Census 2001 and the Annual Business Inquiry 2005 at ward level.

Long-term spatial impacts

There were 13,127 people working at MG Rover in 1998. This number had decreased to 5858 in 2005. Table 1 presents the residential distribution of MG Rover employees in 1998 and 2005. This demonstrates the wide geographical distribution of MG Rover workers in the West Midlands both in 1998 and 2005, suggesting the extent of the regional impact both from the job losses during the period 1998–2005 and from the final closure in 2005. In 1998, the bulk of MG Rover employees lived along a corridor running from the south of Birmingham and extending along the A38 to Bromsgrove, Redditch and Wychavon in the south and Dudley and Sandwell in the west. Around 22% of MG Rover employees lived in the south of Birmingham (the wards of Longbridge, Northfield, Kings Norton, Bartley Green and Weoley) in 1998; the majority of them in both Longbridge (9%) and Northfield (6%). There were also important pockets of employees in other parts of Birmingham where 45% of the workforce lived.

There had been very little change in this by the time of the closure in 2005. The shrinkage in numbers of employees may have been slightly greater in North Birmingham and less outside the city but the continuity in the pattern is remarkable and there is the same spatial distribution around the south west corridor. There are two immediate implications from this. First, while there is a 'local' concentration effect there is also a widely dispersed workforce and the spatial impact is sub-regional rather than local. Second, by the time of the closure in 2005 all of the areas affected by that closure had already been affected by earlier job losses. The MG Rover closure could be seen as a final shock – following on from a period of long decline which had already affected the labour market and other processes and would affect their capacity to adjust to the shock.

The relative importance of the impact of the closure on each neighbourhood and locality emerges from comparing the size of the MG Rover workforce with the number of 16 to 74-year-old employed people in each area in the Population Census for 2001. This is an imperfect comparison because the Census took place in between the two dates, but it gives an idea of the extent of the impact at ward level. In 1998, the MG Rover workforce represented 1.6% of Birmingham's employed workforce and 0.5% of the region's workforce. This figure rose to 3.6% in Bromsgrove. At ward level within Birmingham it represented 4.5% of the workforce in Weoley and 9.4% in Longbridge. These figures increase significantly if we only look at the workforce employed in manufacturing. MG Rover employees represented around 50% of the workforce employed in manufacturing in Longbridge, 40% in Northfield, 30% in Weoley and 20% in Kings Norton, Bartley Green and Bromsgrove. These absolute and relative figures suggest that the closure has had a long-term, sustained impact in and around Birmingham.

Data on MG Rover employees can be disaggregated by types of job for 1998. Hourly workers (74%), general staff (14.8%) and management staff (8.8%) formed the three main categories of the MG Rover workforce. The hourly workers mostly lived in Birmingham (50%), Dudley (15%) and Sandwell (10%). In contrast, executive staff were more dispersed with only 20% of them living in Birmingham, Dudley and Bromsgrove. More than half of the management staff also lived outside these three districts. The pattern for general staff lies between these two extremes and involves a more even distribution regionally: 40% of them lived in Birmingham, 17% in Bromsgrove, 9% in Dudley and 30% were dispersed across the rest of the West Midlands. This demonstrates that the impact of closure on local labour markets is uneven.

Although the concentration effect may have reduced over time it was never as great as in some other industries. A survey of methods of travel by employees at Longbridge and

Table 1. Place of residence of MG Rover employees in 1998 and 2005.

	1998		2005		
	Employees	% of all MG Rover employees	Employees	% of all MG Rover employees	Var. 2005–1998
Birmingham	5977	45.5%	2545	43.4%	−2.1%
Longbridge	1188	9.1%	532	9.1%	0.0%
Northfield	731	5.6%	328	5.6%	0.0%
Rest of South West Birmingham*	1037	7.9%	418	7.1%	−0.8%
Bromsgrove	1556	11.9%	687	11.7%	−0.1%
Dudley	1667	12.7%	766	13.1%	0.4%
Sandwell	937	7.1%	424	7.2%	0.1%
Other local authorities – WM	2474	18.8%	1268	21.6%	2.8%
Not allocated West Midlands	52	0.4%	NA	NA	NA
Total West Midlands	12,663	96.5%	5690	97.1%	0.7%
Rest of UK	144	1.1%	145	2.5%	1.4%
Outside UK	NA	NA	5	0.1%	NA
Not allocated	320	2.4%	18	0.3%	−2.1%
Total	13,127	100.0%	5858	100.0%	0.0%

*Includes Bartley Green, Weoley and Kings Norton.
Source: Calculated from MG Rover database.

another factory at Castle Bromwich (north east of Birmingham) showed that in 1937 only 10% walked to work. Many more were travelling by train, bus or coach (33.5%), private car or motorcycle (16%) and bicycle (13.5%) (Smith 1989). This suggests a wide geographical spread of employees, over 70 years ago. In 2001, around 60% of all commuters used a private vehicle to go to work in the south west of Birmingham; this was roughly equal to the City of Birmingham average but was inferior to the regional average (68.1%). In Dudley and Bromsgrove, these figures rose to more than 70% of all commuters. The proximity of the Longbridge works to the motorway and major road networks around Birmingham and to the south probably made this effect much stronger than with other workplaces. It seems likely that compared with miners or steelworkers in other cities, car workers at Longbridge were not concentrated in particular neighbourhoods and their relatively high incomes enabled them to achieve various positions in the housing market. While some were in the rented sector, the majority of skilled and better-paid workers were owner-occupiers and had traded up and moved further away from original locations near to the factory.

This evidence suggests that the concentrated neighbourhood impact of closure in 2005 was less than anticipated in the immediate aftermath of closure. Even if the local economy was sufficiently depressed and the employability of the workers was sufficiently low that they were unlikely to get other employment, the place effects would not be as strong as initially expected.

Long-term economic impacts

One of the main conclusions from reports on the impact of MG Rover closure is that 63% of the 5300 workers from MG Rover and its suppliers who had registered for Jobseeker's Allowance (JSA) in 2005 were back in work in February 2006 (MG RTF 2006); this percentage had reached 70% later in 2006 (House of Commons 2006, 2007). However, there was concern regarding the remaining unemployed workers as well as those not registering for JSA. As shown above, the impact of the run-down of MG Rover from 1998 to 2005 was absorbed by a wide south west area around the factory. Birmingham, Bromsgrove and Dudley provided the place of residence for 68.2% of the workforce in 2005. In Birmingham, around a third of workers were located in Longbridge and Northfield. This section explores the economic impact of the closure in these areas.

Key statistics for selected areas

Figures from the Census 2001, from the Annual Population Survey and from the Annual Business Inquiry showed that Longbridge, Northfield, Bromsgrove, Dudley and Birmingham display different economic and social characteristics and are different types of neighbourhoods. While Longbridge displays the profile of a 'working-class' neighbourhood, Bromsgrove looks like a 'middle-class' town. Dudley and Northfield are somewhere between these two profiles. Longbridge and Birmingham as a whole have slightly lower levels of employment compared with Northfield, Dudley and Bromsgrove. When compared with the City of Birmingham as a whole and the national average, occupations in Longbridge are biased toward elementary occupations, skilled trades, process plant and machine operatives as well as personal services. In contrast a higher proportion of Bromsgrove residents work in managerial and professional occupations than applies nationally. In Northfield a higher proportion of the labour force comprises workers in administrative and secretarial occupations, skilled trades and process plant and machine operatives. Finally, Dudley displays a mixed pattern, with a higher proportion of its labour force in managerial occupations as well as skilled trades and process plant and machine operatives. In terms of economic activities, Longbridge again displays a different profile with much more involvement in the manufacturing sector (38.1%) than the City of Birmingham average (12.4%). Consequently, the level of service activity is lower – it is mostly concentrated in public administration, education and health. Dudley retains a strong manufacturing sector (16.4% of all economic activities) whereas Northfield and Bromsgrove have around 90% of their economic activities in the service sectors.

Mobility varies across the five areas. A higher proportion of residents from Dudley, Longbridge and Northfield travelled more than 5 km to go to work than in Birmingham as a whole or Bromsgrove. However, more people travelled by public transport (reflecting the City of Birmingham average) in Longbridge and Northfield than in the adjacent districts of Dudley and Bromsgrove.

Finally, using the 2004 Indices of Deprivation (DCLG 2004), Birmingham was ranked 15th most deprived out of the 354 local authorities in England, although in the West Midlands it was the most deprived local authority area (just ahead of Sandwell which was ranked 16th). By comparison, Dudley was ranked 109th and Bromsgrove 293rd. Although most of the most deprived areas in Birmingham were located around the city centre, Longbridge – and to a lesser extent Northfield – also contained such areas.

In summary, the areas that had significant numbers of residents who lost their jobs at the MG Rover had significantly different social profiles. There were unequal impacts on an uneven surface. Following from this, our analysis aims to explore differences that emerge from the interrogation of employment data. Because of the nature of these data we regard this part of the analysis as raising questions rather than providing definitive findings.

Long-term unemployment in selected areas

Although there had been the loss of some 7000 jobs at MG Rover between 1998 and 2005, these areas had seen a declining rate of unemployment over the previous 15 years (Figure 1). They seem to have successfully absorbed the increased labour supply associated with MG Rover's longer decline.

The closure of MG Rover marks a clear break with an important increase in the numbers of Jobseeker's Allowance claimants in most areas in May 2005 (Figure 1). There was a clear increase in JSA claimants from April to May in all our five areas compared with the national average. For example, JSA claimants as a proportion of the working-age resident population increased from 4.4% to 7% in Longbridge; from 3.6% to 5.7% in Northfield; and from 1.6% to 2.8% in Bromsgrove (Figure 1). However, this rate subsequently decreased in these three areas until November 2005. It then started increasing again, this time associated with an increase nationally. These two blows to the economy have meant that JSA claimant rates had not fallen back to their 2005 levels by April 2007, two years after the closure of MG Rover. It seems that the national increase in unemployment was detrimental to the chances of MG Rover employees finding new jobs. This effect was more important in Longbridge and Northfield than in Bromsgrove. The impact seems to have been less important in Dudley where JSA claimants as a proportion of the working-age resident population only increased slightly (from 2.9% to 3.2%) in the period April to May 2005; the fact that it only started decreasing in October 2006 suggests that it was more persistent.

These variations can be linked with the usual occupation of claimants in each area over that period (Figures 2–5). After a sharp increase in the levels of JSA claimants for most of

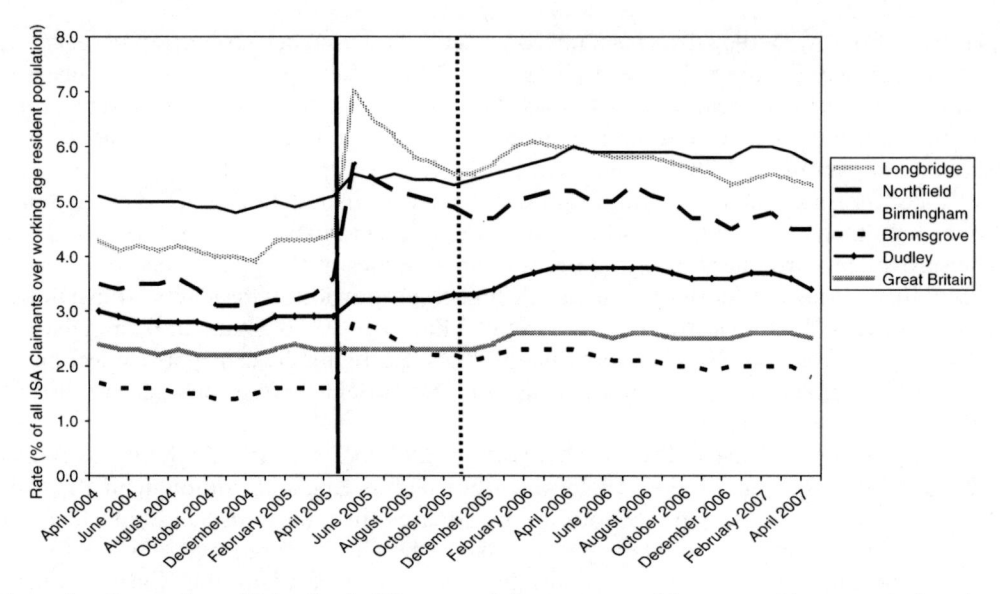

Figure 1. Proportion of Jobseeker's Allowance claimants on working-age resident population, April 2004–April 2007.
Source: ONS claimant count with rates and proportions.

types of occupation from April to May 2005, the numbers of claimants in managerial and professional occupations, skilled trades and process, plant and machine operatives rapidly decreased towards their initial levels in Longbridge, Northfield and Bromsgrove (Figures 2–4). Although the number of claimants in these occupations increased again in later 2005 in line with the national increase, they were almost back to their original levels by April 2007. In contrast, the levels of claimants in sales and customer service, administrative and

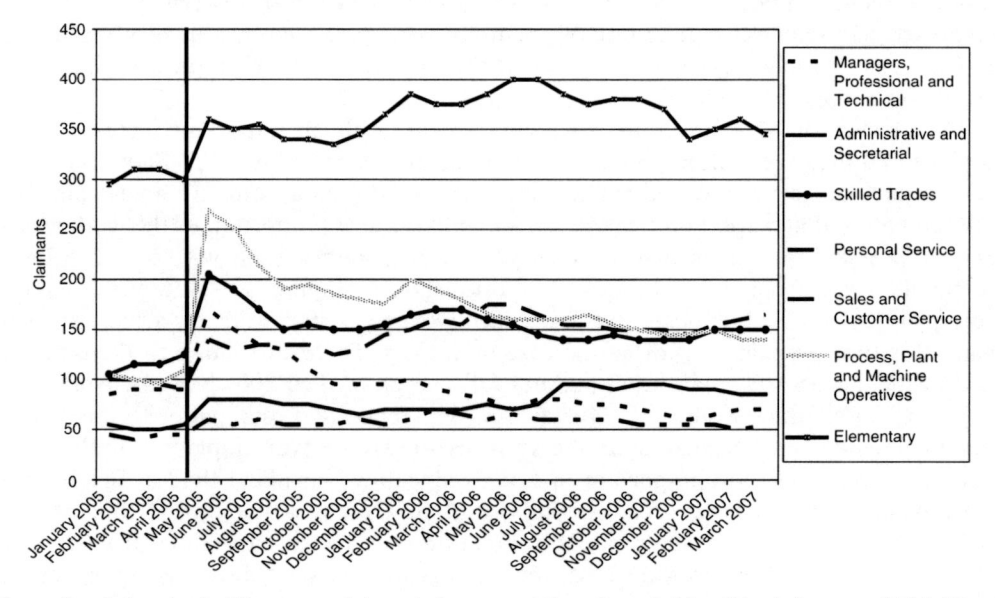

Figure 2. Jobseeker's Allowance claimants by occupation, Longbridge Ward, January 2005–March 2007.
Source: ONS claimant count by occupation.

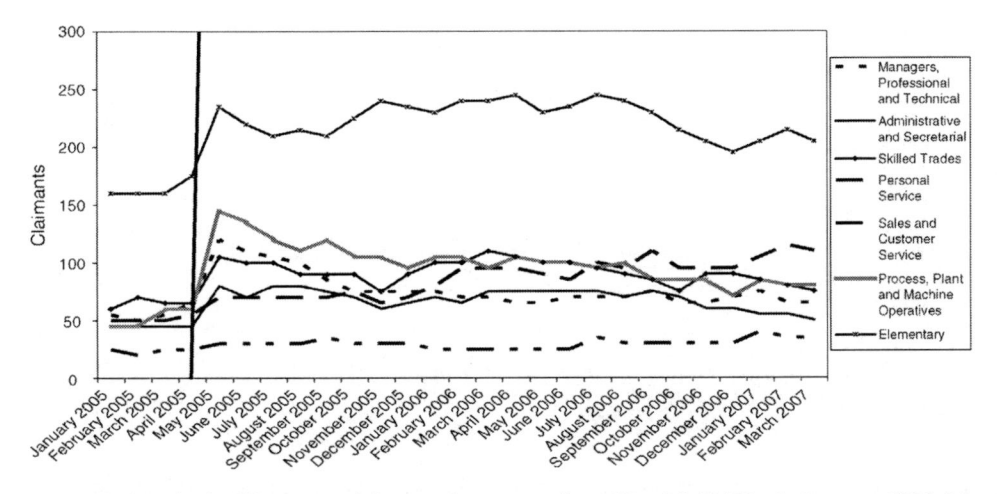

Figure 3. Jobseeker's Allowance claimants by occupation, Northfield Ward, January 2005–March 2007.
Source: ONS claimant count by occupation.

secretarial, and elementary occupations did not decrease significantly and/or increased or remained constant over the period. This pattern is slightly different in Northfield where the number of claimants in administrative and secretarial occupations decreased over the period (Figure 3). Again in Dudley trends were slightly different, with an increase in claimants in most occupational groups and a tendency to remain constant afterwards (Figure 5). Previous reports on the work trajectories of ex-MG Rover workers reported that 50% found work where they were earning a lot less than at MG Rover (Armstrong 2006). We also know that some of them changed occupations with their new job (MG RTF 2006, House of Common 2007). We can suppose that some ex-MG Rover workers may have had a competitive advantage over other unemployed workers in these occupations, creating some difficulties for non-MG Rover workers in finding work.

Figure 6 presents data for people who had been JSA claimants for over 12 months in our five areas and Great Britain. These rates decreased sharply in April to July 2005. This

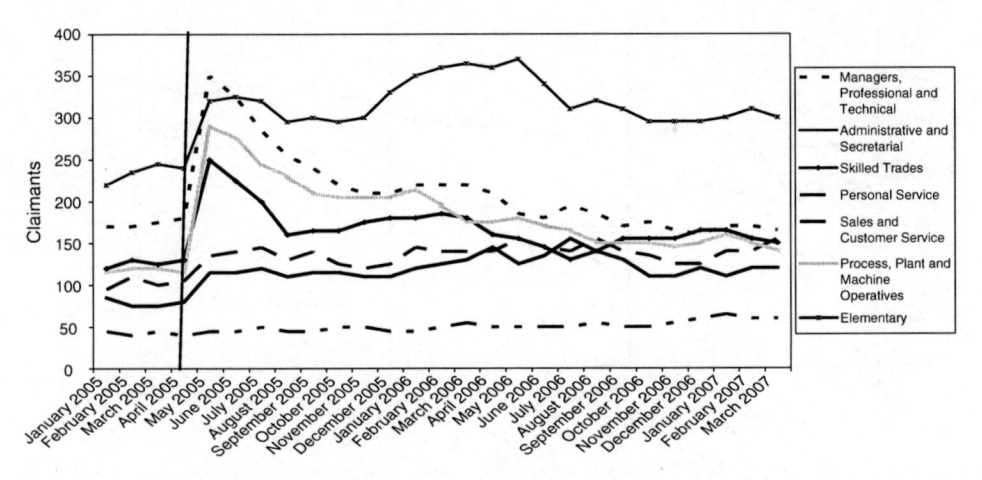

Figure 4. Jobseeker's Allowance claimants by occupation, Bromsgrove, January 2005–March 2007.
Source: ONS claimant count by occupation.

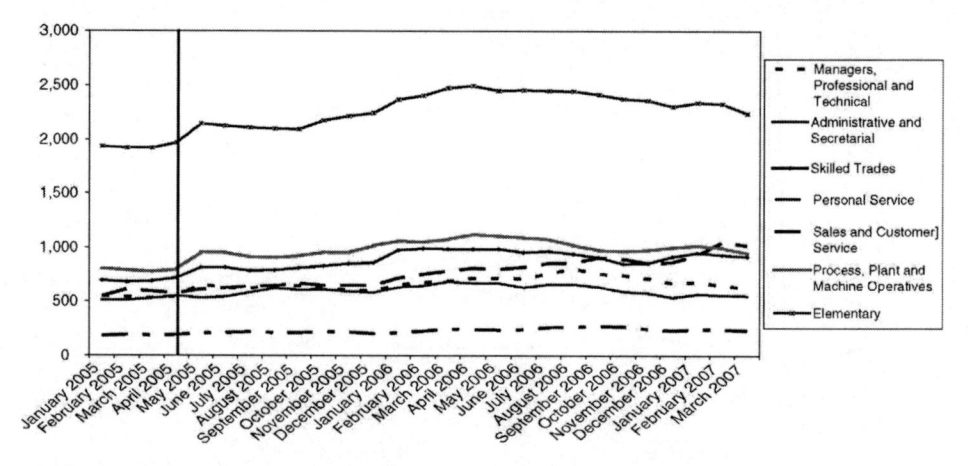

Figure 5. Jobseeker's Allowance claimants by occupation, Dudley, January 2005–March 2007.
Source: ONS claimant count by occupation.

is explained by the increase in new claimants in each area due to the MG Rover closure. However, instead of going back to their levels of 2005 a year after the closure, we observed a sharp increase in the proportion of over-12-months JSA claimants in all areas. For example, from April 2005 to April 2007, these proportions increased from 16.6% to 25.8% in Longbridge; from 17.2% to 24% in Northfield; from 10.3% to 16.3% in Bromsgrove; and from 16.2% to 24.7% in Dudley. This suggests the difficulty that an important proportion of claimants experienced in finding employment over that period – partly reflecting a rising proportion of long-term claimants nationally. However, the increasing difference between the areas referred to above can not be explained by this and appears strange in view of the record of former MG Rover employees obtaining work.

In conclusion, even though a majority of MG Rover workers were back in work a year after the MG Rover closure, labour market activity in our five impact areas was not back to normal in April 2007, some two years after the closure. This is partly because of a national decrease in employment in late 2005. However, our data also suggest increased

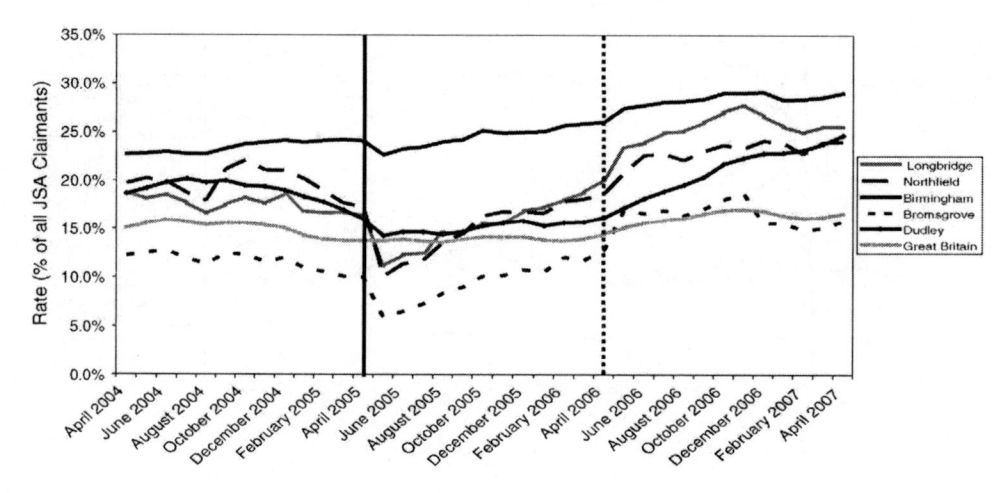

Figure 6. Proportion of over-12-months JSA claimants, April 2004–April 2007.
Source: ONS claimant count by age and duration.

long-term unemployment in areas where former MG Rover workers live. It seems likely that some of these are former MG Rover workers but that there may also be a displacement of less-qualified workers in each area and an increase in long-term unemployment experienced by other workers due to the impact of more-qualified MG Rover workers entering the labour market. The spatial variations in labour market adjustment are also striking with Dudley showing more persistent rising levels of unemployment over the longer term.

Conclusions and policy implications

This paper has provided a discussion of new data related to a major factory closure that has taken place at a later stage than those discussed in much of the literature. This closure is in the motor industry and relates to a factory located on the edge of a city and particularly well served by main roads and motorways. The spatial impact of the closure has been much wider that could have been expected 20 or more years ago or than expected in the immediate aftermath of the closure. In effect, the development of longer-distance commuting and the restructuring of the housing market over recent years has meant that the impact of the MG Rover closure has been relocated and dispersed compared with what would have been the case in the past. The social pattern will not have changed with the impact being experienced most severely by lower-paid workers with less employability and by older workers who will find it more difficult to obtain jobs in the future.

The conclusions from this are that we should be very cautious about dramatizing a very localized neighbourhood effect of a major factory closure. In a period of relative prosperity and in a period where workforces are relatively dispersed, associated with travel to work by car, the impacts will not be as concentrated as in the past. However, we should not swing to the opposite extreme and imply that there is no neighbourhood effect. The evidence points to a wider zone experiencing a relatively concentrated impact. This indicates a dispersal of the economic impact of the closure compared with the past and some other closures, but does not deny that a spatial concentration remains. In addition, although most MG Rover workers had found new jobs within a year of the closure, long-term unemployment rates were not back to their initial levels after two years.

These findings suggest that there are 'second wave' effects from factory closures not picked up by methodologies that focus on short-term impacts or that are wholly focused on tracking individual redundant workers. Whether ex-MG Rover workers stay in their new jobs or whether their availability for work affects the employment of others is difficult to identify. However, recent interviews with local policy-makers in Longbridge and Northfield alluded to a number of ex-MG Rover workers remaining in long-term unemployment due to difficulties over re-entering the labour market, or being in and out of employment because the job they found was unsatisfactory, as well as to ex-workers facing significant mental health problems. It is also evident that other members of ex-MG Rover workers' households have in some cases made major changes in their work and living patterns. This includes partners who previously did not work but now do, and children whose decisions about education and work have been affected. These interviews also indicated increased difficulties in finding new employment among people who were already unemployed because of the competition generated by the arrival on the market of ex-MG Rover workers. The pattern of impact is also not easy to read-off directly from the workforce as this does not include those working in service and other sectors which are affected by the reduced spending power of MG Rover workers. All these elements suggest that there are broader economic impacts on local communities than those identified in many studies.

Future research concerned with spatial and other impacts of factory closure should explore these issues as well as the relationship between place of residence and the location of the factory that has closed.

These findings also have direct implications for policy. These include the need for a broader agenda of coordination and regeneration in the longer term. Richard Burden, Member of the Parliament for the Northfield area, expressed this concern in the House of Commons report on the closure of MG Rover (2007, p. Ev12, Q.47):

> ... there is also a long-term problem in that area and there are people who are out of work in that area or who have got skills problems in that area or who did not work for MG Rover. The family links mean that we need to have a much broader perspective about trying to raise skill levels, aspiration levels and provide help in that part of Birmingham, and I would say north Worcestershire as well.

Regeneration has usually been included in the remit of task forces addressing the consequences of closures in other parts of England (Pike 2005). In 2000, the first MG Rover Task Force had a regeneration focus, which was subsequently taken forward by Advantage West Midlands in its new regional development strategy (Bailey 2003, MG RTF 2005).[2] However, most of these programmes have been targeted primarily at ex-MG Rover workers. Our results suggest that the impact of the closure may have had a broader impact on less-qualified workers in the affected local communities and beyond Longbridge and Northfield. Targeting programmes specifically at redundant workers may reinforce this effect.

Acknowledgements

The authors wish to acknowledge the support of the ESRC under award number RES-000-22-2478.

Notes

1. Under the Labour Force Survey, unemployed people are without a job, want a job, have actively sought work in the last four weeks and are available to start work in the next two weeks, or out of work, have found a job and are waiting to start it in the next two weeks (ONS 2006).
2. A key component here was developing the Central Technology Belt and, within this, a science park at Longbridge. But there was no further regeneration strategy developed following the 2005 closure until October 2006 when Birmingham and Bromsgrove presented a plan to redevelop some of the vacant parts of the Longbridge site to create mixed developments (Longbridge Area Action Plan 2006). In addition, some long-term unemployment strategies were put in place in Longbridge and Northfield in the later stages of the MG Rover Task Force 2005. These were designed to deal with suspected long-term and community unemployment (MG RTF 2006, House of Commons 2007).

References

Amicus the Union, 2006. *MG Rover survey report*. London: Amicus.
Armstrong, K., 2006. *Life after MG Rover. The impact of the closure on the workers, their families and the community*. A report prepared for BBC Radio 4. The Work Foundation.

Bailey, D., 2003. Globalisation, regions and cluster policies: the case of the MG Rover Task Force. *Policy studies*, 24 (2/3), 67–85.
Department of Communities and Local Government (DCLG), 2004. Indices of deprivation. Available from: http://www.communities.gov.uk/index.asp?id =1128440 [Accessed 31 May 2007].
Henderson, R. and Shutt, J., 2004. Responding to a coalfield closure: old issues for a new regional development agency? *Local economy*, 19 (1), 25–37.
Hinde, K., 1994. Labour market experiences following plant closures: the case of Sunderland's shipyard workers. *Regional studies*, 28, 713–724.
House of Commons, 2006. *The closure of MG Rover. Fifty seventh report of session 2005–2006. Report together with formal minutes, oral and written evidence.* Committee of Public Accounts. Ordered by the House of Commons. London: The Stationery Office.
House of Commons, Trade and Industry Committee, 2007. *Success and failure in the UK car manufacturing industry. Fourth report of session 2006–07. Report together with formal minutes, oral and written evidence.* HC399. London: The Stationery Office.
Kirkham, J. and Watts, H., 1998. Multi-locational manufacturing organisations and plant closures in urban areas. *Urban studies*, 35 (9), 1559–1575.
MG Rover Task Force (MG RTF), 2005. *Six months on.* Prepared for submission to the Department of Trade and Industry.
MG Rover Task Force (MG RTF), 2006. *Final update report: the work goes on.* Prepared for submission to the Department of Trade and Industry.
National Audit Office (NAO), 2006. *The closure of MG Rover.* Ordered by the House of Commons.
Office of National Statistics (ONS), 2006. *How exactly is employment measured?* Available from: http://www.statistics.gov.uk/downloads/theme_labour/employment.pdf [Accessed 31 May 2007].
Pike, A., 2002. *Task force and the organisation of economic development: the case of the North East region of England.* Discussion Paper 02/3. Centre for Urban and Regional Development Studies, University of Newcastle Upon Tyne.
Pike, A., 2005. Building a geographical political economy of closure: the case of R&D Co in North East England. *Antipode*, 39 (1), 93–125.
Pinch, S. and Mason, C., 1991. Redundancy in an expanding labour market: a case-study of displaced workers from two manufacturing plants in Southampton. *Urban studies*, 28 (5), 735–757.
Regeneris Consulting (RC), 2005a. *Closure of MG Rover: economic impact assessment.* An interim report. MG Rover Task Force.
Regeneris Consulting (RC), 2005b. *Closure of MG Rover: economic impact assessment.* Stage 2 report. MG Rover Task Force.
Shutt, J., Henderson, R., and Kumi-Ampofo, F., 2003. *Responding to a regional economic crisis: an impact and regeneration assessment of the Selby Coalfield closure on the Yorkshire & Humber region.* Paper delivered to the Regional Studies Association International Conference, Pisa, Italy, 12–15 April.
Smith, D., 1989. 'Not getting on, just getting by': changing prospects in South Birmingham. *In*: P Cooke, ed. *Localities. The changing urban face of Great Britain.* London: Unwyn Hyman.
Tomaney, J., Cornford, J., Whittingham, D., Hayward, S., Pike, A., and Thomas, D., 1997. *Workers' experience of plant closure: the case of Swan Hunter on Tyneside.* Discussion Paper No. 97/1. Centre for Urban and Regional Development Studies, University of Newcastle Upon Tyne.
Tomaney, J., Pike, A., and Cornford, J., 1999. Plant closure and the local economy: the case of Swan Hunter on Tyneside. *Regional Studies*, 33 (5), 401–411.

Risk and return: housing tenure and labour market adjustment after employment loss in the automotive sector in Southern Adelaide

Andrew Beer

Introduction

Economic restructuring is an inescapable feature of contemporary societies as globalisation, shifts in competitive and comparative advantage (Porter 1990) and the emergence of new, and often disruptive, technologies results in the decline of some industries or the closure of enterprises within a still prosperous sector. The processes of industry adjustment raise significant challenges for public policy as governments seek to maintain economic growth, reduce income inequalities and advance the competitive position of their economy on a national and global stage. Globalisation and economic restructuring has had a profound impact on the Australian economy and labour market over the last 20 years and this change has been accompanied by a growth in service-sector employment, a significant reduction in some manufacturing sectors, and changes in the nature of employment, with the growth of part-time and casual employment and falling rates of permanent full-time employment. In Australia, policy settings award priority to the processes of 'adjustment': the encouragement of new industries to replace those that have declined, as well as measures to assist displaced workers find employment elsewhere (House of Representatives 2006). Publicly at least, Australian governments eschew the propping up of failing industries or enterprises but instead focus policy interventions on identifying and encouraging industries with the potential for growth. Workers made redundant are assisted through access to the Australian government's employment assistance scheme – the Jobs Network; through programmes that provide formal recognition of prior learning and/or the upgrading of skills; and through information sessions on applying for employment (Beer *et al.* 2006). The Australian government provides income support to eligible workers and employment assistance, while state governments have primary responsibility for training.

For individual workers the experience of redundancy is mediated by a host of social, economic and demographic processes, including their age, gender, household structure, social networks, skill sets and relative position within the labour market. This paper considers the role of housing tenure on the processes of labour market adjustment following redundancy. It considers the ways in which home ownership has affected the propensity of workers made redundant to find new employment, their willingness to leave their region as either long-distance commuters or migrants in order to secure work, and how they assess employment opportunities with respect to both their quality and availability. These issues are examined through the analysis of two waves of quantitative and qualitative data collected via interviews with employees made redundant by an automotive manufacturer located in southern Adelaide in 2004. The paper begins with an examination of the literature on the relationship between regional housing markets and labour markets, with specific reference to the 'Oswald hypothesis'. It then considers the evidence of the impact of tenure on labour market adjustment in southern Adelaide, before drawing out the implications for public policy.

Housing and labour markets at the regional scale: understanding the relationship

There is a considerable body of literature on the relationship between housing markets and labour markets. At the level of the macro-economy labour markets are seen to drive housing markets (Gallent 2006, Wong 2006) including the demand for dwellings and the price of accommodation. There is also an emerging policy literature on the potential role of housing assistance as a disincentive to engagement with the formal labour market (Dalton and Ong 2005, Wood and Ong 2005, Wood *et al.* 2005). In Australia the available evidence suggests that the receipt of housing assistance in the form of public rental housing or Commonwealth Rent Assistance payment has an impact on the propensity of individuals to find paid employment.

At the regional scale a considerable body of research was undertaken in the late 1980s and early 1990s into the relationship between housing markets and labour markets (see, for example, Bover *et al.* 1989, Muellbauer and Murphy 1990, Allen and Hamnett 1991, Johnes and Hyclack 1994, Doogan 1996). Much of this attention was focused on the impact of housing on regional migration, especially in England where the North/South divide resulted in limited employment opportunities in the north of the country but access to affordable housing, in contrast to the job-rich south where housing was decidedly unaffordable. However, as Randolph (1991) observed, much of this literature failed to provide a coherent explanation of the interaction between housing markets and labour markets at the regional scale because of the tension between the often highly localised nature of housing markets on the one hand, and the broader-ranging regional or national labour markets on the other. Randolph (1991) developed a model of the relationship between housing markets and job markets that was informed by his reading of labour market segmentation and labour market discontinuity theory. This perspective suggests that the employment market does not operate as a single entity, but instead there are a number of discontinuous segments, defined by location, skill levels, experience, ethnicity and race. Randolph (1991) suggested that we can only understand regional housing markets by approaching the topic with a knowledge of how the labour market is organised and segmented; by focusing on the processes of production; by recognising the potential importance of discrimination; by acknowledging that location is significant, and that market segments overlap each other; and, finally, by accepting that specific empirical analysis is needed in order to fully understand each market segment. (cited in Beer 2004, p. 59)

Randolph (1991) also recognised that households – rather than individuals – play an important mediating role in the interaction between housing markets and labour markets. It is the household that ensures that there is no simple relationship between housing and job markets, as individuals in identical labour market positions may have very different household structures which influence their requirement for, and ability to purchase, housing. While this emphasis on the household in determining housing consumption is not new, it does, however, remind us of the complex relationship between economic change and employment outcomes on the one hand, and housing decisions on the other (Beer 2004). Randolph's (1991) perspective also leads us to anticipate that the relationship between housing outcomes and changing labour markets will be complex, that household rather than individual characteristics are determinant, and that both locational factors and housing market conditions will shape outcomes.

There is a second body of literature on housing and labour market dynamics that warrants attention. Using data from across the OECD, but largely drawing upon European examples, Oswald (1996, 1997) hypothesised that regions and nations with higher rates of home ownership tended to have higher levels of unemployment because ownership served as an impediment to mobility within the labour market. That is, that unemployed owner-occupiers were less willing than private tenants to relocate in order to find employment, were less willing to seek employment in distant locations and had a reduced propensity to remain in the labour market, resulting in a greater incidence of persons out of work. Oswald (1996) suggested that a 10% increase in a nation's home ownership rate was likely to result in a 2% rise in unemployment. Oswald placed home ownership at the centre of explanations of the rise in the natural rate of unemployment since the 1960s in advanced economies (Flatau et al. 2002a, p. 1). He argued that large-scale unemployment exists 'because of a secular change that has happened in all but a few Western housing markets – the rise of home ownership and the decline of private renting' (Oswald 1996, p. 2).

Internationally, numerous researchers have investigated the Oswald thesis. Working in Denmark, Munch et al. (2006) concluded that home ownership does reduce mobility in the labour market but does not increase periods of unemployment because home owners are more likely to find local jobs. Green et al. (2002) examined panel data from the USA in order to overcome the problems of aggregation bias. They followed individuals who entered unemployment and after controlling for selectivity bias concluded that 'unemployed individuals in owning households find jobs more rapidly than do unemployed individuals in renting households' (Green et al. 2002, p. 18). Brunet and Lesueur (2003) found some support for the Oswald hypothesis in their analysis of French labour market and housing data. Ahn and Blazquez (2007) analysed data from Denmark, France and Spain, and concluded that Oswald's theory held only for Denmark and that the effect of home ownership on labour market mobility was insignificant in France and absent in Spain.

The Oswald thesis has been tested in Australia for Australian regions and localities (Flatau et al. 2002a) as well as the individual level (Flatau et al. 2002b). The results have been summarised by Bridge et al. (2003, p. 8) who argued:

The analysis of both individual-level and locality-level data supports a rejection of the Oswald thesis for Australia. In fact, in the case of individual level results in particular, the likelihood of someone owning a home appears to decrease (rather than increase) the probability of being unemployed, and, if they become unemployed, of their being unemployed for longer. Both studies find higher rates of unemployment, after controlling for other factors, among public tenants and in localities where public tenants are more concentrated.

It is worth noting, however, that Flatau *et al.* (2002b, p. 2) acknowledged the importance of mortgage status on labour market performance, observing that:

> recent anti-Oswald results are the result of (1) highly leveraged owners having a greater incentive to remain employed and to become reemployed more rapidly than outright owners and (2) those paying below-market rents having a lower incentive to avoid unemployment than become reemployed than those paying market rents.

The context of the broad tenure category is therefore important, as is the distinction between outright owners and home purchasers, and between private and public tenants.

Oswald's thesis around the nature of the interaction between housing tenure and participation in the labour market is significant because it suggests there will be poorer labour market outcomes resulting from large-scale redundancies where the majority of affected workers are owner-occupiers, compared with redundancies where tenants predominate amongst displaced workers. It is important also to draw an explicit link between Oswald's hypothesis and Randolph's insights into spatially and occupationally differentiated labour markets. Randolph (1991) suggests that there are potentially multiple barriers to movement in the labour market and that these barriers operate at a variety of spatial scales. We should therefore expect that labour markets in metropolitan areas operate as discrete segments and that housing tenure will exert a measurable influence on labour market processes in the aftermath of a large-scale redundancy.

Redundancy, housing and labour markets in southern Adelaide

As noted in the Introduction to this special issue, the loss of just under 1200 jobs from an automotive manufacturer was announced in April 2004. The impact of redundancy on the affected workers and their families has been the subject of a large-scale study involving three waves of quantitative data collection and two waves of qualitative data collection over a period of three years (Beer *et al.* 2006). The job losses were associated with the closure of one of the company's two plants in the region – a foundry and supplier of other components – and the restructuring of operations at the assembly plant. Workers were made redundant involuntarily at the former plant, while voluntary redundancy packages were made available at the latter site.[1] The nature of the redundancy process was significant, as those in receipt of an involuntary redundancy package received five weeks of pay for every year of service up to 20 years and then one week of pay for every additional year. Workers who took a voluntary package received three weeks of pay for every year of service up to 20 years and then one week of pay for every additional year of employment. Critically, redundant employees had worked an average of 19 years with the manufacturer (Beer *et al.* 2006), such that many employees left with two years of salary. This level of redundancy payment is generous by Australian standards, with most workers entitled to two weeks of pay for every year of service. In addition, most were mature men aged from their mid 40s to late 50s who lived locally, with the majority either home owners or home purchasers. Some 30% of workers included in the study had lived in their dwelling for five to nine years and a further 28% had lived in their current house for more than 15 years.

These data should be compared with national averages from the Australian Bureau of Statistics which suggests that 40% of all households move address between each five-yearly Census, although residential mobility rates are much lower for home owners compared with renters.

Interviews undertaken within six months of the redundancy (Beer *et al.* 2006) with 374 of the displaced workers revealed that fully 40% were outright home owners, 43.5% were mortgagors, 10% were renting privately and just 2% were renting from the public sector. Some 141 workers – or 54% of those who held a mortgage – indicated that they would use their payout to discharge all or part of their mortgage. As one ex-employee who paid off his mortgage said, 'It's the working man's dream', while another noted:

> I had a mortgage and I thought any money that they give me I (will) pay the mortgage off. That's the best financial thing that I can do with the money, because that's a debt that's costing me, so the best thing I could do is pay that. And not that it paid it off, but it took a big chunk out of it.

A second round of interviews was completed one year after the initial interviews and during that period a further 70 displaced workers used their redundancy to pay off all or part of their mortgage. In total, therefore, some 210 of the 374 retrenched workers interviewed invested funds from their redundancy in acquitting some or all of their mortgage.

In the first set of interviews post-redundancy only 37 retrenched workers indicated that they had moved home since leaving the automotive sector and just 69 respondents – 20% of the total – expected that they would need to move home as a result of their changed employment circumstances.[2] At the second wave of interviews just 29 respondents had moved home in the previous 12 months and fully 81% of workers interviewed believed that they would not need to move home or change their housing circumstances over the next 12 months. Overall the housing market data indicate that retrenched workers were both committed to home ownership and embedded within their region. Many had lived all their lives in southern Adelaide and one third had lived in their current neighbourhood for more than 15 years. At the second round of interviews some 60% of those interviewed indicated that housing costs were not a matter of concern for them.

The Oswald (1996, 1997) thesis suggests that owner-occupation raises unemployment rates by reducing the willingness to relocate to find employment. It can also be assumed that owner-occupants have less incentive to find work because they have the financial resources – including reduced living costs – to withstand extended periods of unemployment or leave the formal labour force. While the data on housing investment and mobility supports the Oswald thesis the critical test for the hypothesis is the relationship between tenure and employment outcomes. This relationship for workers made redundant in southern Adelaide is presented in Table 1 and analysis of these data suggests a more complex set of relationships than a simple 'reading off' of the Oswald thesis would suggest. Interpretation of the data is made difficult by the numerical dominance of outright home owners and home purchasers amongst the workers who responded to the survey. There were 118 outright home owners at the second wave of interviews, 140 persons paying off a mortgage and just 41 private tenants. In percentage terms, private tenants were more likely to be in paid employment at the second wave of the survey, with 51% employed full-time, compared with 27% of outright home owners and 32% of mortgagors. Private tenants also had higher rates of employment in casual work than outright home owners and a comparable rate with mortgage holders. The percentage of private tenants unemployed was

Table 1. Tenure by labour market status, 12–18 months post-redundancy.

	Outright owner N (%)	Paying off a mortgage N (%)	Renting N (%)	Other N (%)	Total N (%)
Self-employed or family business	12 (10.2)	22 (15.7)	3 (8.9)	2 (18.2)	40 (12.7)
Employed full-time	33 (27.9)	46 (32.9)	24 (53.3)	4 (36.4)	107 (34.1)
Employed part-time	6 (5.1)	3 (2.1)	1 (2.2)	0 (0.0)	10 (3.2)
Employed as a casual worker	21 (17.8)	30 (21.4)	9 (20.0)	1 (9.1)	61 (19.4)
Unemployed looking for work	19 (16.1)	18 (12.9)	4 (8.9)	1 (9.1)	42 (13.4)
Not in labour force	27 (20.0)	21 (15.0)	3 (6.6)	3 (2.7)	0 (0.0)
Total	118 (100.0)	140 (100.0)	45 (100.0)	11 (100.0)	314 (100.0)

appreciably lower than for the two owner-occupation categories, with 7.3% of tenants unemployed, compared with 16% of owners and 13% of home buyers.

Critically, the percentage who could be considered to have left the formal labour force, that is those persons who indicated they were retired, engaged in household duties and not looking for work, not working because of a disability or were engaged in the duties of carers, varied appreciably by tenure. Some 22% of outright home owners had left the labour force, 11.5% of mortgagors had done so, but only 7.3% of tenants had left the world of paid work. Clearly, the age of persons in each tenure explains a proportion of the difference, but the gap between the tenures is so profound with respect to participation in the labour market that we can only conclude that there is an appreciable tenure effect. The same argument can be made with respect to those remaining in the labour market: that there are real differences in employment outcomes by tenure, with private tenants more likely to find full-time employment and as likely as mortgagors to find casual employment.

Oswald's (1996, 1997) hypothesised relationship between tenure and unemployment related to the national scale and did not present detailed evidence as to the processes driving this set of outcomes. The in-depth data collected as part of the research into redundancy in the automotive sector in southern Adelaide offer an opportunity to consider these housing and labour market drivers in depth. The quality of employment on offer following redundancy is a critical factor in understanding why the increased incidence of owner-occupation may raise unemployment rates and discourage active participation in the labour market.

Many of the workers, and especially those with fewer formal qualifications, reported difficulties in finding work and poorer working conditions once they found work. Participants in the round of interviews that took place 12–18 months after redundancy were asked a series of questions about their current working conditions and their attitudes to their employment arrangements. Whereas their previous employer only engaged full-time permanent staff, only 107 of the 316 surveyed at the second round of interviews were employed on a full-time basis, while 61 were employed casually and 10 were employed part-time.[3] The remainder had either left the labour force, were unemployed or were self-employed. Fully 225 of the 316 respondents (72%) in the wave two interviews reported that they now earned less when compared with their income prior to redundancy. Only 11% had incomes that matched their wages prior to redundancy and 15% earned more. In many instances those who received higher wages post-redundancy were the more skilled workers – such as electricians. One automotive engineer reported that his income fell from AU$150,000 to AU$71,000.

For the majority of workers made redundant, lower wages were an important component of the lower-quality work available to them. As noted previously, a significant percentage of respondents experienced a reduction in the terms of their employment, namely a shift from full-time employment to part-time or casual employment. Of those working full-time, 15 were employed on a fixed-term contract, eight reported that they did not receive paid annual leave and 11 were not eligible for paid sick leave. The latter two in particular are conditions of employment that Australian workers would normally expect to enjoy. Those who had found employment were asked to assess their current job relative to their previous work in the automotive sector; more than one third indicated that they believed their current job was worse than their previous employment, 25% felt that it was comparable and 44% considered it to be a better job. Across the 316 workers who participated in the interviews undertaken 12 to 18 months after redundancy, 121 had had at least two jobs in the preceding year, 62 had three or more jobs, 26 had four or more jobs, 11 had five, while six had six or more separate employment arrangements. This suggests a very high level of insecurity within the labour market, especially for a workforce that had previously experienced considerable employment stability with a single employer.

Overall there was an appreciable level of disaffection with their new employment, with 14% of employed participants indicating that they strongly intended to leave their current job within the next six to 12 months and a further 17% indicating that they intended to leave. It is worth acknowledging, however, that 43% of respondents strongly intended to stay in their current employment and 19% intended to stay, which suggests that the patterns of employment satisfaction are uneven. Some of the issues raised by workers with respect to their new employment included reduced Occupational Health and Safety standards relative to their former employers; the failure to recognise previously acquired skills and experience; greater pressure to deliver work under short time-frames; poor or absent human resources practices; difficult bosses; and ongoing insecurity in the new enterprises where they work. The final concern was common amongst those who found employment in the automotive sector with component suppliers to the two assembly plants in Adelaide. They felt that having being made redundant once, they were at risk of losing their job again because of continuing uncertainty within the sector – and indeed several had been made redundant on one or more occasions over the previous 18 months.

Finally, it is worth considering the location of employment available to retrenched workers from the automotive sector and how that has influenced labour market outcomes. Southern Adelaide offers an attractive living environment distinguished by proximity to high quality beaches; low density suburbs with well developed public and private gardens; and access to the Southern Vales wine region. It does not have significant large-scale industry and the redundancies from the automotive sector announced in April 2004 significantly reduced the total stock of manufacturing employment in the region. Those seeking further work in the industry – through choice or skills – must inevitably consider employment in northern Adelaide where blue collar employment is both growing and available on a larger scale. Travel to the region from southern Adelaide requires a car journey of up to 80 kilometres and takes an hour or more in peak traffic periods.

Many of the workers included in our study are reluctant to seek work in northern Adelaide either as commuters or by moving to that region to find work. Very few of those interviewed were willing to consider a permanent move to the northern metropolitan area, often giving reasons that reflected either prejudice or uninformed opinion. In-depth qualitative interviews were undertaken with approximately 40 retrenched workers as part of the broader study, and their responses shed considerable light on the motivations driving the employment decisions of this group. For example, one respondent referred to as BG argued that he wouldn't relocate because: 'I think northern Adelaide is the lowest part of Adelaide'.

A second worker – JC – responded to a series of questions around his willingness to move in the following manner:

> Q: And would it be hard for you to leave your house in order to take a job somewhere else like another state or in the north of Adelaide?
> A: Yeah I wouldn't; I like living in this area, the southern area, so I wouldn't really like to move north or interstate, no.
> Q: Would you turn down a job if it meant you'd have to move?
> A: Would I take it?
> Q: Would you turn it down?
> A: Yeah I would, yeah yeah.

A third retrenched worker responded to the same set of questions in ways that reflected both the diversity of responses and the importance of broader household composition and experience.

> Q: Would it be hard for you to leave your house in order to take a job either in northern Adelaide or interstate?
> A: I wouldn't go out the northern side of the town.
> Q: You wouldn't live there?
> A: I was born and bred this side. I don't know, it depends what it was I suppose. I don't really want to leave family.
> Q: You'd be quite reluctant to move outside the southern suburbs of Adelaide?
> A: I haven't really thought about it.
> Q: What would be the reason that you wouldn't move out of the state or other parts of South Australia? Is it family or friends?
> A: Family, friends, yeah.
> Q: And familiar?
> A: Yeah, safe.
> Q: What are the best aspects of living here?
> A: It's relaxing quiet, not too far. You've got Marion (a shopping centre) there, don't know, we just like it here.

The three brief examples given above are indicative of the broader views of respondents. Many of the workers articulated – sometimes in an unformed way – a very strong attachment to their region and to their home (Beer and Thomas forthcoming). That attachment was founded on a long period of residence, family and friendship ties within the region and a perception that the environment in southern Adelaide – physical and social – is superior to the northern metropolitan area. Workers were therefore unwilling to move on a permanent basis, and some indicated that they would move inter-state rather than shift to northern Adelaide. The reality is, however, that most included within our research do not move and many end up as under-employed, unemployed, outside the formal labour market or in lower-wage jobs. While some workers commute to employment in the north, many eschew this option because of the time lost from their day as well as the cost. Workers earning AU$500 per week (before tax) could spend 20–25% of their income on fuel costs in getting to work. For many the wage is simply insufficient to justify the expense. That equation is made less attractive because workers appreciate that the jobs they find in northern Adelaide are likely to be insecure, offer poorer conditions, and may be more demanding than the employment they had experienced previously. Put simply, the returns available to many workers – and less-skilled workers in particular – do not justify the risks that confront them: the recurrence of redundancy; higher living costs associated with long-distance commuting; higher levels of stress and reduced time for family and recreation. It should be noted also that the threat of instability in employment is a strong disincentive for both long-distance commuting and permanent move to a region where the chances of finding employment are greater. Home owners have more to risk and are therefore more likely to become disengaged from employment.

Conclusions and implications for policy

This paper has considered the relationship between housing tenure and employment following a large-scale redundancy within the automotive sector in southern Adelaide. The available evidence suggests that following redundancy private tenants are more likely to remain in the labour market than either home owners or home purchasers and they are also more likely to find full-time employment. The survey data also suggest that owner-occupiers have a higher reserve price for their labour. At this stage the analysis is suggestive rather than conclusive because there is a need to control for both age and occupation, and it is difficult to argue that tenure *per se* influences labour market decisions. Rather, tenure would appear to be correlated with a number of other factors such as the age of the affected worker; their financial resources – including housing wealth but also embracing more liquid assets such as the value of superannuation and redundancy payments; and the degree of embeddedness within the region, including family and friendship ties. Within the context of the debate around the Oswald thesis, tenure may well serve as a surrogate for these other factors which in large measure reflect both a maturing of the workforce and the economies within which individuals make decisions.

The Oswald hypothesis is an important starting point for an investigation of the relationship between employment and housing but a wider, geographically aware, perspective is also needed. Randolph (1991) focused on the spatially and sectorally fragmented nature of labour markets and how the processes and dynamics evident in the world of work are mediated through several filters, including household structure. The qualitative data discussed in this paper supports Randolph's (1991) position because the willingness of individual workers to consider relocation to a region where employment in their industry is more plentiful has been affected by their established prejudices about that region; the importance they place on their existing home and neighbourhood; and, the strength of their family and friendship ties within the region. Their partner's employment circumstances would also be critical. It is interesting that the insights offered by Randolph (1991) and Oswald (1996, 1997) can be seen to intersect in that private-sector tenants may be more willing than owner-occupiers to cut their ties to their region and accept the risks associated with relocation or long-distance commuting.

There are significant implications for policy arising out of the analysis of the relationship between housing and employment outcomes in the aftermath of a large-scale redundancy. The research shows that displaced workers are less spatially mobile than many policy-makers assume, and that the major form of adjustment offered to the workers who were the focus of this research – a generous redundancy payment – may have in fact reduced their willingness to relocate or commute to find work, and thereby lowered their participation in the labour market. This is an important conclusion because redundancy payments of this nature are relatively common within Australian industry. By contrast, the payments offered to workers following the collapse of MG Rover in Birmingham in the United Kingdom in 2005 were far less generous but there was a stronger public sector response that concentrated on providing workers with jobs. This included a relocation payment (Beer and Thomas 2007) and labour market training and, as other papers within this special issue document, the employment outcomes for workers made redundant at MG Rover have been better than those in southern Adelaide. Both Australia and the UK have burgeoning economies and low formal unemployment rates, and South Australia has a growing shortage of skilled labour (Spoehr and Barrett 2005). Ironically, the skilled labour released by the restructuring of the automotive sector in southern Adelaide has, in large measure, become under-employed, unemployed or left the workforce entirely.

There are a number of steps that all three tiers of government in Australia could take to improve labour market outcomes for workers who lose their jobs when a large-scale employer closes or significantly restructures their operations. The Australian and South Australian governments responded to the job losses in the automotive sector in southern Adelaide through the announcement of a AU$45 million package of assistance for workers. Since April 2004 other packages have been announced for workers from the same firm displaced one year later, from Electrolux and General Motors. Some of that assistance has been directed into programmes intended to attract new businesses into South Australia or to help existing businesses within the state expand. This assistance has not been directed at specific regions within South Australia and as this paper has shown, this is a significant failing because retrenched workers – and especially home owners – seek work locally. Australia has been a nation of mass home ownership since the 1950s (Beer 1993) and this tenure pattern is unlikely to change rapidly. Structural adjustment measures need to be sensitive to this reality and direct employment into the regions most affected. In addition, where further employment cannot be secured locally, financial assistance with the costs of relocating or long-distance commuting should be provided and this assistance needs to be at a substantial level to compensate for the perceived risks confronting workers. Such a measure would challenge the established bureaucratic frameworks for assistance, but would deliver improved results in the long term.

Finally, policy settings need to recognise that retrenched workers often have very limited knowledge of the employers and regions to which it is assumed they will move. As this paper has shown, there is a range of social and attitudinal impediments to both residential relocation and re-employment with a new enterprise, and these barriers have become higher for some workers as the deregulation of employment conditions enacted through the Howard government's WorkChoices legislation has introduced far greater uncertainty into the terms of employment. Local governments, coalitions of businesses and state governments should take steps to challenge existing prejudices and help displaced workers make better informed decisions about the employment opportunities available to them. Such actions could help retain skilled and experienced workers in the labour market, raise household incomes at the state and regional level, and enhance the productivity of the economy as a whole.

Acknowledgements

This paper reports on research funded by the Australian Research Council Linkage Grant LP0562288. The author would also acknowledge the assistance of Mrs Louise O'Loughlin in the typing of the tables and Mrs Cecile Cutler in proofreading the text.

Notes

1. There is some suggestion that the packages offered were less than completely voluntary as the closure of some areas of the assembly plant left workers with few options to continue their employment.

2. It is important to acknowledge that there is inevitably a degree of selection bias amongst the persons interviewed as part of our research into the impacts of redundancy in the automotive sector. This bias would encompass inclusion of persons more likely to stay within the region and their current home, while those willing to move in the period immediately after the redundancy may be excluded.
3. Of those employed part-time, two indicated that they would prefer to be working on a full-time basis and eight were not seeking full-time work.

References

Ahn, N., and Blazquez, M., 2007. *Residential mobility and labour market transitions: relative effects of housing tenure, satisfaction and other variables.* Autonomous University of Madrid Foundation for the Study of Applied Economics Working Paper, 2007–05, Madrid.

Allen, J. and Hamnett, C., 1991. *Housing and labour markets: building the connections.* London: Unwin Hyman.

Beer, A., 1993. A dream won, a crisis born? Home ownership and the housing market. *In*: C. Paris, ed. *Housing Australia.* Melbourne: Macmillan.

Beer, A., 2004. On wine, rent and regions: labour market change and housing market processes in non-metropolitan South Australia. *European planning studies*, 12 (1), 57–83.

Beer, A. and Thomas, H., 2007. The politics and policy of economic restructuring in Australia: understanding government responses to the closure of an automotive plant. *Space and polity*, 11 (3), 243–262.

Beer, A. and Thomas, H., forthcoming. Understanding the impacts of employment loss: space, place and public policy. *In*: R. Stough, R. Stimson, and L. Gibson, eds. *Applied geography.* Washington, DC: Enterprise University.

Beer, A., Baum, F., Thomas, H., Lowry, D., Cutler, C., Zhang, G., et al., 2006. *An evaluation of the impact of retrenchment at Mitsubishi focusing on affected workers, their families and communities: implications for human services policies and practices.* Adelaide: SA Department of Health.

Bover, O., Muellbauer, J., and Murphy, A., 1989. Housing wages and UK labour markets. *Oxford bulletin of economics and statistics*, 51 (2), 98–144.

Bridge, C., Cockburn-Campbell, J., Flatau, P., Whelan, S., Wood, G., and Yates, J., 2003. *Housing assistance and non-shelter outcomes, final report.* Melbourne: AHURI.

Brunet, C. and Lesueur, J., 2003. *Do homeowners stay unemployed for longer? A French microeconomic study.* Groupe d'Analyse et de Théorie Economique Working Paper 03-07. Lyon: University of Lyon.

Dalton, T. and Ong, R., 2005. *An audit of Australian and overseas policy initiatives designed to promote housing policy and economic participation goals, research paper 2.* Melbourne: National Research Venture 1, AHURI.

Doogan, K., 1996. Labour mobility and the changing housing market. *Urban studies*, 33 (2), 199–221.

Flatau, P., Forbes, M., Hendershott, P., and Wood, G., 2002a. *Home ownership and unemployment in Australia.* Murdoch University Economics Program Working Paper No. 190.

Flatau, P., Forbes, M., Hendershott, P., O'Dwyer, L., and Wood, G., 2002b. Home ownership and unemployment: does the Oswald Thesis hold for Australian regions? *In*: E. Carlson, ed. *The path to full employment, proceedings, 4th Path to Full Employment Conference.* Newcastle: Centre for Full Employment and Equity.

Gallent, N., 2006. *International reflections on managing growth* [online]. Report of the Housing and Regions Working Group Meeting May 2006, Regional Studies Association. Available from: http://www.regional-studies-assoc.ac.uk/working/reports.asp

Green, R., Hendershott, P., and Liu, Y., 2002. *Home ownership and the duration of unemployment: a test of the Oswald hypothesis.* Unpublished manuscript.

House of Representatives, 2006. *Shifting gears: employment in the automotive components industry.* Standing Committee on Employment, Workplace Relations and Workforce Participation. Canberra: Parliament of Australia.

Johnes, G. and Hyclak, T., 1994. House prices, migration and regional labour markets. *Journal of housing economics*, 3, 312–329.
Muellbauer, J. and Murphy, A., 1990. Regional economic disparities: the role of housing. *In*: A. Bowen and K. Mayhew, *Reducing regional inequalities*. London: National Economic Development Office.
Munch, J., Rosholm, M., and Svarer, M., 2006. Are home owners really more unemployed? *The economic journal*, 116, 991–1013.
Oswald, A., 1996. *A conjecture on the explanation for high unemployment in the industrialised nations: part 1*. Warwick economic research papers number 475. Warwick: Warwick University.
Oswald, A., 1997. *A theory of homes and jobs*. Warwick economic research papers. Warwick: Warwick University.
Porter, M., 1990. *The competitive advantage of nations*. New York: The Free Press.
Randolph, R., 1991. Housing markets, labour markets and discontinuity theory. *In*: J. Allen and C. Hamnett, eds. *Housing and labour markets: building the connections*. London: Unwin Hyman.
Spoehr, J. and Barrett, S., 2005. Employment and workforce development. *In*: J. Spoehr, ed. *The state of South Australia*. Adelaide: Wakefield Press.
Wong, C., 2006. *International lessons on managing decline/change* [online]. Report of the Housing and Regions Working Group Meeting October 2006. Regional Studies Association. Available from: http://www.regional-studies-assoc.ac.uk/working/reports.asp
Wood, G. and Ong, R., 2005. *Housing assistance and economic participation, stage 1 report*. Melbourne: National Research Venture 1, AHURI.
Wood, G., Ong, R., Dockery, M., and Flatau, P., 2005. *Housing assistance programmes and their contribution to poverty and employment traps, research paper 1*. Melbourne: National Research Venture 1, AHURI.

Closure of an automotive plant: transformation of a work-based 'community'

Fiona Verity and Gwyn Jolley

Introduction

This paper focuses on one aspect of 'community' impacts of retrenchment, namely, the implications for work-based community. Understanding complex and shifting dynamics of a movement from paid employment to retrenchment in terms of impact on 'community' is not a straightforward task, in part because interpretations hinge on meaning given to the contested notion of 'community'. As fleshed out in a large volume of literature on this subject, 'community' is a concept associated with a range of ideas, values, associated feelings and experiences and practices (Plant 1974, Nesbit and Perrin 1977, Bryson and Mowbray 1981, Bauman 2001, Blokland 2003). For instance, 'community' is used to describe and invoke connections facilitated through shared territory (work spaces, locality, towns, cities) and social contact and purpose (associations, groups, kinship/friendship relations) and has symbolic and cultural meanings. 'Community' is also put to overt and covert ideological purposes to transmit dominant cultural codes and define boundaries of inclusion (Bauman 2001, p. 148).

A perspective on the much contested notion of community is that, in the words of Blokland, '... communities are networks of social relations' (Blokland 2003, p. 47). Tonnies (1957) wrote of these matters in Germany in the late nineteenth century in theorising about social relations in terms of historical processes of change. Tonnies outlined two constructs or categories of social relations: *Gemeinschaft* ('community') and

Gesellschaft ('society'). He theorised that *Gemeinschaft* 'community' relations are characterised by dense bonds and obligations, interdependence and 'shared mores' (forged through patterns of kinship-relating and/or close living). *Gesellschaft,* or 'associational society' (Cahnman 1973), describes a social structure in industrial capitalism wherein human inter-relations are episodic and contractual (mirroring capitalist market contracts). Here communal attachments and obligations are less intuitively 'known' and reproduced (Tonnies 1957); rather the emphasis is on social relations for the achievement of desired ends. Tonnies distinguishes between 'essential or communal will' inherent in *Gemeinschaft* relations and the workings of 'human rational will' in *Gesellschaft*.

In countries such as Australia, work-based 'communities' take many forms influenced by factors like industry type, the nature and conditions of work (i.e. hours of and at work, organisational values, form and structures), workforce profile and opportunities for work friendships or associations to develop. Class, occupational role, gender and family responsibilities shape experiences. By way of example, research evidence cited by Gray (2003, p. 2) in her work on time availability and social capital indicates a qualitative difference for part-time and full-time working mothers and fathers in experiences of paid-work life and meeting other life demands and responsibilities (i.e. responsibilities for child care, household tasks, wider kinship commitments and maintaining social connections).

There are different perspectives on what an intensification of labour means for work-based community. One thesis is that it leaves little room for friendships or social contacts to develop at work. Another position is articulated by Pocock (2003), for example, that in a context of reduced locality-based and civic 'community', and more time spent in paid work, workplaces become more important as sites for community formation. From this latter position work-related associations (including unions), social clubs and friendships that form at work may spill into connections outside work time. However, as Pocock (2003) and others saliently argue, the social relations generated through twenty-first century work-based 'communities' are extremely fragile because of the transforming nature of production and industrial relation systems (Castells 1997, Bauman 2001). As Pocock (2003, p. 50) bluntly puts it, such social relations are '... conditional on having and keeping a job'.

In elaboration of this latter point, in a context of de-industrialisation many Australian workers have found themselves retrenched. Webber and Campbell (1997) writing in the Australian context a decade ago, note numerous case studies exploring the experiences of Australian workers retrenched from manufacturing industries as varied as the General Motors Holden plant in NSW, a brewery closure in Victoria, and retrenchments at Rowntree-Hoadley Adelaide, the BHP steelworks at Newcastle, and footwear and clothing industries in Victoria. A trend to retrenchment from manufacturing plants has continued. There is also a growing evidence base, confirmed in our study, that retrenchment has psychological, health and economic consequences for retrenched workers and their families. Whilst community impacts may be alluded to, in the Australian context research attention specifically on communal relations in the process of retrenchment has been scant.

In this paper we take up one aspect of what is a multifaceted, multi-experienced and still unfolding tale of 'community' changes through a process of retrenchment. The focus is an analysis of the evolution of a work-based community through examination of the accounts of workers retrenched from Mitsubishi Motors' Lonsdale foundry and the assembly plant at Tonsley Park, both located in Adelaide, South Australia. Specifically we explore the following questions. What is the value and meaning of work-based community to workers retrenched from Mitsubishi? To what extent are work-based social relations maintained? What supports them in continuing? Is there a re/connection with forms of 'community' outside the workplace and if so to what affect? What are some public policy and practice implications to be drawn?

The discussion follows two paths; first we explore how employment at Mitsubishi has offered and facilitated 'community' and the meanings of such 'community' to Mitsubishi workers. The second path is an exploration of changes in 'community' as perceived by workers some time after retrenchment. In both sections of the paper we draw upon the first survey (in a longitudinal study) collected from 373 retrenched workers by members of the research team. This first survey was administered face-to-face immediately before or shortly after workers finished at Mitsubishi, second and third stage data collection was by telephone interview at six months and 12 months post-redundancy. However, we draw mainly on data from in-depth interviews with a random sample of 40 of these respondents that were conducted at six and 12 months post-redundancy. These interviews were audio-taped, transcribed and imported to NVIVO v7 to assist with analysis. Coding was first conducted under question headings, then by emerging themes.

In respect to analysis of multifarious interconnections between paid employment and 'community' it is common to see Tonnies' distinction of *Gemeinschaft* and *Gesellschaft* used as an exploratory window. In this paper we too use Tonnies' delineation as a frame of reference that we supplement for analysis with insights from a combination of classic and more contemporary writers on 'community'. We begin with a descriptive overview of the geographic community in which Mitsubishi Motors is located and a profile of the 'work-based' community at the time of redundancies. This paper is part of ongoing work being conducted by the researchers.

Geographic-based community

At the time of the retrenchments Mitsubishi operated both a foundry and assembly plant in the southern region of Adelaide, South Australia. This region is a large geographic area with a diversity of land use and population characteristics. The foundry was located at Lonsdale in the Local Government Area (LGA) of Onkaparinga that spreads across the outer realms of the southern metropolitan region. This area had already experienced the closure of a nearby oil refinery and other manufacturing job losses. Tonsley Park is the location of the assembly plant on the southern edge of the City of Marion. Marion is a large LGA, which in 2001, had 24% of the population employed in manufacturing industries. Our research has shown that a sizable proportion of our respondents lived within 5 km from their employment at either site, with 40% living in their neighbourhood for more than 15 years.

Work-based community

Prior to the recent retrenchments Mitsubishi had been a secure source of employment for its staff. Operations at the Tonsley Park site commenced in 1964 and the Lonsdale plant, formerly owned by Chrysler, also dates back to this time. Historically both sites have been largely male domains with women employed in areas such as the 'cut and sew', catering and administration areas. The respondents in the study are reflective of the population of workers who exited Mitsubishi in total. They are generally middle-aged to older men, with limited formal education, and largely of Anglo-Celtic origin with two-thirds Australia-born. The UK-born are the largest immigrant group. Most of the participants in the study were married or partnered men and many had lived all their adult lives in the southern region of Adelaide.

As indicated above, stability of employment has been a feature of the Mitsubishi workplace. Table 1 depicts the length of time that survey respondents had been employed at Mitsubishi. Almost 50% of respondents who answered a question about their period of employment at the company had worked at Mitsubishi for over 21 years and a larger proportion had worked there 16 years or more. Nesbit and Perrin (1977) describe 'duration over time' to be a hallmark of *Gemeinschaft*-type social relations, which Tonnies (1957) articulates as close associations developed through ongoing patterns of behaviour.

In the Mitsubishi workplace, bonds or attachments were formed through daily and familiar rhythms of interaction. Here the work organisation provided what Blokland (2003, p. 89) calls the 'framework' for community relationships. For instance, one respondent recalls the bonds developed because co-workers 'talked together at lunch time' and did so repeatedly over many years. Another describes the myriad of connections he had with workmates '... because there were so many people there, you know, it was just like, go to work and you bump into someone and it's like, oh yeah, "Where ya goin', what ya doin'"?' Furthermore, there were many instances where whole families – brothers, sons, cousins, fathers, grandfathers and mothers – worked together at the company. Hence not only did daily patterns of familiar interaction form 'community', but kinship relations are in the mix. A further variable shaping the nature of this work community, as gleaned from workers' accounts, is the shift-work schedule that creates 'separate and regular worlds' bounded and distinguished by time.

Given the factors mentioned above, it is not at all surprising that a high proportion of survey respondents report that almost half or all the people they know are people they worked with at Mitsubishi (see Figure 1). Also congruent with these findings is the dominance of a language of 'friendship' and 'family' used by workers in reflecting upon what they most missed about working for Mitsubishi. This is more than expression of a feeling that the workplace was reminiscent of 'family'. As seen in the following quotes from interviewees these connections were 'family':

> The people would have to be the best. I made some good friends and there was a lot of good people there and still are there. Social aspect was very good.

> The company of the people that you're going to work with, you spend more time with those people in there than what you do with your own family. So I think it was the friendships, the mates ... and I think that's something that you miss because being able to intermingle with those people after you left.

Table 1. Length of employment at Mitsubishi.

	Frequency	%
5 years or less	12	3.2
6 to 10 years	59	15.8
11 to 15 years	59	15.8
16 to 20 years	70	18.8
21 to 25 years	23	6.2
26 to 30 years	25	6.7
31 to 35 years	20	5.4
36 to 40 years	15	4.0
More than 40 years	9	2.4
Total	292	78.3
Missing	81	21.7
	373	100.0

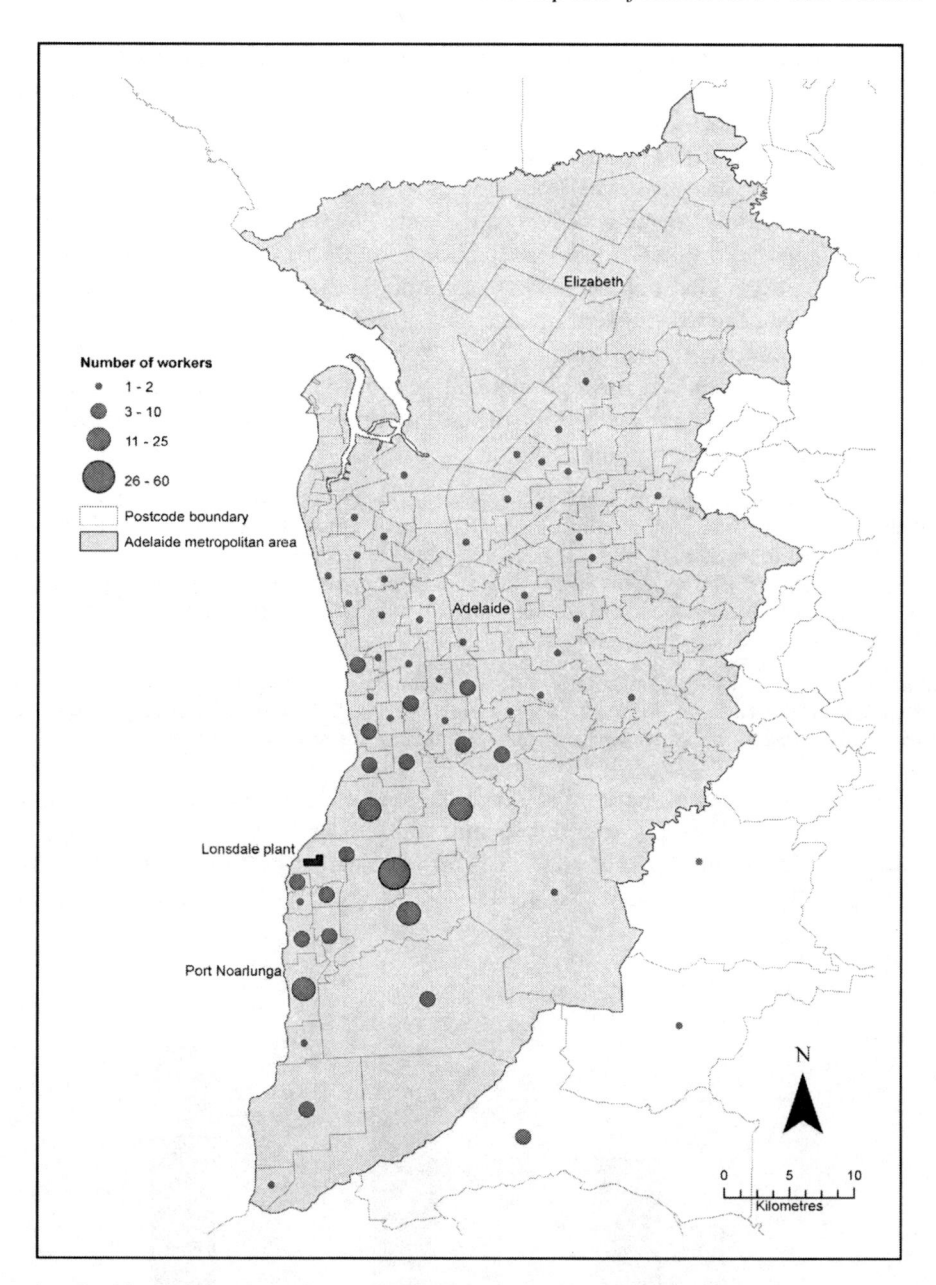

Figure 1. Residential location of survey respondents in metropolitan Adelaide.

It was like being part of an extended family really. Being a shift worker meant I saw more of my co-workers than I did of my family. Also no longer see so much of my co-workers outside of work socially.

In addition to the informal workplace connections developed and reinforced over time, there were a plethora of regular formal and informal social group activities that included participation in social and sporting clubs, picnics, Christmas parties, family events (births, support and care in times of crisis, etc.). As expected in a manufacturing environment there was a high level of union membership, with all but three interview respondents stating that they were union members and 15% of survey respondents reporting participation in a union-based activity in the 12 months prior.

The interdependence of social bonds in a *Gemeinschaft* sense is captured in the following quotes from two interview respondents. The social activities recounted by respondents depict traditional gender social roles: a BBQ for the male toolmakers and Tupperware parties and baby showers for the woman in the 'cut and sew' section. The first respondent, in using the words 'we went outside', conveys the social connections extending outside the boundary of the workplace. As well, both respondents describe interlocking circles of connections enabled through work at Mitsubishi: work connections that spilled into outside social connections which in turn are incorporated into kinship connections; a 'full family' as the second respondent notes.

> We went outside, we went every Christmas, we went out together all of us. We had a party at Mitsubishi, within Mitsubishi at cut and sew. Everybody got a dish and we all sat down. And we were allowed to work a few minutes extra each day the last week so we can have an extended break. We organised parties, some of the girls had postie parties and Tupperware parties, and well got together. Or if somebody had a baby, there would be a group of us going to have a look at the baby.

> Apart from the social club picnics and that, the toolmakers would get together at least once a month and take it turns at different people's places, yeah, for a barbie or a get together. The wives would come along so it's not just the toolmakers. It's sort of a full family.

Not as evident in interview material are recollections of friction or competition amongst members of the workplace community, and this is of note given sociological and psychological understandings that conflict is an inescapable part of 'community' life.

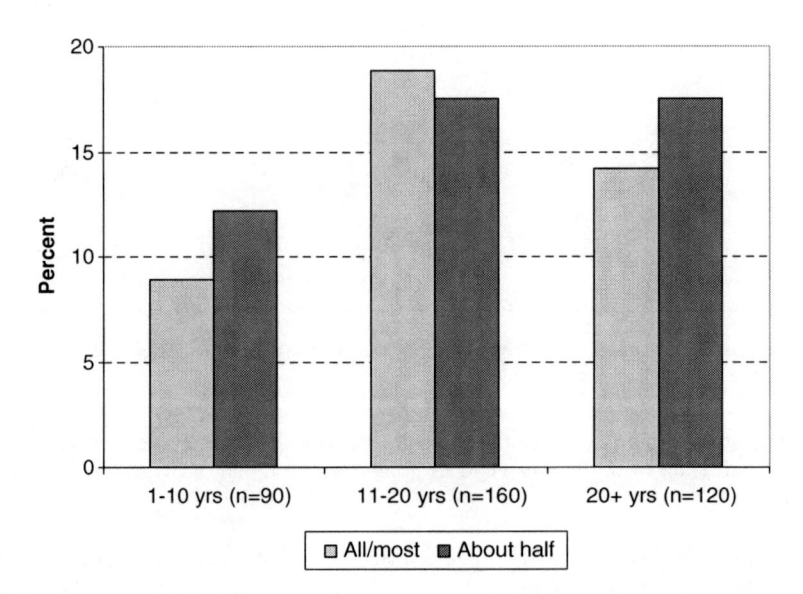

Figure 2. Proportion of respondents reporting that all/most or about half the people they knew were from or through their workplace, by years worked at Mitsubishi.

At face value, the work-based 'community' described by respondents has characteristics of a *Gemeinschaft* community: interactions experienced and patterned within the institution of the workplace and reinforced in social relations outside the workplace. We suggest there were a number of factors that may have enabled this type of 'community' to be maintained: the length and stability of employment, shared cultural connections, kinship connections merging with other attachments within the workplace, the ordered and interdependent nature of the production environment, the nature of shift work in demarcating and binding social groupings, and until these retrenchments, the reach of social connections from the workplace to family and social life outside the paid workplace. Furthermore, the majority of respondents lived in the same geographic community.

Blokland (2003, p. 126) writes that communal attachments arise from '... repetition, socialization and organization' and such processes are evident in the workers' accounts of their interconnections with other workers. It could be argued that the company itself played a role as a container or 'holding environment', to use the psychoanalyst Donald Winnicott's notion, wherein 'community' interactions could develop. Mitsubishi Motors purports to have an explicit 'community-minded' culture, as conveyed in company documentation where they pledge active support to community organisations and community life, both within and external to the workplace. For example, the company provides grants to local groups, sponsoring charities, sporting clubs and arts and cultural activities. In a sense the company has enabled what Nesbit and Perrin (1977, p. 100) wrote about many years ago as '... a corporation-based social life'. On a related point, it is of interest to note an anxiety expressed by some human service providers interviewed as part of the research, about a possible loss of the Mitsubishi's financial support for community development.

What happens to work-based 'community' when work changes?

How then have work-based associations changed post-redundancies? Our research signposts a move away from the *Gemeinschaft* social relations noted above, to a situation more akin to what can be described as *Gesellschaft*, or social bonds that, as Nisbet and Perrin (1977, p. 99) write, are relations '... more tenuous, loose, and less deeply rooted in his (sic) allegiances or commitments'. A tangible sign of this shift is an obvious report of less time in everyday contact. Tonnies (1957, p. 65) suggests *Gesellschaft* relations are evident when people's 'spheres of activity and powers are sharply separated'. In this case a loss of the repetition of contacts within the organisational setting seems to have impeded the maintenance of the relationships that had existed over many years within and outside paid work.

The reasons for this loss of contact, as rationalised by respondents, are many. For some the loss of contacts with friends is due to both the loss of day-to-day contact and the closure of the various Mitsubishi-related social clubs. For others, their own new employment or personal circumstances (including changing working hours) had changed their priorities and/or restricted their time for connections with former friends and workmates. There were other examples where the pressing concern for the retrenched worker had been dealing with financial concerns, or coping with moving away from the southern region, and these matters, rather than maintaining social contacts, had been the main priority. One respondent attributes the change in contacts with former colleagues to be a consequence of losing a sense of common purpose that is generated through the tasks and culture of the workplace. He says: 'I've still got a few contacts with people, but that is not the same because now everybody has got a different vision. A different direction.'

These changes in social relations can be seen in the following interview responses, all from male retrenched workers:

> Working there for 15 years meant I had built up a large group of friends who socialised regularly. We would go to each other's houses, fix cars together, help each other build sheds etc. This has virtually ceased since I left. I work shift work which also interferes with socialising.

> I miss some mates. I miss the social club, we had a very good organisation over there in Mitsubishi. I still pay the fee. I have good memories ... picnics and cinema sessions, we have Christmas dinner next month with shopping day in a couple of weeks. It's a social dinner every year. Because I worked 25 years ... It was good, I was a member in the tennis club over there too. I played, they've got tennis courts.

> But, you know, like the first week I just thought I was on holidays again and then you realise, well, hang on, you ain't going back. I mean, there's a lot of people I don't see anymore and I probably never will see again who I'd like to keep in contact with. But, well one bloke in particular, I used to play golf with him, every time we had a day off we'd go out and play golf. He now works on the other side of town so he doesn't have time to go and play golf.

The extent to which respondents (most of whom are men) report little or no contact with former work mates and friends post-retrenchment is quite striking, especially given the fullness of the former community life they recall. Some respondents talk about wanting to maintain social connections but not being able to overcome the factors pulling people away from each other. For instance, the following respondent saw the loss of key organisers and fracturing of the group members going their 'different ways' as contributing to the demise of an important golfing event:

> It would be like a once-a-year event, you know, a big fun day. We'd book out the whole golf course, and the whole golf course would be entire Mitsubishi people, only ourselves, a great day, and then in the clubrooms afterwards and there'd be awards given out. There was talk of trying to keep it going, but it was, it just couldn't happen because everyone's just gone their own separate ways.

In analysis of these changes we put forward some thoughts. First, the majority of our sample is male and this picture of a shattering of stable and affirming communal connections after retrenchment is congruent with understandings that workplaces are for men a source of social connections, and that men face particular obstacles in maintaining existing relations and navigating new ones after changes in employment. In the light of this it is also not surprising that male respondents report high levels of depression post-retrenchment.

A second point concerns organisational or institutional factors. There was little reported support for the workers as a 'community' leaving a community. Not only did Mitsubishi workers leave long-term employment but they left a family environment of sorts; a 'warm circle', to use Rosenberg's image as cited in Bauman's (2001), p. 10) work on community. It is of note that whilst government and company effort was made to re-attach workers to the labour market and to social security for income support, there was no explicit strategy to consider ways to acknowledge and support social attachments to one another. Whilst this seems curiously to be at odds with the 'community-minded' Mitsubishi Motors corporate culture referred to earlier, we suggest it is consistent with approaches to organisational responses to retrenchment where a pre-eminent task, beyond negotiating payouts, is to attend to dynamics within the workforce that remain, both for productivity concerns but also in terms of managing adjustment to change within the company (Mohr and Dielmann 2006).

Mourning for a loss of relationships developed through work at Mitsubishi is apparent in interview responses. Van Beekum (2006, p. 330) writing on organisational mourning states that there '... is a direct link between the length of the grieving process and the intensity of the bonding'. The interview material cited above indicates, in part, the strength of the relational attachments or bonds that workmates had with one another. Furthermore, many respondents comment that the rituals for saying goodbye, expressing loss and celebrating the connections that had been important over the years, were not adequate. This perspective is seen in the following interview extract from a retrenched male worker who is responding to a question about whether he had experienced a grief process after leaving the company.

> Worker: I think so, and sometimes the grieving was by not seeing people before they left. You know, it was some of the processes of when we were leaving that you didn't get to say goodbye to some of the people and that was a bit of a loss you know if you didn't work in the direct vicinity of, you know. There were a lot of people you never got to say goodbye to them. That was a bit of a loss when you'd spent 17 years with them, you know.
> Interviewer: How did the goodbyes happen?
> Worker: They put on some barbecues, but it was quite funny, you know. Some were good, some were, like I said, you didn't see some people leave. You heard that they left. So-and-so left yesterday. Oh, I would have liked to have said goodbye to them, sort of thing, but yes it was very funny. It was all sorts of ways that it happened ... It was this area's going to have a barbecue and the other area's not going to finish until four weeks time sort of thing, and that was sort of how it happened, and wasn't really, it was just a barbecue. It wasn't a goodbye-type thing, but on the day they'd say okay you five people are going to go through the things today, and it was a bit like a process-type thing. You went into this door and you had this person sign these papers and then wait for them to sign, and once you were out the door you weren't allowed back in ... And if you had to go back in for something, you had to get a security guard escort. That was sort of the bit, very formal. A bit sad, you know, well there was nothing personal about it, you know. They gave you a hat and a CD and said here's your present for leaving sort of thing, and okay yes, thanks.

An absence of meaningful mourning and farewell rituals can lead to what Doka (1993) terms 'disenfranchised grief' where there is little to no public recognition or acknowledgement of the loss experienced and thus the 'legitimacy of the grief'. Doka further contends that disenfranchised grief has negative impacts on the bereavement process that can manifest in emotional and psychosocial health issues. There are also implications for workers not retrenched who are also saying goodbye to members of the 'family' of the workplace; however our data limits what we can say about this.

In this research we also explore if post-retrenchment, there is a re/connection to communal life outside the workplace. There are signs that, for some retrenched workers, the abandonment of work-based community connections has been a catalyst for an uptake of other forms of community (including kinship connections) and social life. Some shift workers made the point that in retrenchment they have been freed from work cycles that had limited their participation in daily family routines. Furthermore, 52 respondents to the survey stated that their new life, or new job, made it easier to take part in social activities. Mostly this was because they now had more time and/or they were working different shifts as these comments below indicate.

> Social life has improved now because I don't work afternoon shift anymore.

> Before spent almost all time with Mitsubishi people, but now feel a whole new world opened up.

Human service providers we spoke with in focus group interviews also expressed a hope that the Mitsubishi Motors retrenchments might enlarge the pool of potential volunteer workers in the southern region. The liberating nature of the retrenchments and the engagement of retrenched workers in voluntary or community work is a theme that will be pursued in forthcoming work.

Conclusion

The discussion in this paper draws on research data about the retrenchments at Mitsubishi Motors, Adelaide to explore the general question of what happens for a work-based 'community' when twenty-first-century capitalist production decisions result in redundancies from a manufacturing plant. A perspective on the much contested notion of community is that, in the words of Blokland (2003, p. 47), '... communities are networks of social relations'. This is a useful description which concords with the accounts of the retrenched workers that the workplace community, as they recalled it, comprised deep social attachments and intensive and extensive networks that had developed over time. These networks were both within and outside the workplace. Further the organisational rhythms of the Mitsubishi institution formed the 'container' or incubator within which these relationships could flourish.

For many of the retrenched workers these social attachments have in large measure been shattered by redundancy. There is a palpable sense of sorrow in the workers' accounts of relationships lost and not easily maintained outside of the workplace. At one level this expression of sorrow is understandable in that the interviews gave an opportunity for workers (predominantly male) to talk reflectively about experiences and feelings of their retrenchment. According to workers, it has been difficult for the workplace connections to be maintained in the same manner beyond retrenchment. Yet there are exceptions, where for some former Mitsubishi workers changes in their workplace community are experienced as liberating. Retrenchment has allowed opened up new possibilities, whether study, retraining, developing a business of their own or forming new relationships.

Our analysis to date suggests that whilst in times of retrenchment and plant closures companies and governments give important and critical attention to employment, training and income support needs, social and 'community' dimensions also need consideration. Such attention would be congruent with government policy focus on community capacity building and community strengthening, increasingly part of policy and programme language across many functional areas (i.e. social welfare, family and community services, education, environment, local government, social and urban planning) (Hounslow 2002). This is evident in Australian governmental initiatives that either directly or indirectly aim to finance or facilitate community capacity-building.

A holistic view of the workplace in terms of the value of work-based social relations is a seemingly neglected aspect in this case example of the retrenchment experience. We suggest there is scope for the human service world to be of assistance in retrenchment-planning and response in terms of psychosocial support, initiatives to support integration (of some form) between economic and social planning, and supports for community capacity-building. On this latter point, it is quite possible that experienced community development workers with skills and knowledge of processes of social relations and community organising may have been able to offer support to a transforming work-based community.

Acknowledgements

This paper reports on research funded by the Australian Research Council Linkage Grant LP0562288. The authors acknowledge the Australian Research Council for funding this research and an anonymous reviewer for helpful suggestions.

References

Bauman, Z., 2001. *Community-seeking safety in an insecure world.* Cambridge: Polity Press.
Blokland, T., 2003. *Urban bond – social relationships in an inner city neighbourhood.* Cambridge: Polity Press.
Bryson, L. and Mowbray, M., 1981. Community: the spray-on solution. *Australian journal of social issues*, 16 (4), 255–267.
Cahnman, W., 1973. Tonnies and social change. *In*: W. Cahnman and E.J. Brill, eds. *Ferdinand Tonnies – a new evaluation.* Brill: Leiden.
Castells, M., 1997. *The power of identity.* Oxford: Blackwell.
Doka, K., 1993. *Disenfranchised grief: a mark of our time.* Queensland: National Association for Loss and Grief Conference Proceedings.
Gray, A., 2003. *Towards a conceptual framework for studying time and social capital.* London: Families and Social Capital ESRC Research Group, South Bank University.
Hounslow, B., 2002. Community capacity building explained. *Stronger Families Learning Exchange Bulletin 1*, Autumn, 20–22.
Mohr, G. and Dielmann, A., 2006. Deep cuts in organisations: building relationships and reductions in staff. *In*: G. Mohr and T. Steinert, eds. *Growth and change for organisations.* Pleasington: International Transactional Analysis Association.
Nesbit, R. and Perrin, R., 1977. *The social bond.* New York: Alfred A. Knopf.
Plant, R., 1974. *Community and ideology.* London: Routledge and Kegan Paul.
Pocock, B., 2003. *The work/life collision – what work is doing to Australians and what to do about it.* Leichhardt: Federation Press.
Tonnies, F., 1957. *Gemeinschaft and Gesellschaft*, C. Loomis, trans., ed. New York: Harper Torch Books.
Van Beekum, S., 2006. The relevance of mourning in organizational development process. *In*: G. Mohr and Steinert, eds. *Growth and change for organisations.* Pleasington: International Transactional Analysis Association.
Webber, M. and Campbell, I., 1997. Labour market outcomes among retrenched workers in Australia: a review. *Journal of sociology*, 33 (2), 187–204.

Auto plant closures, policy responses and labour market outcomes: a comparison of MG Rover in the UK and Mitsubishi in Australia

Kathy Armstrong, David Bailey, Alex de Ruyter, Michelle Mahdon, and Holli Evans

Introduction

Integrating displaced workers – job quality and well-being

Economic restructuring has been an important feature of the UK and Australian economies in the last 25 years. The processes of deregulation, privatisation, technological change and globalisation have combined to reshape the economic landscape across both countries. Some industries have grown, while others have declined. In particular, there has been a dramatic shift away from manufacturing to the services industries; a process which has been typified by a number of high-profile plant closures across both countries (see Chapain and Murie in this issue).

Whilst the overriding labour market policy emphasis in both countries has been a raw focus on transition into 'any job', successful adjustment and well-being requires that issues of job quality should also be addressed. Graetz (1993) found that the relationship between psychological well-being and employment is related to the quality of the employment found. Well-being only improved after re-employment if people went into jobs that they were satisfied with. Similarly it has been found that re-employment into jobs with lower pay or where skills are underutilised does not enhance psychological health relative to that of unemployed persons (Winefield et al. 1990). In contrast, positive psychological health facilitates re-employment following unemployment (Waters and Moore 2002).

Such research illustrates that the issues surrounding reintegration extend beyond merely providing 'jobs' or 'job opportunities' for displaced workers. They extend to job quality as well as income security. This is particularly pressing for displaced workers who are only able to obtain casual or part-time work after redundancy. Indeed, there is evidence to suggest that individuals who subsequently obtain such work can become 'trapped' in precarious cycles of intermittent work and unemployment (Westin 1990) – further adding to their sense of exclusion and deprivation. The demise of secure jobs in traditional sectors and the shift to part-time and casual[1] arrangements is a key reason for growing job insecurity in both the UK and Australia in the past 20 years (De Ruyter and Burgess 2003). Indeed, casual employees now comprise over one-quarter of the Australian workforce (De Ruyter and Burgess 2003). Hence, the issues surrounding plant closure also extend to those of individual health and well-being and prospects for lasting career opportunities, not to mention the effects on the household and wider community.

As such, the employment and well-being consequences of closure are considerable, and need to be explored through longitudinal studies. Yet few studies (e.g. Westin 1990, Leana and Feldman 1995) have explicitly looked at the employment outcomes and the quality of jobs entered into over the longer term. As Leana and Feldman (1995, p. 1385) note, most of the research on plant closure 'has taken as its end point re-employment; when laid-off workers get new jobs, they typically cease to be the focus of further research'. It is the employment-quality impacts of these closures on ex-MG Rover workers in the UK and Mitsubishi workers in Australia that this article seeks to explore. The rationale for this is that the similarities in the profile of ex-workers and the similar problems of adjustment for manufacturing apparent in Australia (Beer et al. 2004) and the UK (Bailey and Kobayashi 2006) provide an excellent opportunity to compare differences in the nature and effectiveness of different policy responses. The following sections describe the policy responses and labour market outcomes of the respective closures in Australia and the UK. In this paper, we focus on one aspect of employment and well-being – the degree of income and employment security of jobs entered into (De Ruyter and Burgess 2003). The paper ends with a comparison of the two cases with a view to expounding some lessons for policy.

The Australian case: Mitsubishi in Adelaide

This section examines the closure of the Mitsubishi Lonsdale plant in Adelaide. The background to the plant's closure and the nature of the policy response is detailed in the introduction to this special issue.

Government policy responses aimed at labour market assistance

When Mitsubishi Motors Australia Limited announced that it was closing its Lonsdale manufacturing plant, along with voluntary redundancies at its Tonsley Park assembly plant, the federal and state governments responded with two main packages of assistance for the 1200 workers affected. The Structural Adjustment Fund for South Australia

(SAFSA) was a pooled fund into which the federal government committed AU$40 million (around £18 million at January 2008 exchange rates) and the South Australian government committed AU$5 million (just over £2 million). The SAFSA was effectively a capital subsidy, offering grants to new businesses wanting to invest in South Australia or existing businesses that wanted to expand their business in South Australia.

The rationale from government for adopting this measure of assistance was that the expansion of business would create new jobs in the region that could absorb displaced Mitsubishi workers. While there have been numerous businesses established on the Lonsdale site through SAFSA funding, the government has been forced to admit that the majority of firms who received grants have not achieved their employment targets. Furthermore, over half of the SAFSA funding went to businesses on the northern side of the city, when virtually all of the displaced Mitsubishi workers lived in the southern region. The main labour market response from government to the redundancies at Mitsubishi was the Labour Adjustment Package (LAP). The federal government committed AU$10 million (around £4.5 million) of funding for the LAP with the state government only contributing a range of services to support the LAP, including financial counselling, CV/resumé preparation and career counselling that totalled AU$383,485 (around £170k).

The AU$10 million funding amounted to approximately AU$10,000 (around £4500) per worker. The LAP was delivered through the privately-run Job Network agencies. The Mitsubishi LAP provided an additional AU$450 per worker to Job Network providers so that they could purchase further services or assistance such as tools, uniform, clothing or training. The LAP was designed to give additional assistance to help displaced Mitsubishi workers find new employment. As part of this assistance all Mitsubishi workers facing redundancy were fast-tracked onto the Intensive Support Customised Assistance (ISCA) scheme. This was an existing programme used to assist long-term unemployed people. This section of the paper focuses on LAP support as the SAFSA scheme has been discussed in more detail by Thomas and Beer in this special issue.

Both government responses in the Mitsubishi case amount to a minor intervention, especially when compared to previous government interventions in the automotive industry, or to the response to the closure of MG Rover in the UK described in the following section. Both the federal and state governments have made it clear that they do not see the role of government to be 'propping up' manufacturing industries that are no longer competitive. The redundancies at Mitsubishi came when the State of South Australia was experiencing a boom in the mining and defence industries. The assumption made by government was that Mitsubishi workers would be able to move seamlessly into jobs in mining and defence. As South Australian Premier Mike Rann recently commented:

> When we saw Lonsdale close, we were able to find jobs for nearly all of the people who wanted jobs because of other things that were happening ... A lot of people who build the actual hulls and things associated with the defence industry will be coming out of car industry jobs.

It is of importance, then, to critically assess these types of claims and examine to what extent successful labour market reintegration (that is, re-entry into permanent, full-time employment) has actually occurred. In addition, given previous research outlined in the introduction, it is vital to assess the quality of these new jobs, as 'good jobs' are linked to better health outcomes providing beneficial long-term effects to the economy.

Labour market outcomes for redundant Mitsubishi workers

This article uses qualitative data collected during the 12 months after redundancy to assess the employment outcomes for Mitsubishi workers made redundant between 2004 and 2005. A total of 373 workers participated in Wave 1 and 315 were interviewed in Wave 2 which occurred approximately 12 months post-redundancy. The findings are part of a longitudinal study into the health, housing and labour market impacts of job losses in the automotive sector within southern Adelaide (see Beer *et al.* 2003). The study as a whole involved three waves of quantitative data collection and two waves of qualitative data collection over a period of 18 months.

It is important to recognise that, whilst at Mitsubishi, all respondents were employed on a permanent full-time basis. However, 12 months post-redundancy only 34% of displaced workers were in full-time employment. Furthermore, over 20% of respondents were in casual or part-time employment, with some 69% of those in casual employment reporting that they would rather be working full-time. These figures indicate a significant level of under-employment among displaced Mitsubishi workers. Many respondents reported they struggled to find full-time employment and had to settle for casual or part-time contract positions. The difficulty these displaced workers faced in finding new employment is illustrated through the fact that 66% of respondents reported that they were unemployed at some stage during the 12 months since leaving Mitsubishi.

Significantly over 30% of respondents did not participate in the workforce 12 months post-redundancy. This included 13% who were unemployed looking for work, 9% who had retired and 4% who were not working because of a disability. This represents a high level of unemployment among displaced workers, especially when compared to the state's unemployment rate which was 4–5% during the same period. Our research suggests that the considerable percentage of workers who withdrew from the labour market hides the true extent of unemployment and under-employment amongst the displaced workers. For instance, 28% of those who had retired said that they would rather be working, but they had been unable to find new employment. A common complaint from respondents was that they were unable to find full-time employment. One respondent remarked, 'casual employment sucks, it's darn hard to get a full-time job', while another commented, 'I'm very frustrated I can't get a full-time job, the pay is a lot less and there is constant uncertainty in not knowing when a contract will end'.

Some 71% of respondents reported that they were now earning less that when employed at Mitsubishi. This is partly a result of the shift from full-time to part-time or casual work for many displaced workers. However, it also reflects the reality that Mitsubishi was recognised as a good employer, who paid above the market rate. Moreover, Mitsubishi also appears to have provided good working conditions for its employees. Most displaced workers have found lower pay and poorer working conditions in their new employment. Of those in full-time employment 31% reported that their current job was worse than their job at Mitsubishi, while 41% of those in casual employment found their current job worse than their job at Mitsubishi. For those in casual employment, when asked the worst thing about their current job, the most common complaint was that they were not getting enough hours or pay.

The number of jobs respondents have had in the 12 months since leaving Mitsubishi also indicates dissatisfaction with new employment. Of those in new employment, many had already had more than one job, with 39% of those who found employment reporting they had two jobs, 20% reporting three jobs and 14% reporting they had more than three jobs since leaving Mitsubishi. This indicates the insecurity of the jobs that displaced workers have entered, with many reporting that they were made redundant again in their new employment, or that they were only employed on a short-term contract and were therefore forced to find other work when that finished. Indeed many respondents reported that they were simply going from one short-term contract to another, as that was the only employment they could find. Many respondents also faced considerable periods of unemployment in between jobs. For instance one respondent reported:

> I've had a few jobs since leaving Mitsubishi ... they were all part-time and contract ... it took me three months to find a job. After nine months of contract it faded out. I found another job six weeks later.

Previous research has shown job security is an important factor in a 'good job' with a positive influence on an employee's state of health (Marmot 2004).

Displaced workers found new employment across a diverse range of industries, though 36% of respondents reported that they were currently working in manufacturing. Other industries where a significant number of displaced workers had found employment included: 11% in retail; 7% in construction; 6% in health services and 4% in agriculture.

Despite the rhetoric from government that former Mitsubishi workers had been absorbed by new employment in the booming mining and defence industries, only 2% were employed at the time of the survey in industries related to mining, and another 2% were employed in industries related to defence. The explanation lies in the fact that displaced workers were not provided with the necessary education and training opportunities to equip them with the skills required to be able to move into employment in the mining and defence industries. No funds were set aside by either federal or state government for re-training or up-skilling redundant Mitsubishi workers, despite the government of South Australia recognising the state was suffering a skills shortage (Government of South Australia 2005). This stands in stark contrast to the £50 million that the UK government put aside specifically for training and re-skilling of redundant workers from MG Rover (MG RTF 2006). Redundant Mitsubishi workers needed greater intervention and assistance from government, in the form of substantial training and education, to enable them to move into the employment being created in growth sectors such as defence and mining.

In Australia the funds for the labour adjustment assistance were channelled into the privately-run Job Network agencies, who were then responsible for delivering assistance to displaced workers in finding new employment. It does not appear that this was an efficient use of resources or an effective policy, given that 38% of respondents reported that they did not use the Job Network providers. Of those currently employed, only 6% reported that they got their job through Job Network agencies. Of those who did use the Job Network provider, their reported experience was one of disappointment and frustration as they felt that the Job Networks were more used to dealing with the long-term unemployed, rather than skilled workers with a long work history. A common complaint was that the Job Network agencies did not put forward suitable jobs. For instance, one respondent reported that:

> they [the Job Network provider] told me that I was over-qualified, that the Job Network didn't have the resources to find relevant jobs for someone like me.

This left a sense of dissatisfaction amongst displaced workers who questioned where the AU$10 million of funding had gone. For instance one respondent reported:

> I'm very disappointed in the number of job opportunities in the southern area. Job Network agencies are absolute rubbish. They abuse us and rip us off. The same agencies don't do a good job ... We are just a commodity and they rip us off big time. We get bad pay and they pocket [the money].

It would appear that the Job Network agencies did not have the resources to deal with skilled workers and that placing redundant Mitsubishi workers on an existing scheme designed to assist the long-term unemployed was an inappropriate response by government. Given that the majority of redundant Mitsubishi workers did not use a Job Network agency and that very few of the individuals who did use them actually managed to find employment through the Job Network agencies, it is evident that the Labour Adjustment Package was not effective in assisting these displaced workers to regain employment. Furthermore, the AU$10 million LAP was divided between the Job Network providers according to how many redundant Mitsubishi workers had signed up with them. The Job Network providers then had the discretion to decide how much money was spent on each individual and for what purposes. This was at best an *ad hoc* system where the Job Network providers were simply the administrator of the LAP, which no doubt led to a considerable amount of the AU$10 million LAP being consumed in administration costs.

Given the skills shortage the state was facing, together with the considerable growth in mining and defence industries, it would have been more appropriate if LAP funding had been redirected to further training or re-skilling opportunities for redundant workers. Lack of training and re-skilling for redundant workers also partly explains why so many former Mitsubishi workers have only been able to find new employment in lower-paid positions with less security of employment, as evidenced by those who could only obtain casual work. While government has claimed the number of Mitsubishi workers in new employment marks the success of their assistance packages, this masks the reality that over 70% of those redundant workers are now earning less than they were at Mitsubishi; that over 20% have gone from permanent full-time employment to part-time or casual employment; that over 30% of redundant workers withdrew from participating in the labour force; and that most of these redundant workers are now faced with insecure employment, many of them having had several jobs in the year after leaving Mitsubishi.

The UK case: MG Rover in Birmingham

This section examines the demise of MG Rover and government policy and subsequent labour market outcomes, utilising the results of two waves of a longitudinal survey of ex-MG Rover (MGR) workers conducted by the Work Foundation (see Armstrong 2006 for a more detailed discussion). The background to the MG Rover closure is covered by Bailey *et al.* (in this issue).

Government policy responses aimed at labour market assistance

Phoenix Venture Holdings (the owners of MGR) went into administration in April 2005, precipitating the sudden closure of the MGR plant at Longbridge, in Birmingham. Immediately, some 5500 MGR workers were made redundant (with several thousand more jobs threatened at suppliers of MGR). As such, the closure of MGR had significant adverse consequences for the West Midlands region, as the firm's turnover accounted for 0.5 to 1% of regional GDP; with £200 million a year alone in government revenue foregone, in addition to multiplier effects within the supply chain (Bailey and Kobayashi 2006).

Much of the immediate policy response to the closure of MGR was that of 'crisis management', focusing on jobs and short-term financial assistance, under the auspices of the Second Rover Task Force (Bailey and Kobayashi 2006). The Rover Task Force comprised organisations including Advantage West Midlands, the Birmingham Chamber of Commerce, JobCentre Plus, the Learning and Skills Council, Birmingham City Council, other local authorities, trade unions, community groups and industry bodies. An aid package worth £176 million was made available, including £50 million for re-training (up to NVQ level 2 skills), £40 million in redundancy payments, a £24 million loan fund to help otherwise viable businesses, and £41.6 million to support ex-MGR suppliers to remain viable. Another £7.6 million was announced by AWM in June 2005 to further assist with supplier diversification (MG RTF 2006).

The focus of the RTF was to facilitate diversification in the supply chain, support ex-MGR workers to find new jobs, and provide assistance to the wider community (Armstrong 2006). A telephone hotline for ex-MGR workers was implemented, in addition to a website providing advice and contact details for MGR suppliers, employees and the local community. A helpline was also established by Birmingham City Council to provide support for local residents. An MGR Jobcentre Plus hotline was launched to provide advice on job opportunities and benefits available. A package of tailored support for suppliers was also developed. Other initiatives included providing travel subsidies for workers having to commute greater distances to work, free training for wives and partners of ex-MGR workers and free training in manufacturing re-skilling (Armstrong 2006). Hence, it is apparent that (in contrast to ex-Mitsubishi workers) there has been significant assistance to ex-MGR workers. However, has this assistance translated into 'successful' labour market outcomes?

Labour market outcomes

In this section we seek to assess the effectiveness of government policy and the consequent nature of labour market adjustment by ex-MGR workers, based on data from both the Work Foundation surveys referred to earlier and data reported by the RTF (2006). The first wave of the survey took place three months after the closure in July 2005 and the second in December 2005. In the first wave, 273 interviews were conducted with ex-MGR workers. In the second wave, 232 interviews (86% of the original sample) were conducted. The demographic profile of the sample was reasonably representative of the MGR workforce according to gender, age, department and length and service.

At the time of the first wave (July 2005), 60% of the sample were unemployed and looking for work. At Wave 1, only a quarter of the sample had found full-time work. Of those who had found a job, 52% liked their new job and considered themselves as doing it for the foreseeable future. However, more than a third (37%) saw their new job as a stop-gap until something better came along. A large number, 25% of the sample, were not aware that MGR workers were entitled to re-skilling in a manufacturing skill. Only 29% of the total sample had taken advantage of the re-skilling opportunity.

Six months after the closure (Wave 2: December 2005) 34% of the survey sample were still unemployed and looking for work. More than half of the sample were now employed full-time; a significant change in the employment status of the sample. Essentially, a majority of those who were unemployed at Wave 1 had obtained full-time work at Wave 2. The numbers of those in education or training, those who were self-employed, or those employed part-time did not change significantly between the two waves (Armstrong 2006). In aggregate, results from the RTF (2006), revealed that by February 2006 (approximately one year after closure), of approximately 6300 claimants resulting directly from the collapse, around 4000 were back in work (90% full-time, in apparent contrast to the case with ex-Mitsubishi workers in Adelaide where some two-thirds of ex-employees were still unemployed 12 months post-closure), 667 were in training or awaiting training, 398 had received training but were still not working, 530 were not working and had not received any training, 443 had unknown destinations and 257 had claimed alternative benefits after claiming Jobseeker's Allowance (MG RTF 2006).

Close to half of the workers (46%) in the Work Foundation survey Wave 2 (Armstrong 2006, p. 18) found themselves doing very different jobs using very different skills compared to when they were at MGR. Although workers had found jobs in a wide variety of sectors, many had found jobs in similar sectors to before (manufacturing and the motor industry) even if they were now using different skills. The sectors where ex-MGR workers had obtained work by February 2006 were (from most to least common): manufacturing; motor industry; transport; engineering; construction; local government; the NHS; government; delivery; retail; security; and financial services (Armstrong 2006, p. 18). On one level, this can be interpreted as a relatively successful policy response in enabling structural change and assisting workers back into employment. However, there has been a high degree of competition for jobs in certain sectors. As one regional development officer commented,

> In this area there [has been] a large influx of ex-Rover workers all vying for the same jobs. I'd say for every job there [were] 50 applicants.

For those individuals still unemployed six months after closure (Work Foundation survey Wave 2), health and poor self-esteem were ongoing issues, particularly for the older workers (unemployment at Wave 2 was highest in the 45–54 age group, at 41%). Those in part-time education or training reported the largest decreases in their state of health. Those who were unemployed were much more likely to report than those employed that health problems were interfering with their ability to carry out normal tasks (Armstrong 2006, p. 19). It was interesting to note that 205 ex-MGR workers who initially claimed Jobseeker's Allowance had since made claims to Incapacity Benefit. This suggests that there appear to have been impacts on the health of unemployed workers in the initial six months following the closure.

Even for those who had regained employment by February 2006, the situation was far from positive; nearly two-thirds of the workers who had found work in October 2005 had a lower salary (MG RTF 2006). Nearly half of the workers in the Work Foundation survey Wave 2 sample (47%, six months post-closure) thought that their current job was worse than their job at MGR (Armstrong 2006, p. 27). It appears that a majority of the low-skilled MGR workers who had been used to 'middling' jobs were now finding that the majority of the employment opportunities were at the bottom of the hourglass (and hence perhaps more akin to the 'casual' employment arrangements that were a common destination for the redundant Mitsubishi workers detailed in the Australian study). The jobs they had at MGR were relatively well paid, considering the skill levels required (again comparable with the Australian study). In part this was a tribute to the effectiveness of unions in collective bargaining, which has traditionally had the effect of improving the pay position of less-skilled/lower-paid workers (Metcalf et al. 2001). For many, working at MGR was a positive experience and it was a workplace where they felt valued and enjoyed their work. Their experience of work is completely different post-MGR. As one worker commented:

> ... family and friends have felt sorry for me because I am no longer able to do a job which I felt pride and job satisfaction in.

As such, the legacy of being part of a highly unionised workforce was not without its problems, in terms of job search. Many survey respondents reported that their experience of job search had been clouded by the perception of potential employers that they were unproductive trouble-makers. As another worker commented:

> I had been talking to one guy at a company which had some openings who had said his management wouldn't be considering ex-MG Rover workers because of the reputation they felt they had, due to the bad press over the years of how Rover workers were meant to be lazy and how they wanted the maximum out while putting the minimum in.

This highlights some of the broader structural problems in the local economy and the difficulty involved in successfully reintegrating displaced workers back into quality permanent employment.

As such, whilst the costs of closure have fallen most heavily on those unable to shift into new employment, it is apparent from the preceding discussion that even those back in work have experienced substantial losses. The majority of workers were now earning significantly less than they did at MGR – £3523 a year less on average for those who were working full-time and on average £10,153 a year less for those who were now working part-time. The anxiety levels associated with this loss were considerable; particularly for those constrained to take part-time work. While those working part-time in the survey sample had a much lower ratio of job applications to job offers compared to other workers, it appeared from their anxiety levels that many were still plagued by financial and other concerns. One could surmise that these workers were not working part-time by choice. Rather, they were accepting what employment they could obtain and as such, were under-employed. One worker commented that: 'I feel uncertain of everything, I don't feel I can plan or commit'. This anxiety appeared to be affecting the families of workers – another worker commented that:

> My wife took it as a bereavement, burst out crying, my young son started bed-wetting again and my daughter became very stressed and highly strung.

Older workers also experienced a larger salary differential than younger workers, perhaps due to the fact that they were no longer being paid for their length of service. Those workers who stayed in the manufacturing sector tended to earn less than those who went into other sectors such as education, health or services.

Thus, despite the rapid policy response to the closure and assistance offered to ex-MGR workers, for a significant group problems remain in facilitating successful labour market transition and well-being.

Discussion: comparative aspects of the closures and lessons for policy

This article has demonstrated that despite the rhetoric of flexible labour markets and successful adjustment from the effects of plant closure for both ex-Mitsubishi and ex-MGR workers, it is evident that the majority of workers in both countries have not experienced an improvement in their labour market status. Rather, for many, the experience of adjustment has been overwhelmingly negative, with a loss of income and a rise in employment insecurity.

Apparent from this study (and previous studies) is that the effects of unemployment could last longer than the period of unemployment itself, and that once a person has been unemployed once, the risk of being trapped in a precarious cycle of further spells of unemployment are increased. Those with a history of unemployment are more likely to be re-employed into insecure and/or poor-quality jobs. Westin (1990) found strong evidence of this in a 10-year longitudinal study of workers affected by of the closure of a sardine plant in Norway. The employment patterns of this group were compared with a group of workers in a 'sister' sardine factory that remained open over the 10-year period. Most notable was the extent to which those who lost their jobs continued to be profoundly affected by the event. Even after 10 years, they spent less time in paid work than those at the 'sister' factory, had consumed considerably more disability benefits – and many had left the labour force for good (Westin 1990). In this context, a lack of active government intervention in the (flexible) labour market would only reinforce the overriding tendencies towards polarisation and exclusion characteristic of liberal market economies such as Australia and the UK (De Ruyter and Burgess 2003).

Governments need to consider how to help the workforce adapt to ongoing changes in industrial structure. A key issue here in both countries is the rapid shift away from mass manufacturing towards smaller-scale high value-added work. For example, services in Birmingham now account for 80% of jobs. These have been quite diverse jobs, with some in high-paying professional services, whilst others are relatively low-paid (often part-time and/or casual) jobs in retail or wholesaling (BSEDF 2005). Unemployment in Birmingham remains high relative to the national average, with a local claimant count of 8.1% against a national average of 2.9% in December 2007 (Birmingham City Council 2008, using ONS figures), concentrated in pockets of deprivation. A real legacy effect is the absence of a 'widespread culture of studying for qualifications' (BSEDF 2005). In both locations (Adelaide and Birmingham), a weak skills base acts as a dampener on economic development. Approximately 22% of the working-age population in Birmingham had no qualifications in 2006, compared to 15% for the rest of the UK (ONS 2006).[2] Similarly, in southern Adelaide the percentage of working-age population with qualifications is significantly lower than the state and national average. This partly explains why despite Australia having near full employment, higher levels of under-employment and unemployment remain in the southern region of Adelaide than other parts of the nation. Hence, evident is the need for a much greater effort in terms of cross-training initiatives in both countries to suit emerging employment opportunities.

A key issue for government then is whether 'bad' jobs can be turned into 'good' jobs. Moreover, can government ensure future closure policies help create high-quality jobs for displaced workers? A more focused and sophisticated effort needs to be made in both countries to improve the wages of the working poor that goes beyond a reliance on the minimum wage. In the UK, the wages of the very low-paid were supplemented with tax credits, with those on minimum wages able to receive the maximum entitlements (see Burgess et al. 2007). This is commendable and has greatly assisted those at the bottom of the labour market. However, more needs to be done to give the lower-paid a genuine living wage and make work pay – an issue not lost on ex-workers themselves, as one ex-MGR worker commented: 'The job I've been offered would make me less well-off than receiving benefits'. As such, regional development agencies need to consider the promotion of high-quality and healthier work as part of their strategies for sustainable economic development. These agencies need to be supported by central government in this direction, which could require a redirection of funding. Indeed, a national agenda for the promotion of higher-quality employment depends on practical delivery at a regional level in both countries.

Finally, the ongoing hollowing-out of manufacturing in both countries suggests a renewed role for industrial policy. It is here that the policy record of both countries is perhaps at its weakest. This needs to be recognised for the development of future industrial policy, given that the latter is now 'back on the agenda' in some sense. An important criticism of the UK government (notably the former Department of Trade and Industry, DTI) was that it took so long to realise that MGR was struggling and then rushed into contingency-planning that focused too much on how to deal with a collapse of the firm (NAO 2006). It was clear to many analysts that MGR was selling off its assets (land, parts business, finance arm and later its intellectual property rights) in an increasingly desperate attempt to continue operations. In fact, the DTI was not capable of recognising this as ongoing monitoring of strategic companies is not what it considered a relevant part of modern industrial policy (Bailey 2003).[3] In Australia, the government similarly appeared completely unprepared as to how to respond to the closure of Mitsubishi at Lonsdale, even though there had been clear warning signs of the imminent closure for years. The government response to the closure of Mitsubishi at Lonsdale was rushed and *ad hoc* and not very effective. Yet despite this, the package of assistance for Mitsubishi has become the standard 'roll out' government response to redundancies that have occurred in Australia such as at Holden Motors, Electrolux and Ford. It is surprising that so little reflection or critical assessment of these policies has occurred within government. As such, there are important lessons to be learnt for industrial policy design and delivery.

Whilst we have focused on employment and income security in this paper, there are other aspects of work and well-being that also need to be explored; for example, issues relating to health, autonomy and discretion in the workplace, and skill use. Hence, further research is required on the employment and well-being implications of plant closure and labour market restructuring.

Conclusion

This paper has provided a preliminary comparative longitudinal analysis of the impact on workers made redundant due to the closure of the Mitsubishi plant in Adelaide and the MG Rover plant in Birmingham. In the Mitsubishi case, given the skills shortage the state was facing, together with the considerable growth in mining and defence industries, it would have been more appropriate if intervention in the form of Labour Adjustment Package (LAP) funding had been redirected to further training or re-skilling opportunities for redundant workers. This opportunity was effectively missed and as a result more workers left the workforce, most notably for retirement, than could have otherwise been the case. The MG Rover case was seen as a more successful example of policy intervention (see also Thomas *et al.* in this issue), with greater funding assistance available and targeted support available, and with more emphasis on re-training needs to assist adjustment. However, despite the assistance offered and the rhetoric of successful adjustment in both cases, the majority of workers have nevertheless experienced a deterioration in their circumstances – particularly in the Australian case where casual and part-time work were often the only work that could be obtained. Even in the UK case, where more funding assistance was offered, a majority of workers reported a decline in earnings and a rise in job insecurity. Job insecurity is one factor known to have a negative influence on well-being.

This suggests that a reliance on the flexible labour market is insufficient to promote adjustment, and that even more active policy intervention is needed especially in regard to further up-skilling. For many, reliance on flexible labour markets only reinforces the polarisation and exclusion referred to earlier. The evidence from Westin's 1990 study casts doubt on the probability of displaced workers finding good-quality jobs in the long term without appropriate government intervention. Hence, there is a need for further longitudinal studies to better understand long-term employment prospects for workers so strongly affected by plant closures as deindustrialisation continues.[4]

Acknowledgements

The authors wish to acknowledge the support of an ARC Linkage Grant, and the ESRC under award number RES-000-22-2478. They would also like to thank the Work Foundation and BBC Radio 4 for their contribution to the UK case study, which draws on the findings of Armstrong (2006).

Notes

1. Casual employment in Australia was traditionally defined as comprising a catch-group of flexible, contingent workers who did not receive annual leave or sick leave (De Ruyter and Burgess 2003).
2. Simply attracting FDI does not help this situation, as inward FDI tends to increase the demand for skilled labour and reduces demand for unskilled labour (see Bailey and Driffield 2007), suggesting the need for a more holistic approach to industrial policy and economic development.
3. It should be noted that the response at the regional level was much more positive, with the local Regional Development Agency *Advantage West Midlands* pursuing a modernisation and diversification agenda in the five years before the MG Rover collapse, which helped suppliers diversify away from the firm and which saved several thousand jobs (Bailey and Kobayashi 2006).
4. Beyond February 2006, virtually nothing is known about the remaining MGR workers still unemployed, the long-term impact of those on long-term benefit, and in particular the impact of the closure on the wider community and stakeholders in the region. Indeed, House of Commons Trade and Industry Committee (2007) notes the wide differences in estimates of employment rates of former MGR workers and the lack of information on the wider impacts of the closure.

References

Armstrong, K., 2006. *Life after MG Rover: the impact of the closure on the workers, their families and the community*. Report prepared for BBC Radio 4. London: The Work Foundation.
Bailey, D., 2003. Globalisation, regions and cluster policies: the case of the Rover Task Force. *Policy studies*, 24 (2/3), 67–83.
Bailey, D. and Driffield, N., 2007. Industrial policy, FDI and employment: still missing a strategy. *Journal of industry, competition and trade*, 7 (2), 189–211.
Bailey, D. and Kobayashi, S., 2006. *Crisis and restructuring in the West Midlands auto cluster*. Institute for Economic Development Policy Discussion Paper No. 2006-06.

Beer, A., Maude, A., and Pritchard, B., 2003. *Developing Australia's regions: theory and practice.* Sydney: University of NSW Press.
Birmingham City Council, 2008. *Unemployment briefing* [online]. Available from: http://www.birminghameconomy.org.uk [Accessed 18 Jan. 2008].
BSEDF (Birmingham and Solihull Economic Development Forum), 2005. *Economic review 2005/6.* Birmingham: Birmingham and Solihull Economic Development Forum.
Burgess, J., De Ruyter, A., Waring, P., and Warnecke, T., 2007. *The minimum wage in three neo-liberal settings: understanding the rationale and the processes.* Paper presented to the British Journal of Industrial Relations '100 Years of the Minimum Wage' conference, London School of Economics, 13–14 December.
De Ruyter, A. and Burgess, J., 2003. Growing labour insecurity in Australia and the UK in the midst of jobs growth: beware the Anglo-Saxon model! *European journal of industrial relations,* 9 (2), 223–243.
Government of South Australia, 2005. *Global horizons, local initiatives: a framework for South Australia's manufacturing future.* Adelaide: Government of South Australia.
Graetz, B., 1993. Health consequences of employment and underemployment: longitudinal evidence for young men and women. *Social science and medicine,* 35 (6), 715–724.
House of Commons Trade and Industry Committee, 2007. *Success and failure in the UK car manufacturing industry. Fourth report of session 2006–07. Report together with formal minutes, oral and written evidence.* HC399. London: The Stationery Office.
Leana, C. and Feldman, D., 1995. Finding new jobs after a plant closing: antecedents and outcomes of the occurrence and quality of reemployment. *Human relations,* 48 (12), 1381–1401.
Marmot, M., 2004. *Status syndrome.* London: Bloomsbury.
Metcalf, D., et al., 2001. Unions and the sword of justice: unions and pay systems, pay inequality, pay discrimination and low pay. *National Institute economic review,* 176 (1), 61–75.
MG Rover Task Force (RTF), 2006. *Final update report: the work goes on.* Prepared for the Department of Trade and Industry.
NAO (National Audit Office), 2006. *The collapse of MG Rover.* HC961 Session 2005–6. London: The Stationery Office.
ONS, 2006. *Labour market profile: Birmingham* [online]. Nomis Official Labour Market Statistics, Office of National Statistics. Available from: http://www.nomisweb.co.uk [Accessed 4 Nov. 2007].
Waters, L. and Moore, K., 2002. Self-esteem, appraisal and coping: a comparison of unemployed and re-employed people. *Journal of organisational behaviour,* 23, 593–604.
Westin, S., 1990. The structure of a factory closure: individual responses to job-loss and unemployment in a 10-year controlled follow-up study. *Social science medicine,* 31 (12), 1301–1311.
Winefield, A., Tiggerman, M., and Winefield, H., 1990. Factors moderating the psychological impact of unemployment at different ages. *Personality and individual differences,* 11, 45–52.

A tale of two regions: comparative versus competitive approaches to economic restructuring

Holli Evans, Andrew Beer, and David Bailey

Introduction

Forced redundancy through the closure of a large-scale manufacturing plant presents a significant challenge for governments and communities. Such closures threaten the livelihoods of hundreds – if not thousands – of households; may depress the demand for goods and services within the region; place greater strain on public-sector resources as well as other service providers; and may call into question the financial credibility of governments (Spoehr 2005). It is inevitable, therefore, that governments respond to large-scale redundancies, particularly in highly visible industries such as the automotive sector. How they react and the outcomes they seek to achieve vary according to the philosophies of government they espouse, the relative prosperity of their economies, the governance arrangements in place at that time, and competing priorities within both the economy and system of government. A critical issue is the balance between centralised and regional responses to industry restructuring, with some governments favouring 'top down' responses while others seek to empower actors at the regional or local level. Importantly, how governments choose to respond provides insights into the wider policy environment and the manner in which economic policy departments interpret, and interact with, the market economy.

Contemporary approaches to economic development at the regional scale draw upon two competing intellectual traditions. Much economic development theory and practice (see Armstrong and Taylor 2000) draws upon the conceptual legacy first popularised by Ricardo (1817) around the economics of *comparative* advantage. The theory of comparative advantage posits that trade between nations generates greater levels of productivity for all parties, resulting in higher incomes and levels of wellbeing. From this perspective, regions should focus their economies on those industries and activities in which they have an advantage relative to others because of natural resource endowments, human capital or other factors. More recently, attention has focused on the issue of sustainable *competitive* advantage which, according to Porter (1990), is the position a firm occupies when the above average profits it enjoys cannot be reproduced by competitors because they reflect advantages intrinsic to the firm. These advantages could include products that are differentiated from their competitors, or the establishment of a superior brand or reputation. Alternatively, sustainable competitive advantage could arise from the business environment in which the firm operates. Porter's (1990) ideas have infiltrated the policies and practice of regional development in the form of 'cluster' theory (Haughton *et al.* 2003, Ffowcs-Williams 2004), with governments and other agencies responsible for the development of regions seeking to establish sustainable competitive advantage through improvements to human capital (the skill-sets of workers), the establishment of agglomeration economies and by developing the capacity of firms within the region to collaborate and innovate. Indeed, innovation is seen to be central to developing competitive advantage which in turn is held up as essential for sustaining advanced economies (Porter *et al.* 2000), especially at the regional scale (Cooke and Morgan 2000, Roberts and Enright 2004). Innovation is argued to generate 'long-run upward development' (Courvisanos 2003) by encouraging capital formation that is inherently place-dependent or embedded. This perspective on the growth of regions therefore emphasises endogenous, rather than exogenous, development; a focus on enhancing the capacity of regions in working for further economic opportunities; the building of skills and intellectual capital within the region; and the provision of appropriate infrastructure that advances the competitive position of the region.

Economic and industrial policies based on the achievement of comparative advantage can be viewed as reactive or responsive, while policies focused on competitive advantage are more proactive and forward-looking. A proactive policy built around developing competitive advantage, as Jacquemin (in Oughton 1997) notes, considers strategies which 'deliberately influence the transformation and the industrial reorganisation of sectors, and nations', noting that 'in many sectors *comparative advantages are based on partially controllable elements*' (our italics). He points to policies that might alter the accumulation of physical and human capital over time, which in turn might alter relative capital endowments. In line with the European Commission, the Department of Trade and Infrastructure (DTI) in the UK has stressed that 'competitiveness increasingly relies on a country's appropriate structures of roles, institutions and processes to enable, organise, and drive efforts to improve business environment and clusters' (Porter and Ketels 2003). Meanwhile, Porter has emphasised the regional scale in such a process: 'competitive advantage is created and sustained through a highly localised process' where 'national competitive advantage ... resides as much at the level of the cluster as it does in individual industries' (Porter 1998a).

How governments respond to the closure of large-scale manufacturing enterprises can be assessed with reference to the competing intellectual legacies of comparative advantage and competitive advantage. Policy responses that look to external solutions, that do not 'privilege' the affected region over others and which assume that an economy-wide process of adjustment will ensue, clearly draw upon the theory of comparative economic advantage. Approaches that are focused more tightly on the needs of the affected region, which seek to encourage innovation within the region's firms and which concentrate on 'adding value' to affected workers within the region are consistent with an interpretation of growth dynamics that reflects notions of competitive advantage. It is also useful to note that over-reliance on a 'comparative advantage' approach in the context of a resource- and mineral-rich environment carries with it the risk of 'Dutch disease' effects which in turn damage manufacturing. This would seem especially pertinent in contemporary Australia, given the volume of raw material exports and the strength of the Australian dollar. The 'Dutch disease' is a term originally used as shorthand for theories intended to explain how a favourable boost to one export sector had a negative impact on other export sectors. In the case of the Netherlands, this was the discovery and production of natural gas, whereas in the UK in the 1980s it was the effect of North Sea oil coming on-stream that arguably led to the over-appreciation of sterling and the hollowing-out of the manufacturing base (see Buiter and Miller 1981, Eastwood and Venables 1982, Neary and Van Wijnbergen 1984). In the case of Japan in the 1990s, Ozawa has argued that a long-term industrial policy which built up some sectors whilst sheltering others led to lopsided trade surpluses, sustained Yen appreciation and ultimately the hollowing-out of the economy (Bailey and Sugden 2007).

The remainder of this paper examines the policy responses used by governments in England and Australia to the loss of jobs in the automotive sector against these two models of understanding regional growth. The paper first examines the response of the UK government to the closure of MG Rover before examining Australian responses to redundancies at Mitsubishi Motors Australia Ltd (MMAL). The paper then compares the two sets of responses and the light they shed on the broader paradigms of government in each nation.

Policy responses to the Rover crisis in the UK industrial policy and competitiveness

The response of government in the UK to the near-collapse of Rover in 2000 and the eventual closure of MG Rover at Longbridge in 2005 must be understood in the context of broader industrial policy developed throughout the 1990s (DTI 1994, 1995). In a series of White Papers the Department of Trade and Industry (DTI) placed competitiveness at the centre of industrial policy in Britain. Upon coming to power, Blair's 'new' Labour Party embraced this approach and launched its own Competitiveness White Paper in 1998. Competitiveness under the Blair Labour government came to be seen as productivity growth (Bailey 2003, p. 68). Industry policy was focused on policies that would raise productivity, including investment in technology and innovation, the promotion of small firms with growth potential, and a more significant focus on 'soft' support such as advisory services, education and training, collaborative arrangements and fostering networks and clusters (Gavron et al. 1998, Wren 2001). While the 1998 White Paper continued to emphasise competitiveness in terms of productivity, it also placed an increased importance on the role of the 'knowledge economy'. The 1998 White Paper states that firms have to 'compete by exploiting capabilities which competitors find hard to imitate', arguing that 'the UK's distinctive capabilities are not raw materials, land or cheap labour [but] knowledge, skills and capabilities' (DTI 1998, p. 6). Influenced by Porter (1990, 1998a,b) the British government supported clusters as a way to promote a knowledge economy and thereby encourage competitiveness.

The emphasis on 'spatial clusters' meant that a regional response became a vital dimension of competitive advantage (Porter 1990, 2003). It led to a decentralisation of industrial policy to the regional level and the creation of Regional Development Agencies (RDAs), who were seen as key agents for implementing competitiveness programmes. The role of the RDAs, in relation to the White Paper, was to 'encourage the exploitation of the science and engineering base; develop links between business and higher education; co-ordinate the development and implementation of innovation and technology programmes; and to disseminate best practice' (Wren 2001, p. 853). The regional level was seen as the most effective level for government intervention and economic management, with support focused on 'clusters of inter-linked sectors with agencies supposedly taking a systemic approach and with the emphasis shifting towards the provision of "soft support" required by firms' (Bailey 2003, p. 69).

The broader context of industry policy in the UK is fundamental in understanding the government's response to the Rover crisis, especially its focus on developing competitive advantage by modernising the auto cluster and diversifying the regional economy. The decentralisation of industrial policy meant that the Advantage West Midlands (AWM) regional development agency played a central role. Advantage West Midlands established economic development strategies which reflected the focus on competitiveness enunciated in the 1998 Competitiveness White Paper and did so through an explicit clusters framework. This was evident in the Regional Innovation Strategy and the West Midlands Economics Strategy. The RIS placed competitive advantage through innovation at the centre of AWM's strategy for regional development, stating that 'in today's global economy businesses gain competitive advantage by constantly innovating ... innovation is profitable change that arises as a result of the exploitation of new ideas' (Advantage West Midlands 1998, p. 2).

The UK government responded to BMW's announcement that it intended to sell substantial parts of the Rover Group by establishing a Rover Task Force (RTF1) that brought together local actors under the leadership of the Regional Development Agency (RDA). The government recognised the crisis that would have befallen the region had Rover closed and the Rover Task Force was established to minimise the damage should the manufacturer close in the future. The Task Force received considerable funding during this period, the £129 million that had been allocated to BMW as a subsidy for production at Longbridge under the Regional Selective Assistance (RSA) programme was instead allocated to the RTF. From 2002 to 2005 funding was provided to the Task Force to safeguard the 24,000 jobs at risk should the Longbridge plant close (Armstrong 2006 p.9). The Rover Task Force focused on modernising the auto cluster and diversifying the supply chain that was dependent on Rover into other sectors.

Modernising and diversifying the automotive cluster

The RTF1 recognised that *modernisation* of the auto 'cluster' was crucial as the West Midlands lagged behind other European automobile supply chains such as those in Germany and especially France (Bailey 2003). Furthermore, it was recognised that too much of the supply base was low value-added 'metal bashing' and that higher value-added production in areas such as electronics was needed (Bailey 2003, p. 75). The *modernisation* programme of the RTF, with £17 million funding, sought to improve the competitiveness of the auto cluster through a range of measures. One of the most successful strategies was the use of the existing programme, *Accelerate*, to offer suppliers to Rover advice on new product and process development; grants for capital investment in plants for new products; and funds for the creation of supplier networks (Bailey 2003, Bailey and Kobayashi 2006, House of Commons Committee of Public Accounts 2006). The RTF also focused on the *diversification* of firms in the auto cluster into other 'clusters', with a long-term aim to 'encourage the application of engineering skills in other industries such as medical and nano technologies' (Bailey 2003, p. 75). Some £19.7 million was used to assist with development costs, while the Small Business Service provided a diversification service.

Part of the diversification efforts of the RTF included a regeneration programme for the regional economy based on the development of 'high-tech corridors' (Bailey and Kobayashi 2006). The RTF commissioned several reports to identify innovative ways to diversify away from the automotive industry. One suggested the establishment of 'high-tech' corridors that could capitalise on the region's existing science and technology base (SQW 2001). The RTF1 Final Report recommended the establishment of three high-technology corridors, one being the Central Technology Belt (CTB), running along the A38 and incorporating Birmingham University and Aston University, as well as the Longbridge site and the Queen Elizabeth hospital. The aim of the high-technology corridors was to promote knowledge-intensive industries in the region (Rover Task Force 2000, Bailey 2003). Bailey has contended that a clusters approach was behind both the modernisation and diversification programmes and that 'the RDA was able to use the RTF to accelerate and legitimise this emerging clusters policy and to extend it further' (Bailey and Kobayashi 2006, p. 14). The adoption of the CTB and other high-technology corridors enabled AWM to link clusters policies with spatial targeting (Bailey 2003). The RTF's recommendation was supported by AWM in its 2004 Regional Economic Strategy (RES), as it was seen as a key mechanism for regional growth and the transition to a knowledge economy (see Ferrari in this issue). Some £9 million from the £176 million package of assistance offered in response to the closure of MG Rover in 2005 was set aside for investment in technology and innovation infrastructure in the three West Midlands high-technology corridors. The RDA also received £42 million for redeveloping the Rover site (MG Rover Task Force 2006). AWM established a company in 2004 to enact the Central Technology Belt strategy and this included the development of the Longbridge site, a feature of which will be the Longbridge Nano Materials Centre, which will be the UK hub for this technology.

The work of the Rover Task Force over the five years from 2000 contained the damage to the region when the automobile manufacturer closed (Armstrong 2006, p. 8, Bailey and Kobayashi 2006). In the first phase the Supply Chain Diversification Scheme assisted 149 firms and helped save 1500 jobs (Rover Task Force 2000, Bailey 2003). The number of suppliers dependent on MG Rover fell from 161 firms in 2000 to 74 firms in 2005, with only 57 of those in the West Midlands (House of Commons 2006). The MG Rover Task Force noted that the supply chain was far better prepared to face the loss of MG Rover business than it had been in 2000 (MG Rover Task Force 2005a). The diverse efforts of AWM led to component suppliers shifting to other activities (House of Commons 2006). Assessments made in 2000 estimated 24,000 jobs may have been lost should Rover close (House of Commons 2006). In the end fewer than 3000 jobs were lost in the supply chain and supply chain closures were limited to just 11 businesses (MG Rover Task Force 2005b, MG Rover Task Force 2006). It is thought that the work of the Rover Task Force between 2000 and 2005 saved between 10,000 and 12,000 jobs (Bailey and Kobayashi 2006, House of Commons Committee of Public Accounts 2006).

Responding to the removal of MG Rover
When MG Rover collapsed in 2005, the government moved quickly to establish a new MG Rover Task Force (RTF2) and provided a £176 million package of assistance. The RDA

was the funding conduit for monies while also coordinating agencies such as Jobcentre Plus and the Learning Skills Council who were responsible for support to former workers (House of Commons Committee of Public Accounts 2006, House of Commons Trade and Industry Committee 2007).

The immediate assistance that the RTF2 gave to suppliers played a critical role in limiting the impact on the regional economy. In the first instance, government produced a £41.6 million package of measures to assist former suppliers of MG Rover to continue trading. This included a Wage Replacement Scheme which provided £50 per day for up to six weeks to assist firms continue operating and avoid retrenching staff. The Wage Replacement Scheme assisted 170 firms keep over 3000 workers employed in the weeks following the collapse of MG Rover. This action saved an estimated 1,329 jobs (MG Rover Task Force 2006, p. 15). Loans were also given to firms who were affected by MG Rover's closure. The Transition Loan Fund assisted 17 companies with a total of £5 million (MG Rover Task Force 2006, p. 7). These measures proved highly successful in allowing businesses to continue, as well as limiting the impact of closure on the regional economy (House of Commons 2006).

The RTF2 implemented a longer-term programme of support that was based upon previous interventions, including the *modernisation* programme that was implemented through Accelerate and the *diversification* programme. There were three main elements to this 'Phase 2' support for suppliers which received £9.6 million of funding. The first was the development of a 'Productivity Alliance', which targeted 25 medium to large automotive companies who were either Tier 1 or Tier 2 suppliers. The aim was 'to improve their competitive position through increased productivity and up-skilling the workforce in a sustainable way' (MG Rover Task Force 2006, p. 19). The programme focused on the dissemination of best practice with the hope that this would lead to improvements in quality, cost and delivery. The programme targeted companies that were long-term members of the supply chain and asked them to second suitable personnel for two years. It was hoped that these skills would be transferable beyond the automotive industry, thereby aiding company diversification and employee mobility (MG Rover Task Force 2006, p. 19). The second element was the Business Support Programme and it was aimed at 140 small to medium-sized automotive companies. It sought to assist them develop and introduce innovative products; penetrate new markets; and gain business by improving their competitive position (MG Rover Task Force 2006, p. 20). Companies were able to procure specialist technical support from R&D organisations and universities to assist in the design and development of new products. Third, an Innovation and Technology Support Programme was set up to encourage the take-up of innovation and technology in the automotive sector. Under this scheme Centres of Excellence were to be developed. The first two announced were in the areas of electronic reliability and design for niche vehicles. The overall goal of these policies was to keep the West Midlands region attractive to vehicle manufacturers and Tier 1 suppliers by strengthening the supply base (MG Rover Task Force 2006, pp. 19–21). These policy interventions are important because, as Donnelly *et al.* (2005) demonstrate, most small to medium firms in the auto sector in the West Midlands lack the capacity to invest in either R&D or up-skilling.

Labour market assistance

The loss of jobs at MG Rover was of particular concern because unemployment rates in Birmingham and the West Midlands were higher than the national average and the manufacturing industry was already in decline (Cowling and Iles 2005, Armstrong 2006).

In 2001 the West Midlands accounted for 20% of jobs in manufacturing (DTI 2001). Eighteen per cent of employment in the region was in manufacturing, 5% more than the UK average (Cowling and Iles 2005). The West Midlands was still seen as the heart of the automotive industry in Britain, with a large percentage of the automotive component sector located within the region (see Bailey et al. in this issue). The potential impact of the closure of MG Rover was therefore considerable.

Recognising the importance of retaining the existing skills base in manufacturing in the region, AWM established a series of incentives for individuals to remain employed in manufacturing and for employers in the manufacturing industry to take on former MG Rover workers. Individuals were entitled to re-skilling to a minimum National Vocational Qualification (NVQ) Level 2 in a manufacturing skill and up to £75 per week for 20 weeks to help those who had to travel long distances for new work. Employers who took on a displaced MG Rover worker were also entitled to have one other staff member trained to NVQ Level 2. A Manufacturing and Engineering Hub, or 'Skills Hub' was also established, providing a job-matching scheme between redundant MG Rover workers and manufacturing businesses in the West Midlands. Employers who took on former MG Rover staff were covered for up-skilling costs as well as receiving a wage subsidy of £50 per week for 12 weeks. The MG Rover Task Force reported that this service had a significant impact in helping ex-MG Rover workers obtain new employment. Direct intervention by Jobcentre Plus and the Learning Skills Council resulted in 751 displaced workers gaining new jobs through the Skills Hub (MG Rover Task Force 2006, pp. 12–13). These were important measures as the viability of manufacturing within the region depended on the retention of the skills base.

The most significant labour market intervention by government was the £50 million of funding set aside for training. Over 4000 displaced MG Rover workers completed an individual skills advice session to develop their own Individual Training Plan. Of these, over 2500 completed vocational training. The LSC also funded approximately 60 individuals to continue with or start a Higher Education programme (MG Rover Task Force 2005b, House of Commons 2006). Of the 4000 individuals back in work, 1111 received training (MG Rover Task Force 2006). This is a substantial labour market intervention, especially when compared to the government response in Australia to the closure of Mitsubishi. However, Cowling and Isles (2005) have pointed out that the growth sectors in the regional economy are public-sector activities or high-technology industries that require a NVQ Level 3 or 4. The economic position of the redeployed workers is therefore insecure unless further training is provided (Armstrong 2006, House of Commons 2007). Moreover, as Ferrari and Burfitt point out in this issue, it is unlikely that former Rover workers will find employment in the knowledge-intensive industries that the 'high-tech' corridors hope to create jobs in.

Policy responses to employment loss at Mitsubishi

In April 2004 Mitsubishi Motors Australia Limited (MMAL) announced the loss of approximately 1200 jobs in southern Adelaide through the closure of its Lonsdale site and redundancies from its Tonsley Park assembly plant. The closure was a profound shock to the region's economy, reducing gross regional product by approximately AU$1 billion (Blandy 2004). It was also symbolically important because the two car manufacturing plants were icons of the region's economy and supported numerous suppliers, as well as many families within the region. As recently as the year 2000 the Lonsdale plant alone employed 2000 workers while MMAL had 5000 employees in total.[1] The loss of employment at MMAL was symptomatic of broader changes in the Australian economy because while manufacturing has been, and remains, an important part of the Australian economy, the industry has declined as a consequence of economic liberalisation, including the reduction of tariff barriers. In the mid 1970s manufacturing employment accounted for 25% of the workforce, but by 2001 it had declined to 12%, even though the value of production had increased (Forster 2003). In South Australia the manufacturing sector still contributes 14% of gross state product, 12% of total employment and 62% of total exports (Government of South Australia 2006). Manufacturing represented 18% of total employment in southern Adelaide at the 2001 Census, reflecting a high degree of dependency on this sector. Moreover, the region has been characterised by lower than average incomes, with a widening gap between average national incomes and those of the residents of the City of Marion and the City of Onkaparinga, the two councils that constitute the region (BITRA 2007).

The strategic priorities of the federal government in responding to the loss of employment at Lonsdale were informed by the neoliberal philosophies that have characterised Australian governments and their engagement with issues of economic development since the mid-1980s (Beer et al. 2005). Importantly, the Howard coalition government had not articulated a formal competitiveness strategy for Australian industry, nor had it recognised the potential impact of regional processes in shaping the wellbeing of businesses. Industry policy was couched in terms of an open, global, and competitive economy, with support for the car industry limited to a single, conventional, industry support programme. The Australian government had previously committed AU$2.4 billion over the period 2000–2005 as part of an industry-wide scheme, the Automotive Competitiveness Industry Scheme (ACIS). The state government provided a range of more direct subsidies to MMAL. From a central government perspective, additional assistance was not justified when other industries were growing more rapidly. Governments adhered to the view that further substantial investment in the industry – and the affected manufacturer – would have had little impact, given the already substantial subventions. In consequence, both the state and Australian governments offered measured assistance in response to the closure of Mitsubishi and neither enunciated an explicit commitment to the well being of the affected region.

The structural adjustment fund for South Australia

The federal government responded to the closure of Mitsubishi Lonsdale by announcing a AU$50 million assistance package for the region (Department of Prime Minister and Cabinet 2004). Some AU$40 million of this package of support went to establishing the Structural Adjustment Fund for South Australia (SAFSA), a pooled fund into which the South Australian government also committed AU$5 million (Invest Australia 2004). The SAFSA was the most significant response by either the federal or state government to the loss of employment at MMAL and we must recognise that it does not fit easily within contemporary paradigms of regional development (Beer et al. 2003b) because the programme consisted of grants – effectively capital subsidies – to firms willing to invest in South Australia. The SAFSA supported firms that were able to make a 'business case' that the injection of additional capital would allow for the expansion of business and would result in a significant number of new jobs. Critically, SAFSA monies were not targeted exclusively on the southern region of Adelaide but rather extended to all of South Australia. Furthermore, the grants did not focus on sectors in which the southern region of Adelaide could have developed a competitive advantage. Indeed, the minimum AU$1 million investment criteria of the SAFSA ensured that most local businesses in the southern region were effectively excluded (City of Marion and City of Onkaparinga 2005). SAFSA funding did not target high-technology industries either. An examination of companies awarded grants shows most SAFSA funding went to low-technology and low-innovation businesses. The single largest grant was awarded to Ingham Enterprises to expand chicken processing in the north of Adelaide. Other substantial grants were awarded to a compost manufacturer and a food-packaging company. Only AU$4.8 million of the AU$45 million SAFSA funding went into business expansions that could be considered 'high-tech'.

It could be argued that the lack of investment in innovation or the 'soft' infrastructure of innovation has not been significant as there has been regional growth through the creation of new businesses on the Lonsdale site. However, there has been a substantial loss of skills from the workforce as a result of the closure of MMAL's Lonsdale site; there is less employment on that site than previously and the value of manufacturing in the region has declined. Our research shows that 12 months post-redundancy, some 35% of former Mitsubishi workers were no longer participating in the labour force as they had retired, could not work because of a disability, or were unemployed (Beer, this issue). Furthermore, the absence of skills development meant that displaced workers were unable to take advantage of the growth in other sectors, such as defence and mining. One South Australian government official remarked

> If you look at our manufacturing sector, large components have transitioned and while we have had the odd shock in terms of downturn in the automotive sector, the economy has absorbed that incredibly well. It has almost been seamless, and those people get absorbed into the economy very, very quickly. (The Weekend Australian 2007)

However, the transition has not been as seamless given that a significant percentage of displaced workers remain unemployed, while others have 'exited' the labour force altogether. South Australia is now facing such a shortage of skilled labour that major projects in defence and mining could be impeded (The Advertiser 2007). Furthermore, as with most programmes of this nature, SAFSA funding has not achieved the employment outcomes forecast (Beer et al. 2003a, Haughton et al. 2003). The federal government acknowledged that the majority of firms who received grants have not achieved their employment targets. This led one newspaper to conclude that the AU$45 million SAFSA was 'creating the wrong jobs in the wrong locations for the wrong people' (Nankervis and Castello 2006).

Overall, SAFSA funding must be viewed as a relatively minor government intervention, especially when compared to the £176 million (the equivalent of approximately AU$525 million) that the UK government provided in response to MG Rover closing. The explanation for this parsimony lies in federal and state governments who believed their interests lay in other sectors and other enterprises.

The Mitsubishi labour adjustment package

The state government of South Australia and the federal government jointly implemented the Mitsubishi Labour Adjustment Programme (LAP), delivered through the federally funded Job Network agencies.[2] The federal government committed AU$10 million to the LAP. Significantly the state government did not commit funds; however, the Department for Further Education, Employment, Science and Technology provided a range of services in support of the labour adjustment package (House of Representatives Standing

Committee on Employment, Workplace Relations and Workforce Participation 2006b, pp. 8, 27). These services included financial counselling, resumé preparation and career counselling. State government support totalled AU$383,485, a modest amount given the scale of the redundancies and their expected impact on the southern region (Government of South Australia 2006, p. 12).

The federally-funded Mitsubishi LAP provided additional assistance to retrenched Mitsubishi employees, beyond the Job Search support normally provided to retrenched workers. The Mitsubishi LAP provided an additional AU$450 per worker to Job Network providers so that they could purchase other assistance including tools, equipment, uniforms or training (DEWR 2006b, Minister for Employment and Workplace Relations 2004a, 2004b). Crucially funds were not set aside for re-training retrenched Mitsubishi workers, despite a skills shortage (Government of South Australia 2005). Only 22 of the 936 individuals who registered for services were placed in full–time education lasting 12 months or more (Government of South Australia 2006, p. 12). Another study indicated that 59% of displaced workers reported that they had plans for further training which could assist their future employment (Beer *et al.* 2006, p. 23). However, only five respondents reported they were full-time students, suggesting that the level of training amongst this group was low despite high interest. Within the Australian federal system such labour market interventions are a state responsibility. Arguably, an appropriate response from the South Australian government was to set aside funds for the re-training of former Mitsubishi workers, liaising with Technical and Further Education, universities and other education providers to develop appropriate skills and training packages. Given the strong growth in the defence and mining industries there was an opportunity to provide training to assist former Mitsubishi workers enter these sectors. Indeed, one of the key recommendations of the recent House of Representatives Standing Committee (2006a, p. 84) report into employment in the automotive and components industry was that future redundancies in the industry should have a labour adjustment programme that focused on 'targeted training to up-skill displaced workers into areas of skills needs'.

Innovation and reaction: policy lessons across nations

Governments in the United Kingdom and Australia adopted contrasting policy settings in response to large-scale redundancies in automotive employment at Longbridge and Lonsdale. As the discussion above has shown, the British government implemented innovative policies that in turn emphasised the building of long-term competitive advantage, the further development of the human capital of affected workers, locally- or regionally-focused solutions to the challenge of redundancy and comprehensive measures to refocus the economy of the region. Critically, the UK government's responses were founded on existing policy settings that embraced Porter's (1990) ideas of competitive advantage and recognised that the future of British manufacturing depended upon the development of high-technology, knowledge-intensive industries. The policy acknowledged that Britain lacked natural comparative advantages – such as resource endowments – and that the nation's long-term economic future was dependent upon the skills and abilities of its workforce, as well as the presence of an innovative culture that accepted change and produced goods and services that were distinct on world markets. The responses of Australian governments to the loss of employment at MMAL stand in sharp relief to the policies and programmes implemented in the West Midlands: government interventions in Australia were reactive, they were not informed by a previously articulated philosophy of economic development and they concentrated on short-term 'adjustment' rather than the longer-term needs of the workforce and the region.

Critically, and unlike the UK, local or regional guidance of government responses was absent, with the package of assistance determined by central government and the allocation of funding to companies determined by a federally-constituted committee. While a regionally-based advisory committee was established in 2004 (Beer and Cooper 2007), it had no influence on the distribution of Structural Adjustment Funds and modest influence on the reshaping of southern Adelaide's economy. Importantly, while the UK government put in place a policy framework in 2000 that reduced the level of risk within the regional economy in the event of MG Rover's closure, no such strategy was in place in southern Adelaide in 2004, despite numerous predictions of the plant's closure over preceding years. Indeed, there is no evidence of such contingency planning even now, despite ongoing media reports on the withdrawal of Mitsubishi Motors Australia Limited as a manufacturer.[3]

The British government developed its policies for the realignment of the West Midlands economy in the knowledge that a successful manufacturing sector was central to the UK's ongoing prosperity. In Australia strategic priorities have been placed elsewhere, especially in the growth of mining and some service industries. South Australia has embraced this change and while the state has been slow to develop its mineral resources when compared with Western Australia and Queensland, the growth potential is considerable. Through the development of new deposits and the application of technology, South Australia has the capacity to develop undeniable comparative advantage in the production of uranium, copper, iron ore, lead, silver and zinc. Moreover, it can do so with relatively modest public-sector outlays when compared with the substantial funds invested by the UK government in reconfiguring the West Midlands to a region of competitive advantage. Indeed, one of the critiques of the UK government's actions following the closure of MG Rover was that not enough has been invested in some key policy domains, especially in funding the training of retrenched workers. This is despite the fact that the UK government introduced a package of measures after the closure of Longbridge more than 10 times the size of the Australian response to Lonsdale's demise and had previously invested an equal amount in anticipation of employment loss. The substantial costs of establishing sustainable competitive advantage remain unattractive to Australian governments enamoured of neoliberal philosophies of government and attached to the notion that there are market-based solutions to virtually all questions of economy and society. The gulf between the policy settings evident in the UK and Australia is stark and in each instance the decisions of governments have established a degree of path dependency that will determine the long-term future of the affected regions. In the West Midlands, the challenge is to make a successful transition to a future based on advanced manufacturing and other high-technology industries. The South Australian economy is set on a track focused on large-scale mining, while southern Adelaide – the region most affected by the loss of employment at MMAL – is likely to become more marginalised economically. Moreover, the economic future of the broader 'region' of South Australia must remain open to question as the mining sector remains subject to the vagaries of fickle international markets, has a low potential for value-adding, is intensely price-competitive and requires little skilled labour.

Finally, it is important to acknowledge that the manner in which governments have chosen to respond in the UK and Australia to the loss of employment in the automotive sector – the twentieth-century industry *par excellence* – reflects the impact of differing paradigms of economic development. The UK response was informed by an adherence to the ideas of competitive advantage while Australia's response was developed within the intellectual framework of comparative advantage. Each perspective led to a distinct model for addressing the challenges of large-scale redundancy. The UK model embraced the need for government intervention in the economy and resulted in a focus on encouraging innovation, improving the skills of the workforce, detailed planning and early intervention within the region. Despite the positive features of the approach used in the UK it is important to acknowledge the challenges that continue to confront the UK West Midlands (see Armstrong *et al.* this issue). There is a need for further training support given the relatively low skill levels of workers leaving the manufacturing sector and the higher skill needs of emerging and growth sectors. In Australia, government action has more explicitly adopted the language and philosophies of neoliberalism and neoclassical economics, resulting in policies with a short-term focus introduced in the absence of previous planning for structural change. Such an approach has been made possible by the presence of alternative economic opportunities within the state, coupled with the assumption – possibly ill-informed – that labour markets and regional economies will adjust. In the medium to long term, the future of the West Midlands and southern Adelaide will reflect these competing paradigms of regional growth and keen observers of public policy should continue to track their relative fortunes in order to better comprehend the advantages and disadvantages of each.

Acknowledgements

This paper reports on research funded by the Australian Research Council Linkage Grant LP0562288 and ESRC Grant RES-000-22-2478. The authors would also like to acknowledge the assistance of Mrs Cecile Cutler in proofreading the text.

Notes

1. At the time of revising this paper (March 2008) the last MMAL plant is about to close with the loss of 980 jobs.
2. The Job Network is a national network of private and community organisations who receive federal government funding to provide employment assistance.
3. Which has subsequently come to realisation.

References

Advantage West Midlands, 1998. *Regional innovation strategy and action plan: shaping our future.* Birmingham: Advantage West Midlands.
The Advertiser, 2007. Rann: we won't prop up industry. *The Advertiser*, 4 July.
Armstrong, H. and Taylor, J., 2000. *Regional economics and policy.* London: Blackwell.
Armstrong, K., 2006. *Life after MG Rover: the impact of the closure on the workers, their families and the community.* London: The Work Foundation.
Bailey, D., 2003. Globalisation, regions and cluster policies: the case of the Rover Task Force. *Policy studies*, 2 (3), 67–85.

Bailey, D. and Kobayashi, S., 2006. *Life after Longbridge? Crisis and restructuring in the West Midlands auto cluster*. Institute for Economic Development Policy Discussion Paper, University of Birmingham.
Bailey, D. and Sugden, R., 2007. Kūdōka, Restructuring and possibilities for industrial policy in Japan. *In*: D. Bailey, D. Coffey, and P. Tomlinson, eds. *Crisis or recovery in Japan? State and industrial economy*. Cheltenham: Edward Elgar.
Beer, A. and Cooper, J., 2007. University-regional partnership in a period of structural adjustment: lessons from southern Adelaide's response to an automobile plant closure. *European planning studies*, 15 (8), 1–22.
Beer, A., Haughton, G., and Maude, A., 2003a. *Developing locally: lessons in economic development from four nations*. Bristol: Policy Press.
Beer, A., Maude, A., and Pritchard, B., 2003b. *Developing Australia's regions: theory and practice*. Sydney: University of NSW Press.
Beer, A., Clower, T., Haughton, G., and Maude, A., 2005. Neoliberalism and the institutions for regional development in Australia. *Geographical research*, 43 (1), 49–58.
Beer, A., Baum, F., Thomas, H., Lowry, D., Cutler, C., Zhang, G., et al., 2006. *An evaluation of the impact of retrenchment at Mitsubishi focusing on affected workers, their families and communities: implications for human services policies and practices, final report to Department of Health*. Adelaide: Flinders University.
Blandy, R., 2004. *A quantitative assessment of the southern economy and the effects of the closures of the Mobil and Mitsubishi plants at Lonsdale and Tonsley Park together with an outline of a strategic response*. Commissioned by the City of Onkaparinga and the City of Marion.
Buiter, W.H. and Miller, M., 1981. Monetary policy and international competitiveness: the problem of adjustment. *In*: W.A Eltis and P.J.N. Sinclair, eds. *The money supply and the exchange rate*. Oxford: OUP.
Bureau of Transport, Infrastructure and Regional Economics (BITRA), 2007. *Regional economic growth, BITRE's taxable income database*. Canberra: BITRE.
City of Marion and City of Onkaparinga, 2005. *Southern Region Economic Diversification Plan draft 2*.
City of Marion and City of Onkaparinga, 2007. *Think south: a new economic future*.
Cooke, P. and Morgan, K., 2000. *The associational economy*. Oxford: Oxford University Press.
Courvisanos, J., 2003. *Innovation for regional communities: a research framework*. Paper presented to the Sustainable Economic Growth for Regional Australia Conference, Gold Coast.
Cowling, M. and Iles, N., 2005. *Sent to Coventry? The re-employment of the Longbridge 5000*. London: The Work Foundation.
Department of Employment and Workplace Relations (DEWR), 2006a. *Supplementary submission to the inquiry into employment in the component manufacturing sector*. Adelaide: Department of Employment and Workplace Relations.
Department of Employment and Workplace Relations (DEWR), 2006b. *Submission to the inquiry into employment in the component manufacturing sector*. Adelaide: Department of Employment and Workplace Relations.
Department of Prime Minister and Cabinet, 2004. *Mitsubishi $50 million federal assistance package*. Media release, 21 May.
Department of Trade and Industry (DTI), 1994. *Competitiveness: helping business to win*. London: HMSO.
Department of Trade and Industry (DTI), 1995. *Competitiveness: forging ahead*. London: HMSO.
Department of Trade and Industry (DTI), 1998. *Our competitive future: building the knowledge driven economy*. London: The Stationery Office.
Department of Trade and Industry (DTI), 2001. *Business clusters in the UK – a first assessment*. London: The Stationery Office.
Donnelly, T., Barnes, S., and Morris, D., 2005. Restructuring the automotive industry in the English West Midlands, *Local economy*, 20 (3).
Eastwood, R.K. and Venables, A., 1982. The macroeconomic implications of a resource discovery in an open economy. *Economic journal*, 92, 825–848.
Ffowcs Williams, I., 2004. Cluster development: red lights and green lights. *Sustaining regions*, 4 (2), 24–33.
Forster, C., 2003. *Australian cities, continuity and change*. 3rd ed. Oxford: Oxford University Press.

Gavron, R., Cowling, M., Holtham, G., and Westall, A., 1998. *The entrepreneurial society*. London: Institute for Public Policy Research.

Government of South Australia, 2005. *Global horizons, local initiatives: a framework for South Australia's manufacturing future*. Adelaide: Government of South Australia.

Government of South Australia, 2006. *Submission to the House of Representatives Standing Committee inquiry into employment in automotive component manufacturing*. Adelaide: Government of South Australia.

Haughton, G., Beer, A., and Maude, A., 2003. Understanding international divergence and convergence in local and regional economic development. *In*: A. Beer *et al.* eds. *Developing locally: an international comparison of local and regional economic development*. Bristol: Polity Press.

House of Commons Committee of Public Accounts, 2006. *The closure of MG Rover. Report, together with formal minutes, oral and written evidence*. HC10013. London: The Stationery Office.

House of Commons Trade and Industry Committee, 2007. *Success and failure in the UK car manufacturing industry fourth report of the session 2006–07*. London: The Stationery Office.

House of Representatives Standing Committee on Employment, Workplace Relations and Workforce Participation, 2006a. *Shifting gears: employments in the automotive components manufacturing industry*. Canberra: Commonwealth of Australia.

House of Representatives Standing Committee on Employment, Workplace Relations and Workforce Participation, 2006b. *Official Committee Hansard*, 1 May.

Invest Australia, 2004. *Structural adjustment fund for South Australia: ministerial guidelines*. Canberra: Invest Australia.

MG Rover Task Force, 2005a. *Closure of MG Rover: economic impact assessment*. Paper prepared for submission to the Department for Trade and Industry. Birmingham: Advantage West Midlands.

MG Rover Task Force, 2005b. *Six months on*. Paper prepared for submission to the Department for Trade and Industry. Birmingham: Advantage West Midlands.

MG Rover Task Force, 2006. *Final update report: the work goes on*. Paper prepared for submission to the Department of Trade and Industry. Birmingham: Advantage West Midlands.

Minister for Employment and Workplace Relations, 2004a. *$10 million labour adjustment package for Mitsubishi workers*, 21 May.

Minister for Employment and Workplace Relations, 2004b. *Job network ready to help retrenched Mitsubishi workers*, 25 June.

Nankervis, D. and Costello, R., 2006. South missing out on $45 million car fund. *The Sunday Mail*, 17 December.

Neary, J.P. and Van Wijnbergen, S., 1984. Can higher oil revenues lead to a recession? A comment on Eastwood and Venables. *Economic journal*, 94, 390–395.

Oughton, C., 1997. Competitiveness policy in the 1990s. *Economic journal*, 107, 444.

Porter, M., 1990. *The competitive advantage of nations*. London: Macmillan.

Porter, M., 1998a. *Competitive advantage: creating and sustaining superior performance*. New York: Free Press.

Porter, M., 1998b. Clusters and the new economics of competition. *Harvard business review*, 76, 77–90.

Porter, M., 2003. The economic performance of regions. *Regional studies*, 37, 549–578.

Porter, M. and Ketels, H.M., 2003. *UK competitiveness: moving to the next stage*. DTI economics paper, No. 2. London: DTI.

Porter, M.E., Hirotaka T., and Sakakibara, M., 2000. *Can Japan compete?* New York: Basic Books.

Ricardo, D., 1817. *On the principles of political economy and taxation*. London: John Murray.

Roberts, B. and Enright, J., 2004. Industry clusters in Australia: recent trends and prospects. *European planning studies*, 12 (1), 99–122.

Rover Task Force, 2000. *Final report and recommendations to the Secretary of State for Trade and Industry*. Birmingham: Advantage West Midlands.

Spoehr, J., 2005. *The state of South Australia*. Adelaide: Wakefield Press.

SQW, 2001. *Regenerating the West Midlands region – a study to consider opportunities for high technology corridors/clusters*. Birmingham: Advantage West Midlands.

The Weekend Australian, 2007. South Australia: on the move. *The Weekend Australian*, 12–13 May, pp. 1–12.

Wren, 2001. The industrial policy of competitiveness: a review of recent developments in the UK. *Regional studies*, 35 (9), 847–860.

Index

Page numbers in *Italics* represent tables.
Page numbers in **Bold** represent figures.

Accelerate programme 112, 114
Adelaide and Birmingham: policy responses 1-5
Advantage West Midlands (AWM) 68, 112; Regional Economic Strategy (RES) 113
pure agglomeration model 13, 14
agglomerations and industrial clusters: typologies 13
Ahn, N. and Blazquez, M. 73
Andrews, C.J. 46
Asian manufacturers: rise 7
assembly capacity: too much 20
assembly line production: Ford 20
Audit Commission 38
Austin Rover 26
Australia: assistance for workers package 80; automobile industry restructuring 5; conditions of employment 77; de-industrialisation 84; globalisation and economic restructuring 71; Government policy responses 96-7; housing tenure and market adjustment 77-81; manufacturing employment 116; plant closure 1; retrenchment from manufacturing 84; shortage of skilled labour 117
Australian Bureau of Statistics 75
Australian Government: Mitsubishi policy responses 115-16; response to Mitsubishi closure 105
automotive cluster: modernising and diversifying 112-13
Automotive Competitiveness Industry Scheme (ACIS) 116
automotive employment: UK regions 23

automotive industry (Western): Japanese production approaches 14
automotive production systems: low wage regions 12; spatially concentrated 12
automotive supply system (Western): diffuse geography 11

Baltimore: harbour front redevelopment 34
Baunman, Z. 90
Beer, A. and Thomas, H. 78, 80
Birmingham: corridor of regeneration 48; deprivation spatial distribution 41; economic context and crisis 35-6; employee travel methods 60, 62; G8 Summit 38; international business tourism 36; KPMG reports 39; renaissance city 34-5; unemployment 40, 114; visitor economy 39
Birmingham and Adelaide: policy responses 1-5
Birmingham City Council 36; helpline 101
black and minority ethnic (BME): Birmingham 41
Blokland, T. 83, 86, 89, 92
Bloomfield, J. 38
BMW: European Commission aid investigation 27; Hams Hall engine plant 22; Land Rover plant investment 27; MG Rover sale ix; Mini production 27; R30 project 27; Rover acquisition 26
Bridge, C. *et al* 73-4
Brindleyplace 37
British Aerospace (BAe) 26
British Leyland Motor Corporation (BLMC) 25

Index

Broad Street Leisure Area 37
Bromsgrove 62, 63
Brunet, C. and Lesueur, J. 73
Bryson, J. *et al* 40
Bullring centre 37, 39, 42
Burden, R. 68
Business Support Programme 114
buyer-supplier firms: concentration 15
buyer-supplier systems: Japanese 10

Cambridge Econometrics *et al* 46
car inventory costs: US and Japan 9-10
Central Business District (CBD) 34, 37; dwellings 40; lower-skilled positions 50
Central Technology Belt (CTB) 45, 48-9, 113; employment target 49
Church, K.B. 28
city living strategy 40
claimant count data 59
Clinton, B. 38
Commonwealth Rent Assistance 72
community: interpretations 83
commuting: long-distance 79
comparative advantage 110; over-reliance 111
competitive advantage 118
Competitiveness White Paper (Labour Party) 111, 112
conditions of employment: Australia 77
Cowling, M. and Isles, N. 115
crisis of cost recovery 21
cycle of doom 26

Daimler Chrysler 5
de-industrialisation 22; Australia 84; negative 22-3; positive 22
Department of Trade and Industry (DTI) 105; White Papers 111
disenfranchised grief 91
displaced workers: integrating 95-6
Doka, K. 91
Donnelly, T. 24
Dudley 62, 63
Dutch disease 111

Eastside project: Birmingham 37-8, 42
economic development strategies: complementary housing 55

economic diversification 3, 47
economic order quantity (EOQ) 9
economic restructuring: comparative versus competitive approaches 109-20; contemporary societies 71; mature industrial economies 1; regeneration x
employee travel methods: Birmingham 60, 62
employment: well-being consequences 96
employment outcomes: Adelaide and Birmingham 80
entrepreneurial model: urban economic development 33-4
European Commission aid investigation: BMW 27
exchange rate volatility 27-8

factory closure: 1980s and 1990s xi; employment and labour market impacts xi; second wave 3
Fiat: GM divorce 20
Flatau, P. *et al* 74
flexible labour markets: UK 21
Flinders University 1
Florida, R. 46
Ford: assembly line production 20; Jaguar and Land Rover sell off 19, 21; West Midlands investment 22
Friedlaender, A.F. *et al* 9

G8 Summit: Birmingham 38
Gemeinschaft (community) 84, 89
geographical-organizational logic 14-15
Gesellschaft (society) 84
global automobile industry 7-9
Gordon, I.R. and McCann, P. 23
government industrial policy 105
government intervention: labour market 104
government policy responses: Australia 96-7; England 100-1
Graetz, B. 96
Gray, A. 84
Great Lakes region: USA 8
Green, R. 73
growth: new segments 20

Haimson, J. 11
Hanry, N. and Passmore, A. 38
Henderson, R. and Shutt, J. 57, 58

high-technology corridors 48
high-technology workforce 49-50; geographical mobility 50; Housing Market Areas (HMAs) 53; housing mismatch 47; population 51
Highbury Symposium 36-7, 40-1; spatial planning objective 36; Third (2005) 40-1
Hinde, K. 57, 58
Holweg, M. and Oliver, N. 20, 26
home ownership: reduced mobility 73
Honda-Rover: joint venture 26
House of Representatives Standing Committee 118
housing consumption 73
housing and job markets: relationship 73
housing and labour markets: regional scale 72-4; Southern Adelaide 74-9
Housing Market Areas (HMAs): Birmingham 47-8, 53; high-tech workforce 53; Longbridge 48
housing market impacts: incoming workers 51-3
Housing Market Renewal (HMR) 47, 54
housing and neighbourhood supply 53
housing policy: implications 53-4
housing and regeneration polices 47
housing tenure: labour market adjustment xi 71-81; type combinations 53
hubs of knowledge 46-7
Hyatt Hotel 36

Iammarino, S. and McCann, P. 13
Indices of Deprivation (DCLG 2004) 63
Individual Training Plan 115
industrial clusters *13*
industrial clusters and agglomerations: typologies 13
industrial complex model 13, 14
Intensive Support Customised Assistance (ISCA) 97
International Convention Centre 36
inventory holding costs 12
inventory management systems 9-11
involuntary redundancy package 74

Jacquemin, A. 110
Jaguar: Birmingham facility 24
Jaguar and Land Rover sell off: Ford 19, 21

Japan: automotive industry structure 14
Japanese overseas subsidiaries 15
Job Network agencies 71-2, 97, 117; redundant workers quotes 99-100; resource gap 100
job security 99
Jobseeker's Allowance claimants 63; by occupation Bromsgrove **65**; by occupation Dudley **66**; by occupation Longbridge **64**; by occupation Northfield Ward **65**; Dudley 65; proportion over 12 months **66**; proportion working-age resident **64**
Just-In-Time (JIT) manufacturing 8; pure form 10; supplier storage 10; supply chain and firm location 11-13; system design 10; Toyota Motor Company 9; Western industry 10

Kirkham, J. and Watts, H. 57
knowledge spillovers 2; geographical proximity 12

Labour Adjustment Package (LAP) 97, 100, 105
labour market: assistance 114-15; impacts 46; leavers 76; neighbourhood impacts 49-51
labour market outcomes: MG Rover workers 101-3; Mitsubishi workers 98-100; Southern Adelaide 77
labour market segments 51-2, 72-3; geographical choices 52; housing consumption 52
Larsson, A. 25
lean paradigm 23
lean production: systems 8; Toyota 20
Leana, C. and Feldman, D. 96
Leather, P. *et al* 54
location theory: optimal location problem 12; transportation costs 12
Loftman, P. and Nevin, B. 38
Longbridge 54, 62, 63; economic traditions 46; Housing Market Areas (HMAs) 48; job losses 59; science park 3
longitudinal surveys: ex-workers xii 4

The Mailbox 37
McCann, P. 9

McCann, P. and Shefer, D. 13
McCann, P. and Sheppard, S.C. 13
manufacturing employment: Australia 116; job losses 1971-81 West Midlands 36; West Midlands 35
Marion: Adelaide 85
MG Rover: anatomy of failure 25; employees dataset 59; exchange rate volatility 27-8; former employees 49; government response 113-14; life under BMW 26-7; Longbridge x; *national champion* 25-6; overview ix; Phoenix 28-9; policy intervention 4; policy responses 111-12; UK case 100-3; unionised workforce 103
MG Rover closure: dispersed workforce 67; economic impacts 62; long-term impacts 58-9, 60-2; neighbourhood effect 67
MG Rover employees: data 60; employment rates post-closure 66-7; geographical distribution 60; health problems 102; labour market outcomes 101-3; lower paid work 102, 103; negative legacy 103; place of residence *61*; Population Census (2001) 60; re-employment 102
MG Rover UK and Mitsubishi Australia: comparison 95-105
minimum wage 104
Mitsubishi: Australian case 96-100; *community* 85; length of employment *86*; Lonsdale plant xii; secure employment 85; state and federal assistance 5; survey respondents **87**; workplace friendship **88**
Mitsubishi employees: full-time employment 98; government rhetoric 99; labour market outcomes 98-100
Mitsubishi Labour Adjustment Programme (LAP) 117-18; funding 118
Mitsubishi redundancy study 85-92, 98-9; *family* connections 86; *family* quotes 86-7, 88; golfing event 90; grief process interview 91; interview responses 90; length of employment 86; post-redundancy employment 98; respondents 85; union membership 88; worker connections 89-90
Monterverde, K. and Teece, D.J. 9
Munch, J. *et al* 73

NANCE code employment figures: West Midlands 22

Nanjing Automobile Corporation 58; MG plant Oklahoma 29; MG Rover assets 28-9; MG sport car 21; MG TF small-scale production 29
National Indoor Arena (NIA) 36
National Vocational Qualification (NVQ) 115
Nesbit, R. and Perrin, R. 86, 89
new model: platform-sharing approach 21
Newstartmag website: Birmingham renaissance 34
Northfield 62

Occupational Health and Safety standards 77
Office Deputy Prime Minister: urban renaissance quote 34
original equipment manufacturers (OEMs): location behaviour 11-12; production processes 11; suppliers' proximity 10
Oswald, A. 73, 79
Oswald Hypothesis xi, 73, 75, 76, 79; Australian data 74
Our towns and cities - the future (Urban White Paper) 34
Owen, G. 25

Peugeot-Citröen: disappointing sales 20-1; Ryton plant 21
Phoenix Venture Holdings 100
Pike, A. 57, 58
Pinch, S. and Mason, C. 57, 58
plant closure: Britain 57-8; comparative aspects 4, 103-5; policy lessons 118-20; studies 1970s and 1980s 57; study background 4-5
Pocock, B. 84
Porter, M. 110
psychological health: unemployed persons 96

quality cost and delivery (QCD) 24
Quality of Place: The North's Residential Offer (Llewelyn Davies Yeang) 46

Randolph, R. 72, 73, 74, 79
Rann, M. 97
post-redundancy: male depression 90; multiple jobs 98-9
redundancy payments 79

redundancy process: involuntary and voluntary 74
redundant workers: commuting barriers 78-9; interviews Southern Adelaide 75, 76-7; lower paid work 77; mortgage repayments 75; qualitative interviews 77-8
Regenerating the West Midlands region: a study to consider opportunities for high technology corridors/clusters (SQW) 48
Regional Development Agency (RDA) 46, 112
Regional Economic Strategy (RES) 48
Regional Innovation Strategy 112
Ricardo, D. 110
Roberts, B. and Enright, J. 110
Rosenberg, G. 90
Rover Task Force 45, 48, 59, 68, 101; modernisation programme 112; regeneration programme 113; results (2006) 102
Rover-Honda: joint venture 26
Rowthorn, B. and Wells, J.R. 22
rust belt cities: US 36

Safety standards and Occupational Health 77
Shanghai Automotive 28; Nanjing Automobile Corporation takeover 21, 29; Rover intellectual property 29
Sheard, P. 10
Shutt, J. *et al* 57, 58
skills: mismatch 1; outdated 1
Skills Hub 115
Smyth, H. 38-9
social attachments: redundant workers 90, 92
social network model 14, 15, 24
social relations: constructs 83-4; *Gemeinschaft* (community) 84; *Gesellschaft* (society) 84; types xi 4
South Australia: government funding 97; mineral resources 119
Southern Adelaide: housing and labour markets 74-9; job losses 115-16; labour market outcomes 77; labour market realities 78-9
spatial costs 12
Structural Adjustment Fund for South Australia (SAFSA) 96-7, 116-17, 119; Lonsdale site 97; recipients 117

Sunderland: shipbuilding 58
supplier-assembler proximity 11
first-tier suppliers: greater role 29; research and development 24; West Midlands 21-2
second-tier suppliers: West Midlands 22
supply chain: integrated network ix 2; location adjustment ix 7-15; spatial structure 10; traditional Western 10
Swan Hunter: Tyneside 58
Symphony Hall 36

Tata: City Rover 28; Jaguar and Land Rover 21
tax credits 104
taxonomy of cluster types: automotive industry 13-14
tenure by labour market status *76*
Thatcher, M.: privatization 26
third revolution change through flexibility 20
Tilson, B. 23
Tomaney, J. *et al* 57
Tonnies, F. xi 83, 84, 85, 86, 89
Total Quality Management (TQM) 8
Toyota Motor Company: hybrid vehicles Australian bid 1; Just-In-Time (JIT) manufacturing 9; lean production 20
transactions-cost: approach 2; framework generic cluster types 14; taxonomy 9, 12-13
Transition Loan Fund 114
Tully, J. and Berkeley, N. 23-4, 24

unemployed persons: psychological health 96
unemployment: Birmingham 104; precarious cycle 104
University of Birmingham: workforce survey 51, 52, 101, 102
urban economic development: entrepreneurial model 33-4
urban renaissance 34; high-profile examples 34; selective 35

Van Beekum, S. 91

Wage Replacement Scheme 114
Webber, M. and Campbell, I. 84
The Weekend Australian (2007) 117

West Midlands: British automotive industry core 22; cluster policy 25; industrial structure 35; key statistics 62-3; long-term unemployment 63-7; NANCE code employment figures 22; workforce *49*

West Midlands auto cluster ix-x 19-30; diversity and challenges 23-4; firm groupings 24; global industry shifts 20-1; inter-regional network 23; local level restructuring 21-3; luxury branded niche production 21; second-tier suppliers 22; first-tier suppliers 21-2

Westin, S. 104, 106
Williams, K. *et al* 25, 26
Winnicott, D. 89
Wolf, M. 27
Womack, J.P. *et al* 20
Wong, C. 46
work-based *community*: Australia 84; impacts 83-92; post-redundancies 89-92
WorkChoices legislation 80
workforce: Housing Market Area Birmingham *50*; skills loss 117; weak skills 104